CHINA'S ECONOMY
WHAT EVERYONE NEEDS TO KNOW®

ARTHUR R. KROEBER

OXFORD
UNIVERSITY PRESS

OXFORD
UNIVERSITY PRESS

Oxford University Press is a department of the University of Oxford. It furthers
the University's objective of excellence in research, scholarship, and education
by publishing worldwide. Oxford is a registered trade mark of Oxford University
Press in the UK and certain other countries.

"What Everyone Needs to Know" is a registered trade mark
of Oxford University Press.

Published in the United States of America by Oxford University Press
198 Madison Avenue, New York, NY 10016, United States of America.

© Oxford University Press 2016

Cataloging-in-Publication data is on file at the Library of Congress
ISBN 978–0–19–023903–9

5 7 9 8 6 4
Printed by RR Donnelley, USA

CHINA'S ECONOMY

WHAT EVERYONE NEEDS TO KNOW®

CONTENTS

PREFACE: WHY THIS BOOK?

This book is an effort to explain how China's economy got to where it is today, where it might be headed in the coming years, and what China's rise means for the rest of the world. It is intended to be useful to the general reader, who has an intelligent interest in China and its global impact but not necessarily a specialized background in either China or economics.

An economy is a complicated organism, which does not easily lend itself to description by narrative, as one might tell the story of a person's life. It is more like a jigsaw puzzle—to be precise, a three-dimensional jigsaw puzzle, in which the shapes of the pieces keep changing. Rather than a fixed structure like a molecule, a skyscraper, or a mathematical equation, an economy is a set of fairly solid institutions and fairly fluid arrangements created by people to enable them to get the goods and services that they want. The nature of these institutions and arrangements is largely determined by the political bargains made among the important groups in a society. As the composition, relative power, and interests of these groups change over time, so do the economic arrangements. In other words, considerations of political practicality usually trump those of economic efficiency. For economic policymakers, this means that they must make do with second- or third-best versions of their ideal recipes. For analysts, it means that describing an economy is more of a historical art than a natural science. To the extent it is a science, it is more physiology than physics.

China is also a complicated organism. It is arguably the oldest state in the world, whose geographic core has been governed almost continuously by a rationalist bureaucracy since the late sixth century C.E., when the famous examination system was established. The centuries of accumulated knowledge about the craft of running an enormous, nominally centralized but practically quite fragmented polity doubtless continue to play an important role in the country's political and economic governance. Just how is hard to describe or quantify, but any outside observer should start with a measure of respect for the durability and resourcefulness of this governing ethos. At the same time, the nation of China as we know it today is quite young, dating from the establishment of Communist Party rule in 1949, and both its political organization and economic development strategy were based on extensive borrowings from abroad. Knowledge of the parallels and precedents of Soviet Russia and the neighboring "developmental states" in East Asia are essential to understanding how China got to where it is.

Proceeding from these biases, I have organized this book to touch on all of the major topics needed to gain a comprehensive understanding of how China's economy works and why it is built the way it is. At the same time I will sketch out the main currents of its evolution since 1979, when Deng Xiaoping inaugurated the period of what he called "reform and opening," and what I and most other analysts loosely refer to as the "reform era."

The opening chapter sets the context by laying out China's general political economy arrangements. Chapters 2 through 4 describe the sectors of economic activity—agriculture, industry, and the construction of cities and infrastructure—that were successively most crucial to China's economic development story between 1980 and 2010. Chapters 5 through 8 analyze what one might call the "nervous system" of the economy: the organization of business enterprises and the fiscal, financial, and energy systems. Chapters 9 through 11 attempt to bring the discussion down to a more human level and present what are likely to be the most pressing issues of the coming decade: changes in demographics and the labor market; the emerging consumer economy; and the social problems most likely to upset the central political bargains, namely inequality and corruption.

The last two chapters return to the stratosphere and take on the two large questions that dominate current public debates about China. Chapter 12 examines China's chances of making a successful transition from the "resource mobilization" type of growth it has enjoyed since 1979 to the "resource efficiency" type of growth that is now required. The final chapter assesses what China's rise to economic power means for the rest of the world.

To fit all this material into the confines of a book succinct enough to enlighten the reader without burying her under a hail of data and qualifications, I have naturally had to simplify a great deal, although I hope not in a way that will cause specialists to cringe at every page. A particular peril of this sort of work is that it can leave the impression that China's economic development has been the working-out of a master plan designed in advance and supervised at every point by wise officials with an exact knowledge of the consequences of all their actions. This is of course absurd: China's economic story, was created by fierce battles between rival groups, decisions taken under emergency conditions with imperfect information, the belated and partial rectification of past errors, and the constant swirl of a billion people seeking personal advantage. Readers hungry for this sort of detail should consult the suggestions for further reading at the end of the book. In public, Chinese officials like to describe the economic reform process as "crossing the river by feeling for the stones." The metaphor is accurate, but overly pastoral. In private, an official once admitted that economic reform was more like "walking a tightrope over a bottomless pit—and the rope behind you is on fire." It is worth bearing that picture in mind as you read ahead.

ACKNOWLEDGMENTS

This book is the result of more than a dozen years spent in Beijing immersed in questions about China's economy and society. It could not have come to life without the help of many people. Among the most important are past and present colleagues at the *China Economic Quarterly* (CEQ) and Gavekal Dragonomics, who have done much of the research that has guided my thinking and provided continuous intellectual stimulation over many years: Chen Long, Cui Ernan, He Yuxin, Rosealea Yao, Janet Zhang, Tom Miller, Thomas Gatley, Simon Cartledge, and especially Andrew Batson, who read the entire manuscript with an unsparing eye, provided many important ideas and sources, and rectified numerous errors. No one in our Beijing office, including me, would have a job for long without Alanis Qin's superb ability to keep us all afloat on the bitter sea of Chinese bureaucratic procedures. Joe Studwell, CEQ's founder, opened his door to me and then graciously let me adopt his brainchild. Louis-Vincent Gave's business talent helped me turn a hobby into a profession, and his good-heartedness gave me the time I needed to finish the work.

Others who read various chapters and whose critiques made the book much better include Ian Johnson, Zha Daojiong, Bob Kapp, and Stephen Green. In the background are the eminent teachers who have generously shared their insights over the years and made me a better student: most notably Nicholas Lardy, Carsten Holz, Pieter Bottelier, Ezra Vogel, and Barry Naughton. Cheng Li of the Brookings Institution's John L. Thornton Center and the directors of the Brookings-Tsinghua Center, Wang Feng and Qi Ye, have afforded me many valuable opportunities to interact with scholars in the United States and China.

Scott Parris at Oxford University Press invited me to undertake this project, and did so on the kind recommendation of Thomas Rawski and Loren Brandt. Liu Beicheng, Yang Yuanying, and Tang Lu taught me most of what I think I know about how China really works. Long ago Charles Fishman taught me how to be a journalist, then more recently bet that I would not meet my deadline, which ensured that I did. Deborah Seligsohn brought me to China in the first place and over many years shared her enthusiasm and knowledge with boundless generosity; I am greatly in her debt. Finally, Elizabeth Knup gave good cheer, unflagging support, and the benefit of her own capacious knowledge and judgment throughout the year of writing. Thank you all.

1

OVERVIEW

CHINA'S POLITICAL ECONOMY

What Is China's Political System and How Does It Affect the Economy?

China is a bureaucratic-authoritarian one-party state, in principle highly centralized but in practice substantially decentralized. Understanding China's unique and resilient political system is a prerequisite for making sense of the country's economic past, present, and future. So to begin, we will examine the three main features of the governance system in turn.

First, China's system is *bureaucratic-authoritarian*. This means that it is not a democracy, like the United States and most other high-income developed countries. But it also means that it is not a dictatorship—that is, a country ruled by a single person or small group of persons, in which the personal authority of the dictator or junta supersedes that of all bureaucratic institutions. Types of dictatorial states include the purely personal dictatorships in many African countries; military juntas such as those that ruled Brazil and other Latin American nations in the 1960s and 1970s, or Myanmar until recently; and hereditary quasi-monarchies within Communist states, of which the main examples are the Castro family in Cuba since 1959 and the Kim family in North Korea since 1946.

China's system, as it has evolved since 1978, differs markedly from all these dictatorial types. Ultimate authority resides not in the individual leader but in the Communist Party, which sits atop the political system; directs the operations of the government and military; and selects leaders who are subject to term limits, mandatory retirement ages, and more or less formal requirements to obtain consensus from the rest of the senior leadership group on major policy decisions. (This senior leadership group may include retired officials. For instance, President Jiang Zemin continued to play an important behind-the-scenes role for at least a decade after his formal retirement in 2003.) These limitations are not fully institutionalized but seem to operate consistently most of the time.[1]

An important difference between China and most other authoritarian regimes is its method of leadership succession. Because of the highly personal nature of authority in dictatorships, leadership transitions are tricky. The simplest solution is to have power go from one family member to another, as in a traditional monarchy. Or it can be transferred from one member of a small ruling oligarchy to another, as in some military dictatorships. Often it is necessary to wait for the death of the old ruler before the new one can be installed. Sometimes succession occurs earlier, not through a formal process but by coup d'état.

China, almost uniquely among modern authoritarian regimes, has achieved three successive transfers of power from one living leader to another unrelated one. (Only Vietnam has done better, with four leadership transitions since 1991.) These transitions are complex because the top Chinese leader holds three concurrent positions: General Secretary of the Communist Party, Chairman of the Central Military Commission (which controls the army), and State President (a mainly ceremonial role that confers ultimate control of the government). A leader must hold all three positions—but especially the first two—in order to exercise full control of the state.

At the Fourteenth Party Congress in 1992, Deng Xiaoping, who had been China's paramount leader since 1978, retired along with several other octogenarian leaders and transferred control of the party, military, and government to a new president, Jiang Zemin. At the Sixteenth Party Congress in 2002, Jiang retired and ceded control of the party and government to Hu Jintao; he did not give up chairmanship of the Central Military Commission until two years later. At the Eighteenth Party Congress in 2012, Hu retired and the new president Xi Jinping assumed control of the party, government, and military.[2]

This record of leadership transitions distinguishes China from not only virtually all other modern authoritarian states but also from the Soviet Union, the state that in many respects it most resembles. All leadership transitions in the Soviet Union's seventy-four-year history occurred only after the death of the old leader or by coup d'état. China's mechanism for leadership transition means that the Chinese state is more stable and resilient than other authoritarian states. Along with other institutional procedures—notably the mandatory retirement rules that force top leaders to step down around the age of seventy, and other officials to retire by the age of sixty-five—it also ensures that there is a constant circulation of new personalities and ideas in government and that the system does not get captured by old leaders resistant to change.

Second, China is a *one-party state*. The important thing here is not the obvious fact that the Communist Party is in effect the sole legal party,[3] but the *nature* of the party. Rather than a tiny cabal of secretive leaders, it is a vast organization of some eighty-six million members (more than 5 percent of the nation's population) that reaches into every organized sector of life including the government, courts, the media, companies (both state-owned and private), universities, and religious organizations. Top officials in all these organizations are appointed by the party's powerful Organization Department.

"A similar department in the US," writes journalist Richard McGregor in his book *The Party*, "would oversee the appointment of the entire US cabinet, state governors and their deputies, the mayors of major cities, the heads of all federal regulatory agencies, the chief executives of GE, Exxon-Mobil, Wal-Mart and about fifty of the remaining largest US companies, the justices on the Supreme Court, the editors of the *New York Times*, the *Wall Street Journal* and the *Washington Post*, the bosses of the TV networks and cable stations, the presidents of Yale and Harvard and other big universities, and the head of think-tanks like the Brookings Institution and the Heritage Foundation."[4] The party no longer tries to control the minutiae of every individual's life, as it did during the Maoist era, but it does seek to directly control or heavily influence every sphere of *organized* activity. The party exercises its control in a flexible, not a dogmatic way, and this flexibility helps explain its resilience amid the rapid changes in China's economy and society.

Another source of resilience and responsiveness is the encouragement and management of large flows of information between local governments and the central authorities in Beijing, and the conversion of that information into policies that address problems on the ground. Much foreign commentary focuses on the ways in which the party censors and controls the Internet and other media. This censorship is real, pervasive, and in many respects harmful. Yet the party has tolerated an explosion of conventional and online media, and has invested heavily in Internet infrastructure, because it finds media reports helpful in gaining information on problems that local officials would prefer to conceal. Beyond this, both the party and the central government commission enormous amounts of research, including ground-level surveys, via state-controlled think tanks and universities. This information feeds into a sophisticated policy-formation process in Beijing. The most visible manifestation of this process is the Five-Year Plan, which has evolved far beyond its original purpose of setting production targets in a command economy into an ongoing procedure for converting information from the grassroots into policy and adjusting policies as conditions change.[5]

Finally, China is *formally centralized, but in practice highly decentralized*. The formal centralization is easy to see. Unlike a federal system such as the United States, there is no division of powers between the central and provincial governments; the same party controls the bureaucracy at all levels of government; and the party's central Organization Department in Beijing appoints the senior leadership of all provinces and many cities. Many crucial laws or policies, notably the famous "one-child" population control policy,[6] have been enforced with a high degree of consistency across the whole country.

As any visitor can attest, however, the reality on the ground is that local governments enjoy a high level of discretion and autonomy. One measure of decentralization is the share of government expenditure that takes place at the subnational level. A 2004 International Monetary Fund (IMF) study found that, in the period 1972–2000, this figure averaged 25 percent for democracies and 18 percent for nondemocracies. For China, the average figure for 1958–2002 was 54 percent; and by 2014 it had risen to a staggering 85 percent. As scholar Pierre Landry noted, "controlling for its level of economic development, one would expect the PRC to be one of the most centralized countries [in the world]. Instead, China's observed level of decentralization is consistent with the behavior of a federal democracy!"[7] We will return to the details of China's fiscal system in chapter 6. For the moment it is enough to observe that China's level of fiscal decentralization is unusually high by any standard, and extraordinary for an authoritarian country.

Two other dimensions of decentralization are worth noting. First, even when China was a centrally planned Communist economy (roughly from 1956, when private enterprises were abolished, until 1979, when Deng Xiaoping's "reform and opening" period began), it was in reality less centrally planned, by far, than the Soviet Union, the state on which it was explicitly modeled.

In 1979, central planners in China controlled the allocation of just 600 commodities and the prices of a few thousand, compared to the 60,000 commodities and millions of prices determined by state planners in the USSR. Chinese local governments had enormous authority in allocation of key commodities: in the late 1970s, localities allocated 50 percent of cement, 40 percent of coal, and 25 percent of steel. In the USSR, distribution of these crucial items was determined almost entirely by the central government.

In 1979 the Soviet Union had 40,000 state-run factories, many of which were run from Moscow, whereas China had 883,000, of which 800,000 were controlled by city and county governments. In the Soviet Union, factories with at least 1,000 workers accounted for three-quarters of industrial output and employment; in China, more than 60 percent of output came from small factories with less than 500 workers. Decentralization of production partly resulted from China's immense geographic diversity and its relatively poor transportation links. But it was also a deliberate strategy pursued by Mao Zedong, who believed that China's best insurance against attack by the Soviet Union or the United States was a system that ensured that production of both daily necessities and military equipment could continue even if one or more major industrial area were wiped out.[8]

Thus when Deng Xiaoping began his economic reforms in 1979, he inherited an economy that was already quite decentralized, and he exploited this in the design of his reforms, which stressed local experimentation and a high degree of latitude for local officials in interpreting and executing central directives. This policy was also explicitly enshrined in the creation of "special economic zones," which created rules on taxation and business investment that were far more liberal than for the rest of the country (see chapter 3).

This leads us to the apparent paradox of Chinese governance: an apparently centralized, one-party authoritarian state presiding over a dynamic, decentralized economy. In the modern era no such combination has lasted very long. Authoritarian regimes that succeeded in maintaining a high degree of centralized control, such as the Soviet Union, succumbed to economic stagnation and ultimately to political collapse. Regimes that prioritized economic growth and permitted a higher degree of decentralized decision-making were forced to open up their political systems, as South Korea did in 1988 after twenty-seven years of military dictatorship. No wonder foreign observers have predicted for decades that China's mix of authoritarian politics and economic dynamism could not possibly last.[9] So far, these predictions have been wrong. Why?

What Has China Learned from the Failures of Other Communist Countries?

One way of describing China is as a "transitional" post-Communist economy. This means it is making a transition from a centrally planned economy to a more market-driven one. It does not necessarily mean that the Communist Party gives up political power. Most Eastern European countries are examples of nations that combined an economic transition from plan to market with a political transition from Communist authoritarianism to multiparty democracy. Russia is an example of a country that tried, and failed, to make an economic transition without a full political one. China and Vietnam are examples of countries trying to make an economic transition while maintaining the Communist Party's monopoly on political power.

The first key to understanding why China has not lapsed into economic stagnation or evolved into a democracy is to examine the lessons its leaders learned from the failure of other Communist states, notably from the traumatic collapse of the Soviet Union in 1991. In the early 1990s, China's political position seemed very shaky. Protests in Beijing's Tiananmen Square in the spring of 1989 swelled at their height to over a million demonstrators, who denounced official corruption, runaway inflation, and the lack of political freedoms. The Communist Party under Deng Xiaoping restored order at the cost of a bloody crackdown and the house arrest of Zhao Ziyang, who until late May that year had been the party's top official and had spearheaded many of the economic reforms of the 1980s. In the next two years China suffered economic sanctions by the United States and other Western countries, and its economic growth rate sagged to an average rate of 4 percent in 1989–1990—a recession compared to the 10 percent average growth rate in the prior decade. Conservative officials blamed the political unrest on Deng's reformist economic policies. The country was diplomatically isolated and in economic and political lockdown.

Meanwhile, the rest of the Communist bloc was crumbling with a speed unimaginable just a few years earlier. Communist regimes in the USSR's satellite states in Eastern Europe all disintegrated by early 1990, and by Christmas 1991 the Soviet Union itself had fallen apart: the Communist Party lost power after a failed coup against Mikhail Gorbachev, fourteen republics from Lithuania to Kazakhstan declared independence, and Boris Yeltsin installed himself as the non-Communist president of a reduced Russian Federation.

In such circumstances, it was easy to imagine either that China would be the next domino to fall, or that the party would tighten its grip on power by crushing dissent and reining in the economic reforms that had proved so politically disruptive. In fact it did the opposite. By 1991 the economy was picking up steam again, and in early 1992 Deng launched a masterstroke with his celebrated "southern tour." Accompanied by senior military leaders, he visited the hot spots of economic reform in south China, beginning with the special economic zone of Shenzhen, right next to Hong Kong, which had been the laboratory for his boldest experiments. On the trip he held a meeting with senior military leaders and the head of the national security services, in which he bluntly declared, "Whoever is opposed to reform must leave office."[10]

This message was intended for Jiang Zemin, whom Deng had appointed head of the party after the Tiananmen uprising, and who was sitting on the fence between Deng's reformers and the conservative camp. In effect, Deng was telling Jiang: "I am still the power behind the throne, I have the military on my side, and I order you to get off the fence and restart economic reforms. If you don't, I will throw you out and find a more obedient lieutenant." Jiang complied, launched a new round of reforms, and over the next five years economic growth surged by an average of more than 12 percent a year.[11]

An old revolutionary, Deng was as committed as anyone to the preservation of the party's monopoly on power. But he gambled that the best way to preserve that monopoly was to run a dynamic economy that boosted living standards at home and raised China's international prestige and leverage. He reasoned that a better-fed population, proud to live in a China that was once again "standing tall" in the world, would in the long run be more supportive of Communist Party rule than people living in a stagnant economic backwater. Economic reform must come first, and political reform—if ever—a distant second. Or in his own words, plastered prominently on billboards throughout China in the 1990s: "Development is the only iron law."[12] In this respect he differed diametrically, and self-consciously, from Gorbachev, who began with political reforms in the hope that they would help unblock bureaucratic resistance to economic reforms. Deng, long before Tiananmen, declared Gorbachev to be "an idiot" for putting political reforms ahead of economic ones.[13]

Deng's judgment about the importance of strong economic growth was later validated by a series of studies of the collapse of the USSR conducted by party scholars in the 1990s. These scholars concluded that the Communist Party of the Soviet Union (CPSU) fell for four main reasons:

- The economy did not grow fast enough, leading to frustration and resentment, and this failure resulted from insufficient use of market mechanisms.
- The CPSU's propaganda and information systems were too closed and ideologically rigid, preventing officials from getting accurate and timely knowledge about conditions both inside and outside the Soviet Union.
- Decision-making was far too centralized, and hence far too slow.
- Once reforms started under Gorbachev, they undermined the core principle of the party's absolute monopoly on political power.[14]

These findings have continued to inform Chinese policymaking over the past two decades. Unlike Western analysts, who see a fatal contradiction between a dynamic economy and a tightly controlled political structure, Chinese leaders see the two as complementary. Tight political control provides the stability within which economic activity can be decentralized; and the resulting rapid economic growth in turn enhances the party's legitimacy for having "delivered the goods" of higher living standards. With strengthened legitimacy, the party's grip on power becomes more secure, and most people find the risk of switching to another, untried system to be unacceptably high.

The ideas that economic growth is the key to sustained political power and that a government's legitimacy can just as well spring from economic growth as from democratic elections are not uniquely Chinese creations. They are also common in China's successful East Asian neighbors, whose experiences Chinese leaders have studied closely since the beginning of the reform era.

What Has China Learned from the Successes of Its East Asian Neighbors?

When China began to emerge from its period of Maoist isolation in 1979, government officials and scholars began to travel around the world. They quickly found that, in economic and technological terms, China had fallen far behind not only the established Western powers but also several of its smaller neighbors in East Asia: Japan, South Korea, and Taiwan. All three countries had experienced sustained economic booms since emerging from the wreckage of war in the early 1950s. By 1979 Japan was already the world's second-biggest economy and seemed poised to wrest global technological leadership away from the United States. South Korea, under the inspired, draconian, and occasionally manic leadership of President Park Chung-hee (1961–1979), had risen from being the poorest country in Asia to a nascent industrial powerhouse. Most embarrassingly, Taiwan, a poor agricultural province in 1949 when the defeated Nationalist government of Chiang Kai-shek took refuge there after losing the civil war to the Communists, was now a thriving middle-income country on the verge of becoming an important exporter of electronic goods.

The developmental achievements of East Asia are now well known, in a general way, but the significance and uniqueness of its achievement are still insufficiently appreciated. Generating sustained rapid economic growth over many decades is hard; leap-frogging from poverty to the club of the richest nations—"catch-up" or "convergence" growth—is a rare feat. A study of catch-up economies found that between 1970 and 2010, only fourteen countries managed to increase their per capita income relative to that of the United States by 10 percentage points or more. Seven of these were peripheral countries in Europe that presumably benefited from spillover effects from the great postwar European economic boom and from the progressive economic integration within the European Union. Another was Israel, which probably also benefited from proximity to Europe. The other six were all in East Asia, and by far the biggest gains in relative income were in Taiwan, South Korea, and Japan. During this period the only countries in the entire world to jump from "poor" (defined as 10 percent or less of US per capita GDP) to "rich" (50 percent of US per capita GDP) were Taiwan and South Korea (see Table 1.1).[15]

Table 1.1 Successful Catch-up Growth Countries: Per Capita GDP at Purchasing-Power Parity, Percent of US Level

Country	Pre-1970 low (%)	2008–2010 Average (%)	Increase in percentage points
Asian exporters			
Taiwan	9	68	+59
Japan	21	72	+51
South Korea	10	58	+48
Malaysia	9	29	+20
China	2	18	+16
Thailand	5	19	+14
Peripheral Europe			
Austria	44	99	+55
Spain	29	68	+39
Greece	29	65	+36
Finland	45	79	+34
Portugal	19	48	+29
Italy	40	69	+29
Israel	34	60	+26
Romania	10	25	+15

Source: Adapted from Batson (2011).

What accounts for the unique success of East Asian economies, compared to all other non-European developing economies? One persuasive explanation is that Japan, Taiwan, and South Korea all adopted varieties of a model called the "developmental state," a term coined by economist Robert Wade in 1988. Subsequent research has suggested that the successful East Asian developmental state economic-growth model has three pillars: land reform, export manufacturing, and financial repression.[16]

"Land to the tiller" agricultural reform. This generally means breaking up big estates or plantations and creating a class of rural smallholders. In populous countries with an unconstrained supply of rural labor, per-acre yields on small owner-cultivated farms are much higher than on plantations tilled by tenant farmers or wage labor. These higher yields create a significant agricultural surplus, and since farm ownership is fragmented, it is much easier for the state to capture a large share of this surplus than it would if it were dealing with politically powerful big landowners. The resources thus captured provide the seed capital for state-led investment in basic industry and infrastructure.

Export-oriented manufacturing. The basic reason why poor countries are poor is that they lack the technological capital that rich countries have, which makes output per worker dramatically higher. To get rich, poor countries must therefore undertake a process of "technological catch-up," in which they acquire technology from rich countries and use it to accelerate the productivity of their own workforce. Exports help this catch-up process in two ways. When a country is poor, foreign technology is expensive and must be paid for in scarce hard currency. Exports (initially of agricultural products, handicrafts, and cheap manufactures) can earn the foreign exchange needed to buy the capital equipment that enables higher-value production.

Later, when the country has an established industrial base, exports provide a handy, and much cheaper, way of ensuring that the country's production techniques keep pace with improvements in global technology. If you are selling your goods on world markets, you must compete with producers from all around the world and cannot benefit from market rules rigged in your favor. The only way to keep up is to make sure that your technology (which includes not just machines but also management techniques, supply-chain control, and other "soft" technologies) is reasonably close to the global standard. Export manufacturers engage in a constant process of upgrading their technology—through purchases, licensing agreements, reverse engineering, or outright theft of intellectual property—in order to stay competitive and gain market share. Producers who rely mainly on the domestic market often have less incentive to invest in technology, since they may find it cheaper to use political influence to have the local market rigged in their favor.

Financial repression. This refers to a set of practices to control financial markets so that the state can direct capital to the sectors favored by its development strategy. These typically include:

- Regulated low interest rates, so that the cash flows from economic growth are not captured by "rentiers" living off interest income, but instead subsidize borrowing to fund state investments in infrastructure and corporate investments in industry.
- A tightly managed and typically undervalued exchange rate to make the country's exports cheaper on global markets.
- Capital controls, to prevent companies and rich individuals from siphoning off national wealth into investments abroad, and instead to compel profits to be reinvested in the domestic economy.

With many variations driven by local political institutions, Japan, South Korea, and Taiwan implemented these core elements with rigor. (By contrast Southeast Asian neighbors such as Thailand, Malaysia, and the Philippines followed the script halfheartedly, which helps explain their less impressive results.) This often required them to resist intense lobbying by advanced countries such as the United States, and multilateral institutions like the World Bank and International Monetary Fund, who pressed for freer exchange rates and more open financial markets.

Despite—or rather because of—their refusal to kowtow to the self-interested free-market fundamentalism of the rich countries, these three East Asian nations generated the fastest economic growth of the second half of the twentieth century: each saw average real GDP growth of 8 to 10 percent a year for three decades before slowing down. Scholars of economic history were not surprised. The "East Asian development model" is an adaptation of the strategy advocated by German economist Friedrich List (1789–1846), which in turn drew inspiration from the "American System" created in the early United States by Alexander Hamilton and Henry Clay. The United States and Bismarck's Germany (which adopted much of List's program) were the two most successful "catch-up" economies of the nineteenth century. Japan's first modernization drive, which turned it from an agrarian feudal state to Asia's first industrial power in the decades after 1870, more or less copied the German model.[17]

As we will see in our subsequent discussions of agriculture (chapter 2), industry (chapter 3), and finance (chapter 7), China adopted all of this program by breaking up the Mao-era communes into small owner-tilled plots, aggressively promoting export manufacturing, and repressing its financial system in order to fund large-scale investments in infrastructure and basic industry. For the moment, however, it is worth considering two important ways in which China's development strategy since 1979 has differed from that of its neighbors.

First, China has relied far more heavily on state-owned enterprises (SOEs). In postwar Japan the state set the rules and controlled the resource flows, but most of the companies and banks were privately owned. South Korea's banks were mainly owned by the state, but most of its large companies were private *chaebol* conglomerates. Taiwan had a much larger stable of companies owned either by the state or by the ruling Kuomintang Party; all the big banks were (and still are) state-owned. But there was also a very large body of private small- and medium-sized enterprises (SMEs) that spearheaded the island's drive into export markets. And many of the state- and party-owned enterprises were privatized in the 1980s and early 1990s.

Because of its Communist heritage, China began its high-growth era in 1979 with virtually all assets in state hands, and thirty-five years later China still has by a wide margin the biggest state sector of any major economy. As noted above, China's political system hinges on the Communist Party having an outsized influence on all organized activity, and corporations are no exception. A secondary factor is that economic officials of the reform era inherited a country virtually without legal or regulatory systems. They therefore found it convenient to regulate via the enterprises they controlled, rather than through the impotent regulatory agencies. The implications of China's unusually high and persistent degree of state ownership will be explored further in chapter 5.

The second big difference between China and its East Asian models lay in the extensive use of foreign direct investment (FDI). FDI played virtually no role in the postwar development of Japan, South Korea, or Taiwan. In China, it was central. One of the ground-breaking economic reforms of the early 1980s, the establishment of special economic zones, was specifically designed to lure in foreign companies to set up export manufacturing factories. Foreign direct investment became virtually a mania after Deng's 1992 southern tour, and annual inflows surged from an average of $2 billion in the preceding decade to $37 billion in 1992–2001.

Another surge after China's 2001 entry into the World Trade Organization carried annual inflows of greenfield investment up to over $100 billion a year by 2010; the numbers are even higher if one includes reinvestment of profits. From 1993 to 2002, new FDI inflows accounted for about 10 percent of all fixed investment in China, although this figure has since fallen to under 4 percent. One of the enduring impacts of this is that, even today, nearly half of all Chinese exports—and three-quarters of high-technology exports—are produced by foreign firms. This is utterly different to the other East Asian countries, whose exports are virtually all recorded by domestic firms.

What accounts for this extraordinary surrender of economic sovereignty, which has led many Chinese critics to complain that China was simply renting out its vast army of cheap workers to foreign capitalists, who grew rich on the proceeds?[18] One reason is that, in the aftermath of the Mao era and the chaos of the Cultural Revolution (1966–1976), China found itself in a position of extreme technological backwardness. It therefore required a strategy for rapid import of foreign technology. The first approach was a massive program of plant imports, initiated in 1977 and carried out in fits and starts for another decade or more. This had some successes, but the nation's ability to import plants was constrained by the availability of foreign exchange to buy them. Moreover, the import of plants on a turnkey basis is intrinsically self-limiting because only physical technology is imported. The intangible technologies of management and engineering techniques and supply chain management, which come from the more diversified investments of entrepreneurs, are lacking.

To gain access to these intangible technologies, direct investment by foreign firms was needed.

The same could have been said about postwar Japan, South Korea, and Taiwan, and yet they did not permit substantial FDI. In the 1970s South Korea even did the opposite: shutting down foreign-invested joint-venture automobile plants as part of an ultimately successful drive to build up domestic car champions. Why could not China have done the same? The best explanation is political. Japan, South Korea, and Taiwan were part of the United States' alliance structure in East Asia. They therefore benefited from immense programs of technical assistance, educational exchanges, and essentially unfettered access to America's gigantic market. This gave them the financial and intellectual resources to continuously upgrade their technological base, without the need to invite foreign firms in. China, on the other hand, lay outside the US alliance structure, although there was an alignment of convenience with the United States from the late 1970s until 1989, driven by a shared strategic desire to contain the Soviet Union. China would never enjoy the kind of privileges that its East Asian neighbors extracted from the United States. Moreover, after the collapse of the Communist bloc in 1989 and of the USSR itself in 1991, the logic of strategic alignment with the United States evaporated. To keep up the flow of technology, a more liberal FDI policy was required.

Another factor is simply timing and luck. Japan, South Korea, and Taiwan all began their industrial takeoff in the period 1950–1980, when production chains were essentially national, and international trade consisted either of raw commodities or of finished goods. After 1980, advances in transport and logistics technology made possible the internationalization of production chains. China, with its abundant low-cost labor force, proximity to the existing production chains of East Asia, and access to one of the world's greatest ports in Hong Kong, was thus perfectly placed in both time and space to become a major location for outsourced manufacturing. There is no evidence—and it is barely conceivable—that this outcome was the strategy of Chinese reformers in the 1980s. It was more in the nature of a lucrative opportunity that presented itself, and that policymakers decided to accept, along with all its various consequences.

The interlocking roles of industrial policy, exports, and FDI will be explored further in chapter 3. For now, two observations emerge from this discussion of China's emulation of its East Asian neighbors. First, China's development occurred within an entirely different geopolitical and security framework, and China's position as an isolated and independent geopolitical actor continues to exert a strong influence on its economic policies.

As members of the US alliance network, Japan, South Korea, and Taiwan benefited from US assistance and market access in ways not always available to China. They were also inevitably compelled to adopt democratic political systems that met the approval of their patron. Japan's political system was imposed by the American occupation in the aftermath of World War II.

In Taiwan, the move to representative democracy was a strategic choice made by leader Chiang Ching-kuo in the 1980s in response to the US decision to normalize relations with Beijing (and hence sever formal diplomatic ties with Taipei). Chiang believed that in order for Taiwan to retain its autonomy in a region increasingly influenced by a fast-growing China, it had no choice but to align itself as fully as possible with American political and ideological values.[19] Similarly, South Korea's military dictatorship was tolerated by Washington during the Cold War, but would not likely have outlasted the fall of the Berlin Wall by very long, even had it not crumbled in the face of embarrassing student-worker protests ahead of the 1988 Summer Olympics in Seoul. By contrast, China's position outside the US alliance structure means that it has no need to accept the liberal-democratic framework.

The other observation is that in many respects China's economic policies (like those of other countries) have been driven by the need to react to crises or opportunities of the moment; decisions were often taken with incomplete information and no sense of what the long-term consequences might be. So while we may rightly discern, after the fact, some kind of underlying logic or coherence in the trajectory of economic strategy and policy, it would be a serious mistake to believe that this coherence arises from the working out of a "grand plan" that was conceived ahead of time and executed consistently. When we talk of the economic "strategy" of Chinese leaders, from Deng Xiaoping right down to Xi Jinping, it is good to bear in mind their own description of the process as "crossing the river by feeling for the stones": an uncertain process of experimentation, guided to be sure by certain broad aims and principles, but without any preordained path.[20]

Who Runs Economic Policy?

Our discussion of China's economic strategy inevitably invites the question: Who are the strategists? We can address this from two angles: personalities and bureaucratic structures. As noted above, China is a bureaucratic-authoritarian state, and the role of institutions in shaping economic policy directions is large. But in China's political system, the personal authority of the leaders is usually even larger. So let us start with a brief review of the key economic decision-makers since the beginning of the reform era in 1979.

A popular view is that from December 1978, when Deng Xiaoping became China's paramount leader, until October 1992, when he retired from the Politburo, Deng was the sole architect of economic policy. This is not really true. Throughout his leadership, Deng had to contend with a powerful rival, Chen Yun, who had a large base of support among conservative officials and in the state planning system, which he had created in the 1950s and continued to oversee in the 1980s. Although Deng had overall management of national affairs, in economic matters he and Chen were of almost equal influence, and they were referred to as "two tigers on one mountaintop." Chen was an important counterweight to Deng, who often favored bold reforms without calculating their long-run impact. The development of economic reforms during the Deng years is best seen as a balancing act between the adventurous Deng and the look-before-you-leap Chen.

Deng also left most of the details of execution to lieutenants. The most important was Zhao Ziyang, who vaulted from a position as the reformist party secretary of Sichuan province (1975–1980) to that of prime minister (1980–1987) and finally to general secretary of the Communist Party (1987–1989), before being put under house arrest in the wake of the Tiananmen Square protests. Throughout his tenure, Zhao was an influential advocate of market-oriented reforms.

After Deng retired, leadership of the country fell into the hands of President Jiang Zemin. Continuing the precedent set by Deng, Jiang left the management of the economy mainly to his prime ministers: Li Peng (through 1997) and Zhu Rongji (1998–2003). The conservative Li Peng generally put political stability ahead of economic growth, but his influence gradually waned as it became clear that Zhu, his first vice premier, was a more innovative policymaker and a very tough politician. Zhu, who had been handpicked by Deng, was vice premier and head of the central bank from 1993 through 1997 and tamed the inflation that had frequently exceeded 20 percent in the preceding decade. In his one term as premier, he masterminded the reorganization and downsizing of the SOEs, recapitalization and reform of the banking system, privatization of the housing market, and China's long-delayed entry into the World Trade Organization. Zhu is widely considered the most effective economic leader in the history of the People's Republic.

The practice of leaving economic management mainly in the hands of the prime minister continued during the two terms of the next leadership team, President Hu Jintao and Premier Wen Jiabao (2003–2012). Although the economy experienced rapid growth during this period (an average of 10.5 percent a year, compared to 9.9 percent in the prior decade), Wen was widely criticized as a weak premier who failed to push through key economic reforms, tolerated bloat in the SOEs and rampant official corruption, and left the nation saddled with enormous debts after two rounds of economic stimulus following the 2008 global financial crisis. He did, however, oversee important agricultural reforms and the creation of a modern social welfare system.

Partly in response to this perception of weak leadership, the next president, Xi Jinping, made clear that he, not his premier Li Keqiang, would be the main architect of economic policy for the next ten years. The reform blueprint published after the Communist Party's November 2013 plenary meeting appears to have been written under Xi's close personal supervision. Xi has also appointed himself the head of most of the "leading small groups" that the party uses to coordinate top-level policy decisions, including the finance and economics group. Xi's highly centralized approach to economic policymaking is a departure from the usual practice over the prior three decades of the top leader delegating much of this authority to lower-level leaders. But it also comes in the context of a much more complex, developed, and powerful bureaucracy than existed in the early reform era. So we must now consider policymaking from an institutional perspective.

In other countries, we generally think of economic policy as moving from top-level strategies, devised by the president or prime minister and his or her key advisers, into implementation by key agencies such as the central bank, the Ministry of Finance, perhaps an economic or trade ministry, and sometimes an economic planning commission. In China the picture is more complicated, because several levels of bureaucracy exist between the top leaders and the specialized agencies. And because these extra levels lie mainly within the party structure, their activities are often cloaked in secrecy.

At the top of the pyramid of Chinese power sits the standing committee of the party's Politburo. (Figure 1.1 shows a diagram of China's leadership structure.) This group, which at present consists of seven members, is the nation's core leadership, and the most important decisions require consensus within this group—although of course the views of the top leader carry a lot of weight. The standing committee sits inside the broader, twenty-five-member Politburo, which meets several times a year and ratifies many major decisions. For instance, the mid-2014 plan to overhaul the nation's fiscal system (discussed in chapter 6) was announced by the Politburo—and not, as one might expect in other countries, by the premier or the minister of finance.

Next in line below the Politburo are the "leading small groups," which the party organizes to coordinate policy on major issues. Membership in these groups typically includes a range of officials holding government or party posts in a variety of agencies. They may also have a permanent office staff whose job is to manage the paper flow and distill the group's discussions into specific policy recommendations for the party leadership. There are at present eleven leading small groups, of which six are headed by Xi Jinping.

Lower still is the State Council, chaired by the premier, which is the highest organ of the government and roughly equates to the cabinet in other countries. But its structure is different: in addition to the heads of all the government ministries and agencies, it has several state councilors—senior officials who outrank ministers, some of whom carry the additional distinction of vice-premier rank. The full State Council meets just twice a year; most of the time its standing committee (the premier and the state councilors) act on their own, in consultation with the Politburo.

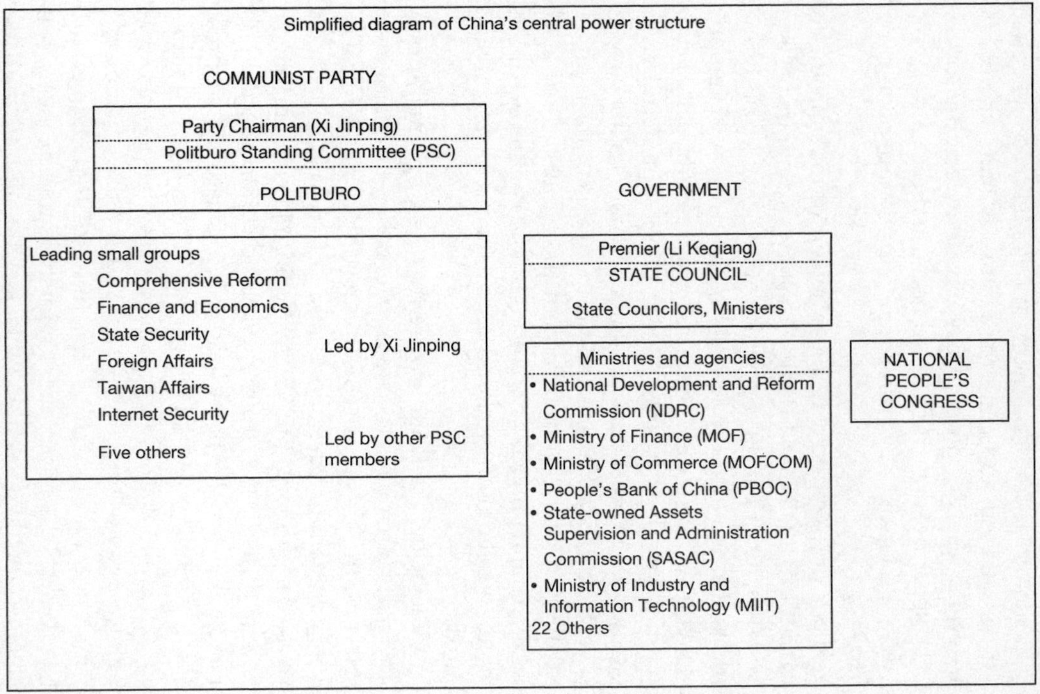

Simplified diagram of China's central power structure

COMMUNIST PARTY

Party Chairman (Xi Jinping)
Politburo Standing Committee (PSC)

POLITBURO

Leading small groups

Comprehensive Reform	Led by Xi Jinping
Finance and Economics	
State Security	
Foreign Affairs	
Taiwan Affairs	
Internet Security	
Five others	Led by other PSC members

GOVERNMENT

Premier (Li Keqiang)
STATE COUNCIL

State Councilors, Ministers

Ministries and agencies
- National Development and Reform Commission (NDRC)
- Ministry of Finance (MOF)
- Ministry of Commerce (MOFCOM)
- People's Bank of China (PBOC)
- State-owned Assets Supervision and Administration Commission (SASAC)
- Ministry of Industry and Information Technology (MIIT)

22 Others

NATIONAL PEOPLE'S CONGRESS

Figure 1.1 Organization Chart of Party and Government

Below the State Council are the ministry-level bodies, of which the most important for the economy are the National Development and Reform Commission (NDRC), a descendant of the old State Planning Commission; the Ministry of Finance (MOF); the Ministry of Commerce (MOFCOM, which also handles foreign trade issues); and the People's Bank of China (PBOC), the central bank. As this quick sketch suggests, a key difference between China and other countries is that officials like the finance minister or central bank governor are less powerful than elsewhere, because they are in fact relatively low-ranking. As in all systems, of course, politically savvy individuals can punch above the weight of their bureaucratic rank.

A final word of caution: this outline of the formal structures of power depicts a centralized system, with a lot of power concentrated at the top. This is formally true, but remember what we said earlier about China's decentralization. Top leaders in theory wield a lot of power, but in practice this power is constrained. Central government ministries often act as virtually autonomous fiefdoms (as do the biggest SOEs), and visitors from foreign governments often remark that the degree of insulation Chinese agencies enjoy from one another is unusually high. Moreover, for all the scope that a visionary leader may have to push his economic agenda, success or failure is often determined by the acts of China's provinces, whose leaders can also be important economic decision-makers.

What Influence Do China's Size and Population Have on Economic Development?

It is an obvious fact, but it bears repeating: China is the world's largest nation by population (1.4 billion) and its fourth largest by area, with a geographic size almost identical to that of the United States. Its size presents China with an unusual set of constraints and possibilities. These are summed up in a motto frequently cited by one of China's leading economists, Justin Lin, who attributes it to Premier Wen Jiabao: "When you multiply any problem by China's population, it is a very big problem. But when you *divide* it by China's population, it becomes very small." The point is simple, though easy to miss: China's size means that any challenge it faces—unemployment, environmental degradation, social unrest, you name it—exists on an almost unimaginably large scale. But it also means that the resources available to tackle the problem are gigantic. The difficulty lies in marshaling all those resources and deploying them effectively.

This observation illuminates a common feature of China's economy in both the Maoist and reform eras: the main goal throughout has been to *mobilize* resources. Maximizing the *efficiency* with which those resources are used has always been a secondary concern. This often distresses economists from rich countries, where virtually all economic growth and improvement in living standards comes from efficiency improvements. Visitors to China observe the waste and inefficiency visible everywhere, and often conclude that the economy will soon hit a crisis. These predictions have so far been wrong, not because observers are wrong about the degree of waste, but because they fail to realize that in a country of China's size, such waste can be irrelevant so long as it is a by-product of an effective process of meeting basic needs. To cite a simple example: in *each year* of the decade 2000–2010, China had to create over 20 million new jobs (nearly equivalent to the entire population of Australia), and build 8 million new urban housing units (six times the annual average housing completions in the United States during that period and four times the peak rate during the US housing bubble), just to meet the basic employment and shelter needs of its population. It is hardly surprising that during this scramble many fairly useless jobs were created and many housing units built that had to wait months or years for buyers.

This is not to argue that China's growth had to be wasteful and inefficient, or that this level of waste can go on forever. Other, more efficient (and probably slower) growth paths were certainly viable. The point is simply that China's enormous size gave its leaders the option of a high-speed growth model that emphasized quantity over quality. There is growing evidence that this phase of "extensive" growth is drawing to a close and that in order to maintain fast growth into the 2020s, China must shift to a growth model that emphasizes efficiency rather than scale. This transition will be difficult (see chapter 11).

A second implication of China's size is that it had much more latitude to conduct large-scale trials of policies before rolling them out nationwide. The country has thirty-one province-level jurisdictions,[21] of which the smallest (Tibet) has a population of 3 million and the largest (Guangdong) 104 million—about the same as Mexico. The average province has a population of around 45 million, roughly that of Spain. In many respects it is thus appropriate to think of China as a continent-sized assemblage of countries. The formal structure in which these provinces operate is a centralized polity run from Beijing, not a federal system like the United States or Germany. But in practice, provincial officials have a lot of leeway to run things as they see fit. Since the late 1970s, national leaders have consciously exploited the advantages of this local autonomy by either tolerating or explicitly authorizing policy experiments in particular cities or provinces. As a result, China has the luxury—unavailable to smaller countries—of testing out new ideas on a relatively large scale. Successes can be replicated elsewhere, but failures do not damage the national system. This makes a trial-and-error style of policy formulation more viable.

The flip side, of course, is that local leaders often feel free to pursue their own agendas, whether or not these conform to the national strategy. One high-profile example is the automobile industry. Since the early 1990s Beijing has had a policy of concentrating production in three big state-owned car makers, emulating the triumvirates that rule the US and Japanese car sectors. This policy has utterly failed, and one reason is that many cities have set up their own car makers in defiance of the central plan. The car market (since 2010 the world's biggest by volume) has grown fast enough to accommodate a plethora of low-end producers, and provinces used protectionist measures to promote sales of locally made cars and prevent "imports" of cars produced by other companies in other provinces. In this instance, Chinese consumers may have benefited from an increased number of low-cost options. But other consequences of local economic decision-making power—notably China's extraordinarily high rates of environmental damage—are distressing.

When Leaders Must Choose between Boosting Economic Growth and Maximizing Political Control, Which Do They Choose?

To answer this important question, let us first summarize our discussion of China's political-economy arrangements. China is a bureaucratic, authoritarian, one-party state that in principle is run by a centralized command structure in Beijing, but in practice is often highly decentralized—necessarily so because of the country's great size and population. The Communist Party's discipline and absolute control of the bureaucratic appointment system throughout the country prevent China from splintering apart and enable the formulation and implementation of coherent economic strategies. The basic economic strategy pursued since the late 1970s combines two approaches: the "East Asian developmental state" model of state-led industrial development; and a "transitional" model of gradual transformation of the original Communist centrally planned economy into a more market-oriented one. The Chinese Communist Party has learned from the failure of other Communist countries (notably the Soviet Union) that sustaining rapid, broad-based economic growth is essential to maintaining its grip on power.

So far so good. But this leads to an obvious question: What happens when the Communist Party's two main objectives—maximizing economic growth, and keeping itself in power—collide? If forced to choose between one or the other, which would the leaders pick?

This question lies at the heart of what one might call the liberal-democratic critique of the Chinese system. Analysts in rich democracies like the United States (and liberal analysts within China) observe that virtually all of the world's richest countries have democratic, or at least relatively open, political systems. They also observe that authoritarian regimes in general tend to put their own survival ahead of the economic welfare of their citizens. Regimes as diverse as the Soviet Union, Francisco Franco's Spain, and Hosni Mubarak's Egypt, not to mention more extreme examples like North Korea, all chose economic stagnation or worse rather than risk fostering the economic freedoms that might lead to demands for political ones. Meanwhile, authoritarian regimes that did put a premium on broad-based economic growth, such as Park Chung-hee's South Korea or Pinochet's Chile, tended to shift to democracy once the original strongman was out of the way. The conclusion is that China's leaders will eventually be forced to choose between opening up their political system, or keeping a grip on power and letting the economy wither.

Chinese leaders have rejected this choice, with success: in fact the present leadership under Xi Jinping has combined an ambitious economic reform program with a campaign to tighten the party's political control. The reason is that they see economic growth and political power as complementary, not contradictory. The uncontested power of the party makes possible vigorous economic development policies that would be hard to sustain in a more open system; in turn, economic success is the main source of the party's legitimacy. Moreover, party leaders have long recognized that in the international arena, national power is a direct result of economic might.

But of course many individual economic reforms require the state to give up some power. Streamlining the SOEs means a big reduction in the state's ownership of assets. Financial liberalization means cutting the government's ability to direct capital to its favored projects. The enduring dilemma of party-driven economic policy is *how much* and *what kind* of power are Chinese leaders willing to sacrifice, in exchange for *how much* and *what kind* of economic growth? There is no one-size-fits-all answer. On several occasions, the leaders have accepted some erosion of state power in order to keep the economy humming. This willingness was visible in the original reform decisions in the late 1970s and early 1980s, as well as in the reforms of the 1990s and early 2000s that involved eliminating most state-controlled prices, opening up to foreign investment, and privatizing many SOEs. The one instance when economic growth was sacrificed for political control was in the crisis of 1989, and as we have seen, once political control was reestablished the focus quickly returned to economic reform.

An important question today is whether Xi Jinping is willing to trade some reduction of state control for greater economic efficiency, or if he is simply trying to solidify the party's authority at all costs. His initial two years focused mainly on measures to tighten political control, including an anticorruption drive, in part designed to break up rival political networks, and campaigns to firm the party's grip on the media and civil society. He also launched significant economic reforms, most scheduled for completion around 2020. But progress on most reforms has been slow, and critics argue that even if they are completed they will do little to reduce state power and boost economic dynamism. The balancing act between economic vitality and political control is a tricky one. In the first 35 years of the reform era, China's leaders did an impressive job of maintaining this balance. How much longer they can keep it up is uncertain, and there is growing concern that Xi has tipped the scales in favor of political control, at the expense of economic growth.

2

AGRICULTURE, LAND, AND
THE RURAL ECONOMY

Why Did the End of Agricultural Communes Jump-Start China's Growth in the 1980s?

It may seem odd to begin our discussion of a great industrial economy with agriculture. In China today, agriculture accounts for only 9 percent of gross domestic product (GDP), while industry and services each comprise more than 40 percent. But nearly half the population still lives in rural areas, and more than a third of the national workforce—about 300 million people—till the fields. Because of the large number of people still engaged in farming, considerations of rural welfare, and the balance between rural and urban interests, remain important constraints on development policies.

Moreover, from a historical perspective, it makes sense to start with agriculture because economic reforms began with the privatization of farming in the late 1970s. This was no accident. Agriculture was then the biggest sector of the economy, accounting for 37 percent of GDP and nearly three-quarters of all employment; it was natural for reforms to kick off there.[1] And as we saw in our discussion of the East Asian development model, getting agriculture right has proved to be the essential first step for successful industrialization.

On the eve of the reform era, in 1978, China's countryside was overpopulated and impoverished thanks to two decades of bad policy. Beginning in the mid-1950s, private ownership of farmland was abolished and agriculture was organized under communes, which in turn were divided into smaller collective units called "brigades" and "work teams." These communes were instructed to produce as much grain as possible, with little scope permitted for vegetables and other cash crops, and the state procured this grain at low prices designed to minimize the cost of staple foods for people living in cities. Stringent internal passport controls adopted at the same time made migration from the countryside to the city virtually impossible, except for soldiers who were recruited from the countryside and later demobilized to cities.

The consequences of these policies were uniformly bad. Rural income growth was glacial: only 1 percent a year in real terms from 1957 to 1978. Per capita production of grain, at about 300 kilograms, was no higher in 1978 than it was in 1955, and output of oil seeds (an essential product since virtually all cooking in China involves frying in oil) fell by about a third during that period. And because of restrictions on mobility, the rural share of the national population, at 82 percent, was actually higher in 1978 than it had been in 1958.[2]

Between 1978 and 1983, the entire basis of the agricultural economy was changed by the adoption of the "household responsibility system." The origins of this shift lay in a village in Anhui province, where a group of farmers got together in secret and signed an agreement to dissolve their collective and divide up their farmland into individual plots. This innovation rapidly spread, and the province's party secretary, Wan Li, realized he was facing a powerful popular revolt against an immiserating system. Rather than crush it, he decided to promote this land-to-the-tiller reform. The party secretary of Sichuan province, Zhao Ziyang, made a similar decision.

At the national level, the December 1978 party plenum that launched the reform era raised agricultural prices and gave a blessing to rural collectives experimenting with different ways of management, but it still condemned private farming. By 1980, however, Zhao Ziyang had become premier and Wan Li was vice premier in charge of agriculture policy. Together they rammed through a national policy to disband the communes and return to family farming. By the end of 1982 virtually all agricultural collectives were gone, and family farmers had been assigned rights to cultivate individual plots of land.

The effect on agricultural output and farm incomes was spectacular. By 1984 grain output was over 400 million tons, a third higher than it had been just six years before; production of oilseeds and cotton sustained annual growth rates of 15 percent; and meat production was growing by 10 percent a year. Rural per capita income more than doubled between 1979 and 1984. Per capita cash savings by rural families rose from essentially zero in 1979 to 300 renminbi (Rmb) by 1989. Rapid gains in agricultural output and incomes continued throughout the 1980s, as farmers continued to diversify their crops and apply new technologies that increased yields. Use of chemical fertilizer, which had risen gradually in the 1970s, tripled between 1978 and 1990. So did the use of farm machinery, notably pumps, small tractors, and food processing equipment.[3]

Agricultural reform had benefits that went well beyond the improvement in farm yields and income. Because of their higher incomes and greater incentives for investment, farmers became important sources of demand for basic industrial sectors such as fertilizer and farm equipment. As their cash incomes rose, their bank savings also grew, and these funds were available for lending to nascent manufacturing enterprises. And as farmers were able to determine for themselves the value of their labor, increasing numbers began to seek off-farm wage labor to supplement their incomes. This combination of factors helped set off China's first wave of entrepreneurial industry, the township and village enterprises.

What Role Did Township and Village Enterprises Play in China's Economic Development in the 1980s and Early 1990s?

Township and village enterprises (TVEs) are business enterprises formally owned, or informally sponsored, by local "collectives," that is, by township and village governments. They are not considered state-owned enterprises (SOEs); SOEs are owned by central, provincial, and city governments. The state's ownership rights were exercised, until the 1990s, through influence over investment budgets and, since 2003, via a set of formal shareholding agencies (see chapter 5 for details). The TVEs are free of these constraints, and in fact their shareholders may be either local governments or private individuals.

The TVEs took off in the 1980s for two reasons. First, as we noted above, there was rising demand from newly well-off farm households for a wide range of goods, and a growing supply of willing workers for factories producing these goods. Second, TVEs offered a convenient structure for combining entrepreneurial energy with government patronage, which was essential to ensure access to capital.

Small-scale enterprises in China were thus spared the common fate of such firms in other post-Communist "transition" economies, where lack of access to capital was a severe constraint on growth.[4]

By 1985, employment in collectively owned TVEs had hit 40 million, and employment in all forms of rural enterprises was about 70 million. A decade later, rural enterprises employed 18 percent of the national labor force and produced one-quarter of GDP. (Collective TVEs accounted for about half these figures.) This represented the peak of the collectively owned TVE model. Over the next several years TVEs faced intense competition from more efficient, reformed SOEs and from private enterprises in urban areas. By 2004 the large majority of collectively owned TVEs had been privatized, mainly through buyouts by firm managers. Although statistics continue to refer to TVEs, most of these are better considered to be private firms that are simply based in rural or semirural areas.[5]

The TVEs played several important roles in industrial development in the early years of the reform era. They laid the foundations for the extensive production of consumer goods, since they rapidly expanded beyond producing goods for farm households into a broader range of consumer products, including fans, bicycles, kitchen appliances, and so on. The TVEs also created space for what was effectively private enterprise in a transitional period when private firms were formally discouraged. And they provided the first large-scale mechanism for the transfer of excess agricultural labor into the modern industrial economy. They declined in relative importance after the mid-1990s because urban private-sector firms were finally large enough, and enjoyed enough regulatory support, to take over these roles.

Why Did Rural-Urban Inequality Grow after 1989?

The reforms of the 1980s started in the countryside, and they disproportionately benefited the rural population. Prices for agricultural products rose quickly, as did opportunities for off-farm wage employment in TVEs; in consequence, rural incomes grew faster than urban ones. This was a welcome corrective to the prior decades of urban bias, but it did not last. Among the varied reasons for the shift from rural-focused reforms of the 1980s to urban-focused reforms of the 1990s, the political disturbances of 1989 were a crucial hinge.

The demonstrations in Beijing's Tiananmen Square and in other Chinese cities in the spring of 1989 had several causes. A background condition was that the 1980s were a period of great intellectual ferment, during which discussion of alternative political systems was widespread and to a surprising degree tolerated by the government. (The central government even had its own office for studying political reform.) For the first time since the 1949 revolution, Chinese students and scholars began to travel abroad in large numbers, and they were attracted by the much higher living standards and greater political openness that they found not only in the United States and Europe but also closer to home in places like Japan and Hong Kong.

Against this backdrop, a number of specific grievances caused discontent. The rapid rise in food prices translated into inflation that routinely hit double digits; in late 1988 and early 1989 it was running at 20 to 30 percent. Although urban incomes were also rising fast and the urban standard of living had improved noticeably since 1980, many urban households felt that rising prices made their gains precarious. Students coming out of urban high schools and universities faced poor employment prospects, as the SOEs struggled to create enough jobs and private companies labored under heavy regulatory restrictions. The most common form of private firm was the *getihu* or household enterprise, which by law could have no more than seven employees. And there was widespread anger over corruption by government officials, in particular the practice of buying up goods at low state-plan prices and reselling them for a big profit on free markets. All these resentments boiled over into the demonstrations, which the government finally crushed on June 4, 1989 as the army dispersed protesters, killing thousands of them.

As reformers in the Communist Party and government regrouped over the next few years, they coalesced around a strategy that shifted the center of reform energy back into the urban arena. Unlike in 1978–1980, when the party made a series of explicit and conscious decisions to favor rural areas by raising farm prices and permitting private farming, this was not an overt or advertised move to raise urban incomes relative to rural ones. But there can be little doubt that party leaders drew from 1989 the lesson that the greatest threat to the regime's hold on power came from the cities. So it was necessary to concentrate on reforms that would raise living standards there. The background of key personnel also shaped this decision.

Major reformers of the 1980s, notably Wan Li and Zhao Ziyang (who was premier from 1980 to 1987 and then party general secretary in 1987–1989 before being deposed as a result of the Tiananmen disturbance), had cut their teeth in the provinces, addressing rural problems. The central figures of the 1990s, President Jiang Zemin and Zhu Rongji (who was vice premier and financial czar from 1993 to 1997 and then premier until 2003) were both former leaders of Shanghai and had mainly dealt with urban issues.

Throughout the 1990s reforms in the cities accelerated, while the countryside entered a period of relative stagnation. The government restructured SOEs and the financial system and promoted private enterprise. Restrictions on labor mobility were relaxed so that it was easier for workers to move to the cities for wage labor; but their families were prohibited from moving, and the burden of providing social services for these migrant families remained in the countryside. Prices for manufactured goods (produced mainly in cities) were liberalized; government procurement prices for grain and some other agricultural goods remained capped. At the same time provinces were ordered to maximize production of grain, at the expense of cash crops that farmers could sell at higher prices on free markets. Most consequentially, beginning in 1998 the urban housing stock controlled by SOEs was privatized, ultimately delivering gigantic windfall gains to the urban households who bought housing at well below its market value. By 2003 urban households had won unrestricted rights to own, buy, sell, and mortgage real property. To this day rural families enjoy no such property rights (see chapter 4 for a discussion of housing privatization.) Taken together, these policies created a widening chasm of inequality between rural and urban households. The average urban income rose from 2.2 times the average rural level in 1990 to 3.2 times in 2003.[6]

How Did the Government Address the Rural-Urban Inequality Problem in the 2000s?

The administration of Hu Jintao and Wen Jiabao, which took power in late 2002, sought to correct the urban bias in policy and boost rural incomes. It launched a broad range of policies to address the problems of the *sannong* (*nongye, nongcun, nongmin*: agriculture, villages, and famers). Grain procurement prices were hiked, and taxes on agricultural produce were abolished in 2006. The government promoted large investments in rural roads and infrastructure as well as in food-processing plants that could provide off-farm employment. Beginning in 2006, it began to rebuild rural social service networks, which had disintegrated in the previous two decades of reform. The nine years of compulsory education were made free for rural residents in 2006. In 2007, a new rural cooperative medical system was launched, providing basic health insurance, and the minimum income guarantee was expanded from urban to rural areas. In 2009 a rural pension scheme guaranteed farmers, for the first time in Chinese history, a cash income after they were too old to do farm labor.

These policies had a large and beneficial impact on both rural incomes and agricultural production. The ratio of the average urban income to the average rural income stabilized at 3.3 times in 2007 and then began to fall (see Figure 2.1). By 2013, virtually all rural residents had some kind of health insurance, up from 13 percent in 2000, and about 240 million people, or nearly 40 percent of the rural population, were covered by pensions.[7] Total grain output, which fell from over 500 million tons in 1999 to just 430 million tons in 2003, steadily climbed, and in 2013 it exceeded 600 million tons for the first time. Real growth in agricultural value added, which grew at less than 3 percent a year in 1997–2003, accelerated to nearly 5 percent a year in the subsequent decade.

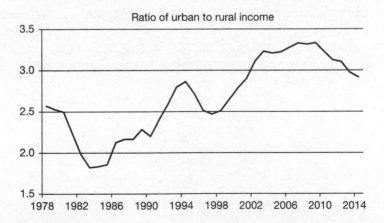

Figure 2.1 Urban vs Rural Incomes

Note: Urban per capita disposable income vs rural net income

Source: NBS/CEIC.

This improvement in agricultural fortunes prompts a few observations. First, it qualifies the common judgment that Hu Jintao and Wen Jiabao were weak and feckless leaders under whom reform stagnated and China suffered a "wasted decade." These criticisms typically come from urban elites, who tend to ignore rural issues. The reversal of the decline in agricultural production, and the establishment of a comprehensive (albeit basic) social safety net in both urban and rural areas, were both major achievements.

Second, it is clear that agricultural and rural reforms have played an important role in the impressive reduction in absolute poverty China has achieved over the last three decades. Between 1981 and 2011, the number of people in China living in what the World Bank defines as absolute poverty sank from 840 million to 84 million— from 84 percent of the population to 6 percent (see Table 2.1). Some of this decline came from moving people into higher-wage occupations in the city, but given that about half the population still lives in the countryside, improving rural livelihoods was also crucial.[8]

Finally, the history of the reform era shows that it is quite difficult, and perhaps impossible, for policy to maintain a balance between serving urban and rural interests. The first decade of reform delivered disproportionate gains to the countryside; the reforms of 1989–2003 skewed heavily in favor of the cities. The Hu/ Wen decade was more balanced, but the renewed emphasis on rural concerns prompted pushback from urban lobby groups, who have succeeded in framing China's development challenge over the next two decades as one of urbanization. Yet even under the most optimistic urbanization scenario, China twenty years from now will

Table 2.1 China's Progress in Poverty Reduction: Number and Percent of People Living on $1.25 a Day or Less (2005 dollars at PPP)

Year	Millions	% of total
1981	840	84
1990	689	61
2002	359	28
2011	84	6
30-year reduction	−756	−78 pp

Source: World Bank Poverty and Equity Databank.

still have 400 million people, or nearly 30 percent of its population, living in the countryside. Tension between urban and rural interests will continue to be a headache for Chinese policymakers for many years to come.

Do Chinese Farmers Own Their Land?

Chinese farmers do not own their land, but they do generally have long-term contractual rights to use it. The issue of rural land tenure is one of China's most intractable policy problems, and the chasm between rural and urban property rights is one of the most important sources of inequality in wealth and income.

When farms were first decollectivized in 1978–1983, farm households typically got the right to farm a specified plot of land for one to three years. By the mid 1980s, household farm assignments were generally extended to fifteen years. But these rights were insecure. The land was still owned by "the collective" (that is, by the village as a whole), and it was common for the village authorities to reassign plots of land within the contract period. Sometimes reassignments were made for good reasons, such as changes in family size. But the power of reassignment also meant that if you got on the wrong side of the village party secretary, you could suddenly find yourself farming a new and inferior plot. This uncertainty over how long they would have the right to farm a particular piece of land meant that farmers were reluctant to make large capital investments.

The government has devoted significant energy to lengthening and strengthening farmers' land use rights. The standard contract term for agricultural land was extended to thirty years in 1993, and this term was written into the Land Management Law of 1998. The Rural Land Contracting Law of 2004 specified that use rights had to be set down in a formal contract and that the village authorities could not arbitrarily reassign land before the end of the contract period. Reassignments are permitted with a two-thirds vote of the village assembly. The 2007 Property Law established that farmers' land use rights are private property rights.

These laws have been implemented with varying degrees of rigor. According to a 2010 survey by the land-use rights organization Landesa, a bit over 60 percent of farm families have land-rights certificates, and about half have formal contracts. These improvements in the security of ownership have increased the incentives for farmers to make costly, productivity-enhancing investments, such as putting in permanent greenhouses or more advanced irrigation systems. They have also made it possible for agribusinesses to take out long-term subleases on groups of neighboring plots and begin to develop large-scale mechanized agriculture.[9]

Yet even as the government was bolstering farmers' land rights, it was also working hard to ensure that the monetary value of those rights stayed as low as possible. For one thing, it continued to insist that ownership of the land itself resided in the collective, which meant that individual farmers had no right to sell or mortgage their land. For another, it tolerated the practice of city governments acquiring large swaths of nearby rural land for a modest sum, then reselling it to property developers for a large markup. This meant that virtually all the profit from converting low-value agricultural land to high-value urban land went not to rural families, but to city governments and urban property developers (who also reaped huge gains from the housing and offices they built). The sums involved were staggering. The World Bank estimated that in 1990–2010, local governments expropriated land from farmers for a total of Rmb 2 trillion less than its market value (US$320 billion at the present exchange rate). If farmers had received the full market value of their land, and enjoyed normal investment returns, they would now have an additional Rmb 5 trillion (US$800 billion, or 8 percent of GDP) in household wealth.[10]

One motive for this "cheap land" policy was of course to enable the growth of cities, since by the early 2000s the government had come round to the idea that the way to maximize economic growth was to move as many people as possible as quickly as possible off the farm and into higher-productivity urban jobs. Another, somewhat contradictory concern was that if farmers were free to sell their land, they might be cheated by sharp-eyed speculators. In other words, it was perfectly fine for farmers to be cheated out of the fair value of their land by government buyers, but not by private buyers.

To appreciate the full impact of this policy on wealth and income distribution, one must understand the great discrepancy between rural and urban rights to real property. Urban land is all owned by the state, in the same way that rural land is owned by collectives. When an urban family buys a house, it is really buying a long-term leasehold, typically for seventy years.[11] Other than the length of the term, this may not sound much different from a farmer with a thirty-year use right on his farmland. But in practice the difference is enormous. The farmer has no right to sell his land to someone willing to pay a high price in order to convert it to a more valuable use. All he can do is sublease his cultivation rights. An urban homeowner can sell his property to anyone, for whatever price the market will bear. As more and more people move into the cities, the value of a given piece of urban real estate almost invariably rises, and the urban homeowner is perfectly free to realize that increased value. Since China has no capital gains tax, all the profits from the sale of a house go straight into his pocket. A farmer can own the rights to only one piece of land for personal cultivation; an urban resident can buy as many houses as he can afford, generating rental income or using the property as security for a mortgage to finance a small business.

Finally, as we will explain in chapter 4, millions of urban households were allowed to buy formerly state-owned housing units, at far below their market value, during a 1998–2003 housing privatization program. They were later allowed to resell these houses at market prices. The aggregate value of the capital gain they were allowed to harvest was about Rmb 4.5 trillion—more than twice as much as the already large amount farmers lost due to local government expropriation in 1990–2010. In sum, the property rights of rural and urban residents followed exactly opposite paths: farmers have been forced to *sell* their land for far less than it is worth; while city dwellers (some of them anyway) were allowed to *buy* property for less than it was worth and pocket all the resulting gains. This inequity in property rights may be the single biggest cause of the huge wealth and income inequality between urban and rural areas.

What Is Being Done to Improve Rural Land Rights?

The injustices imposed by the rural land tenure system have long been recognized by Chinese scholars, and the government has begun to undertake reforms to correct them. These efforts have been aided by the belated recognition that the helter-skelter urbanization of the last decade needs to be replaced with a more orderly process, and that city governments must learn to finance themselves in more sustainable ways than by buying up farmland cheap and selling it dear.

Reforms of rural land tenure are subject to two major constraints. One is that the collective ownership of rural land remains sacrosanct. This principle was explicitly reaffirmed by the Third Plenum reform decision document in 2013 and by subsequent rural policy statements. This means that the simplest and best solution to the rural land problem—giving farmers the same kind of strong private property rights that urban homeowners enjoy, and that farmers in most of the rest of East Asia have had for decades—is off the table.

The second constraint is the "red line" on arable land: a policy in place since 2006, which states that the total amount of cultivated land in the country may not fall below 120 million hectares. The rapid conversion of rural land to urban use over the past two decades means that arable land is only just above this red line. In practice this means that any future increase in urban land area must be offset by conversion of wasteland or rural construction land back into land for cultivation.[12] This "red line" is in turn a function of national food-security policy, which we discuss below.

Within these strictures, the central government is pursuing several reforms to create a healthier rural land economy. These reforms fall into three baskets: stronger land rights for farmers, promotion of mechanized large-scale agriculture, and "townization" of rural areas.[13]

Improved land use rights. The Third Plenum decision and subsequent policy documents stress the need to improve the registration of rural land and to strengthen farmers' right to buy, sell, and mortgage use rights for agricultural land on the open market. A key issue here is registration: property rights over land cannot be effective unless the boundaries of land plots are surveyed and the boundaries and property owners set down in a public registry. Slightly more than half of China's rural land is registered. Completing registration for all rural land is likely to take at least another decade and is complicated by the fact that many family holdings are fragmented among several noncontiguous plots. Another thorny issue is ensuring that women's property rights are protected. About 90 percent of registered rural land is in the name of the male head of household, leaving most rural women at risk of destitution if they divorce.[14]

Large-scale agriculture. For most of the reform era, the government resisted efforts to create large-scale, mechanized farms. The chief reason was that the family farm was considered to be the main rural social-safety net. If a family fell on hard times, or a migrant family member was laid off from a city job and unable to find work, one could always fall back on the family farm for shelter and basic sustenance. With the increase in permanent migration to the cities, and the rollout of rural pension, healthcare, and minimum-income programs, this rationale has weakened. The Ministry of Agriculture now advocates a move to larger-scale farms, and this is one factor behind the desire to make rural land more marketable. Larger-scale farms can be created by agribusinesses buying up the use rights to many plots of land from individual farmers and consolidating them into a single operation; and this is occurring in some places. But it is likely the government will prefer the development of cooperatives, under which farmers pool their land, put it all in a joint-stock company, and issue shares to each farmer based on the value of the land he put in. Farmers could then decide to stay inside the cooperative and maintain an agricultural lifestyle, or sell their shares and move on to something else.

Townization. This refers to the practice of consolidating scattered villages into more concentrated rural towns. Villagers are moved from their original settlements into new, higher-density towns; the original village is demolished and the land returned to cultivation. This results in a net increase in cultivated land, since the new town occupies less land than the villages it replaces. Farmers retain the use rights to their agricultural land and can continue to farm it if they like; but the assumption is that a majority will prefer to transfer the use rights to their land and start working in urban jobs. This policy is an effort to continue the gradual urbanization of the rural populace, but in a way that maintains or increases the supply of farmland.

Can China Feed Itself?

A final question about the rural economy is whether China can feed itself, or if it even needs to. This question is of great importance not only to China but also to the rest of the world, because if China starts to import food on a large scale to feed its population of 1.4 billion people, the impact on global prices could be great. From time to time one reads scare stories about how China's ravenous appetite for imported food will lead to ruinous worldwide food price inflation, or intolerable pressure on the world's scarce supply of arable land.[15] Chinese policymakers also worry about this question because they see the need to import food as a national security risk, and also because they recognize that the sudden entry of huge Chinese demand into global food markets could lead to costly price rises.

The first thing to observe about these concerns over China's impending food crisis is that they have been frequently expressed for the past twenty years, and so far have always proved wrong. The pessimists have consistently underestimated China's ability to raise production of key agricultural products and livestock. Today China produces 50 percent more grain, three times as much oilseed, and six times as much meat as it did in 1980 (see Figure 2.2). China already enjoys fairly high yields of most crops: its per-acre output of rice and wheat is among the highest in the world. But the

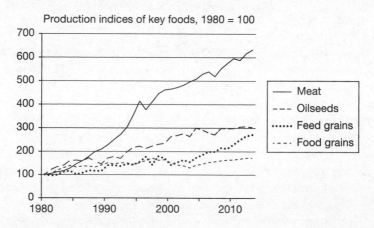

Figure 2.2 Food Production Indices
Source: US Department of Agriculture.

scope for increase—through increased mechanization, improved land management techniques, and higher-yielding varieties—is in some cases still considerable. The biggest opportunity lies with corn (important mainly as feed for livestock), for which China's average yield of six tons per acre is well above the figures for Brazil, India, and Southeast Asia, but below the eight to nine tons achieved in North America.

On the demand side, China's total food consumption may grow, but probably not by much. The average Chinese today consumes nearly 3,000 calories a day, an ample diet. South Korean consumption leveled off at about this level in the early 1990s. In Japan, average daily calorie intake has actually fallen over the past twenty years, as the population aged. Given that China's population will replicate Japan's aging experience over the next twenty-five to thirty years, a large further increase in calorie consumption is unlikely.

Of course the composition of diet matters too: as societies grow richer, they consume more meat, and this indirectly pushes up demand for grain, because the creation of a pound of meat requires many pounds of feed-grain. Yet China's consumption of the preferred meat, pork, is already quite high at around eighty pounds per person per year; this is about 30 percent higher than the figure for South Korea and only slightly below the ninety pounds at which Taiwanese consumption topped out in the 1990s.[16]

China is thus not likely to cause a worldwide food Armageddon. It is probable, however, that growth in demand will outstrip growth in domestic supply, leading to an increase of imports. This poses a challenge for the government, which for national security reasons has long maintained a policy of 95 percent self-sufficiency in grain. This policy has been relaxed somewhat in recent years. China still supplies more than 95 percent of its need for cereals (principally rice, wheat, and corn). But its self-sufficiency ratio on its broader definition of grain—which includes beans and potatoes—has fallen below 90 percent, mainly because of a huge increase in imports of soybeans since the late 1990s. It is likely that within a decade China's grain self-sufficiency will fall below 85 percent, with greater imports of both soybeans and corn thanks to higher demand for animal feed. Soybean and corn producers in the Americas and Eastern

Europe will probably be able to supply this demand. China is also actively encouraging its agricultural firms to invest in farmland in Africa and South America, both to increase the total global supply of agricultural land and to ensure that China has secure sources of supply as its import needs grow.[17]

3

INDUSTRY AND THE RISE OF THE EXPORT ECONOMY

Why Did China Become Such a Big Manufacturer and Exporter?

China's emergence as a great industrial and exporting power is one of the truly world-changing economic events of the last two decades. In the late 1970s China accounted for little of the world's industrial production and less than 1 percent of its trade. By the end of 2014 it was the world's leading manufacturing nation, and its biggest exporter, accounting for 12 percent of global exports and 18 percent of manufactured exports (see Figure 3.1).[1] It is now the hub for a global production network that begins with design studios in the United States and Europe; proceeds through producers of specialized components and raw materials in East and Southeast Asia; and ends up in China, where designs, materials, and components are brought together in finished products that are then sent all around the world. How did this transformation occur? Historical advantages, lucky circumstances and good policies all played a role.

Taking a very long view, one might argue that China is simply returning to the central position in manufacturing and trade that it enjoyed for perhaps a thousand years before the Industrial Revolution. Economic historians have shown that, as late as 1800, China accounted for about one-third of world GDP, had market-based systems of domestic manufacturing and trade at least as sophisticated as those in Europe, and dominated global trade in pre-modern manufactures such as silk textiles and ceramics.[2] China's enormous trade surplus resulted in a drain of silver currency from Europe; it ultimately led to the Opium War of 1840–1842, which established that China's traditional strengths were no match for the

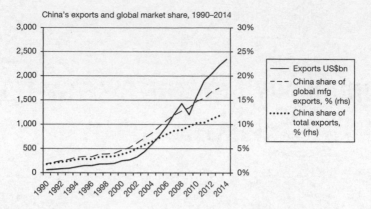

Figure 3.1 Exports

Source: NBS, WTO for global share.

new technologies spawned by the Industrial Revolution in Europe.[3] Over the next century, Europe and North America fully industrialized, but China failed to do so. Once it started to industrialize and adopted an open trading system in the early 1980s, the advantages that led to its pre-nineteenth-century eminence—a large, relatively well-educated population and well-established traditions of manufacturing and commerce—kicked in once more.

These "deep" historical advantages are real. But they would not have done China much good without more specific and immediate factors. As a comparison, until the eighteenth century India's economy was almost as large as China's, and it dominated global trade in cotton textiles.[4] Like China, it has a large population and centuries of commercial and manufacturing tradition. Yet since the 1980s its industrial and trade development has lagged; in 2013 its exports were only about one-seventh of China's, and it runs a persistent trade deficit of over $100 billion a year. Clearly some other things have gone right for China in the last thirty years. This is where lucky circumstances and good policy come in.

The lucky circumstances include:

- **Good neighbors:** The successful export-driven development of Taiwan, South Korea, and especially Japan gave Chinese policymakers an easy-to-follow template for industrial development.

- **Hong Kong:** When China started its reforms, Hong Kong was already a world-class port and trading hub with modern legal and financial systems. This gave Chinese manufacturers quick access not only to global trade routes but also to much of the "soft" infrastructure needed for a modern economy.[5]
- **Timing:** China was fortunate to open up to trade just at the moment when the shipping container, invented in the 1950s, was beginning to make possible the creation of global production chains, spanning multiple countries, through steep reductions in long-distance shipping costs.
- **A "killer app":** By the late 1980s, culturally similar Taiwan had established a sophisticated electronics industry, which moved en masse to China in the late 1990s, creating a world-class electronics manufacturing base almost overnight.

Whether consciously or not, Chinese policymakers recognized these opportunities and exploited them to the utmost. Two policy orientations stand out. The first is embedded in the slogan Deng Xiaoping and his colleagues invented to describe their economic program: *gaige kaifang*, or "reform and opening." Deng recognized that reforming the domestic economy would be quite difficult without an ever-greater openness to trade and investment. So time and again he and his successors adopted policies that maximized opportunities for exporters, from the opening up of special economic zones (SEZs) in the early 1980s to joining the WTO in 2001.

The second was the strong emphasis on building infrastructure, especially ports, roads, power plants, and telecommunications networks, which made life easier for manufacturers up and down China's long coastline. The result was that, by the early 2000s, China had a unique and probably unrepeatable combination of low, developing-country labor costs and good, almost-rich-country infrastructure. This created an irresistible platform for export-oriented manufacturers. A further infrastructure drive in China's interior in the 2000s helped knit together the internal market, bringing closer to reality the old but elusive dream of "a billion Chinese customers." (Details of infrastructure development can be found in chapter 4.)

The confluence of historical advantages, good luck, and good policy produced an unusually powerful economy. Yet as we go through the steps by which China built up its industrial and trading might, it is also worth bearing in mind some of the limitations of the Chinese model. One is that the heavy reliance on direct investment by foreign multinationals meant that certain sectors, and the majority of export production, wound up captured by foreign firms. Another is that low labor costs, good infrastructure, and a large market of price-conscious domestic consumers led to a business model described below as "80 percent of the quality at 60 percent of the price." This is a perfectly viable business model, but it does mean that Chinese firms are at a disadvantage in trying to move up into the highest-value niches and in developing first-class innovative capacity.

What Has Been China's Strategy for Developing Its Industry?

As we outlined in chapter 1, China's industrial development since 1978 can be considered the result of two long-term processes: the *transition* away from a Communist command economy to a more market-driven system; and the gradual adoption of an *East Asian developmental strategy*, similar to those of Japan, South Korea, and Taiwan. The first process involved a steady reallocation of resources away from the state and toward the private sector. The second involved a continuous refinement of a large state role in economic management via policies aimed at maximizing exports: "industrial policies" to promote particular sectors, and strong centralized control of the financial system. We cannot view China's industrialization as the result *simply* of pro-market reform policies, or *simply* of an effective top-down developmental strategy. It was both.

This industrialization process also had a uniquely Chinese characteristic, not shared to the same degree by other East Asian developmental states or post-Communist transition economies: an unusually heavy reliance on foreign investment. This reliance was strong up to about 2006; since then the government has shifted to policies that aim to reduce dependence on foreign investment and build up the capacities of domestic firms. It is worth exploring in detail the ways in which industrial policy has evolved since the beginning of the reform era.

What Was Deng Xiaoping's Industrial Policy?

When Deng Xiaoping took power at the end of 1978, he inherited an industrial economy that, thanks to decades of Maoist central planning, had two core problems. First, it was overly reliant on capital-intensive heavy industry, while production of consumer goods was minimal and supplies of basic goods like clothing, bicycles, and electric fans were rationed. This went against China's basic factor endowments: as a poor country, it had relatively little capital, but plenty of cheap labor. It would therefore be more logical for the economy to be structured around labor-intensive light manufacturing. Second, virtually all industry was in the hands of SOEs, who had few incentives to improve their efficiency.

After much trial and error, and with no very clear plan or strategy, economic policymakers devised an approach with the following elements:

- A shift from capital-intensive heavy industry to labor-intensive light industry.
- A focus on light industrial exports to generate the foreign exchange needed to import capital equipment.
- The establishment of special economic zones (SEZs), allowing foreign companies to set up factories on preferential terms.
- Price reforms, to reduce the power of central planners and increase the role of the market.
- Increased tolerance for private enterprises.

The first two policies represented an embrace of the East Asian development model, with its emphasis on labor-intensive exports of consumer goods as the first step on the ladder to long-term economic growth. The last two (price reform and more private enterprise) were the tasks required for a successful "transition" from a Communist to a more capitalist economy. The one in the middle (SEZs) was borrowed from another reformist Communist country, Yugoslavia, but eventually morphed into a uniquely Chinese invention, the foreign direct investment (FDI)-driven growth model.

Implementation of these reforms was chaotic, and proceeded in fits and starts, thanks to constant battles between reformers led by Deng Xiaoping and conservative officials led by Chen Yun. But over a decade, the results were impressive. Between 1978 and 1990, the share of consumer goods whose prices were set by the market went from zero to 70 percent; overall industrial output rose sixfold; the SOE share of industrial production fell from 78 percent to 54 percent; and annual exports sextupled, from about US$10 billion to US$62 billion. In the first decade of reforms (1979–1988), the economy grew at an average annual rate of 10 percent a year, about the same as Japan during its "miracle" industrial takeoff period in the 1950s.[6]

How Did Industrial Policy Change under Jiang Zemin and Zhu Rongji?

Impressive as the early gains were, China still faced problems as the reform era entered its second decade. Reforms had unleashed a huge wave of pent-up consumer demand, and inflation soared above 20 percent in 1988–1989. Partial price reform meant that many products had two prices: a low plan price and a high market price. Many officials profited by buying up goods that were in short supply at cheap plan prices and reselling them on the free market. Popular discontent over high inflation and rampant official corruption were two important causes of the political protests that rocked Beijing and other Chinese cities in the spring of 1989, ending in the massacre of thousands of demonstrators around Tiananmen Square. And overall, China was still a poor country.

In the immediate aftermath of the Tiananmen massacre, conservative leaders brought reforms to a halt, and growth slowed. But in early 1992 Deng Xiaoping made his famous southern tour, which kick-started a new, aggressive reform phase. The next decade set China firmly on course to becoming a major industrial and trade power. Price reform accelerated: by the end of the 1990s, 95 percent of consumer goods, and 90 percent of agricultural commodities and producer goods, were purely market-priced (see Figure 3.2). Better financial management brought inflation under control. Beginning in the mid-1990s, an SOE reform program dramatically reduced the number of state enterprises and state-sector workers, and it also greatly increased opportunities for private companies, especially in manufacturing.

The most noteworthy characteristic of this second reform phase was the strong emphasis on enticing foreign companies to invest in China and building up export industries. FDI—which had run

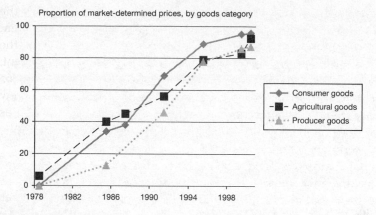

Proportion of market-determined prices, by goods category

Figure 3.2 Price Reform

Source: Adapted from Lardy 2014.

at $2 to 3 billion a year in the 1980s and mostly consisted of small-scale Hong Kong manufacturers moving their factories across the border to the neighboring Shenzhen SEZ—exploded after Deng's southern tour, peaking at $45 billion in 1997. Between 1994 and 1997, FDI accounted for nearly one-sixth of all fixed investment in China. Much of this FDI went into export manufacturing. Between 1990 and 2001 China's exports more than quadrupled, from $62 billion to $266 billion, and by the end of that period more than half of the country's exports were produced by foreign firms.

Why Did Industrial Policy Become More Statist under Hu Jintao?

During the administration of president Hu Jintao (2003–2012), industrial policy took on a decidedly more statist tinge, as the government promoted large-scale infrastructure projects, provided additional protections for SOEs, and slowed the pace of market reforms. Nonetheless, FDI and exports grew even more rapidly than in the previous decade, not because of anything the government did but because of a perfect storm of favorable conditions. China's entry into the WTO in late 2001 gave it expanded access to world markets; the relocation of much of Taiwan's electronics-assembly capacity to the mainland enabled China-based exporters to benefit disproportionately from the explosion in global demand for computers and cell phones; and the world economy grew by 5 percent a year in

2003–2007, well above the long-run average. Between 2001 and 2008, China's exports grew at an astonishing rate of 27 percent a year, rising sixfold from $266 billion to $1.4 trillion.[7]

Government industrial policy, though, did not focus on export promotion. Its main concerns were to consolidate the state sector, facilitate infrastructure, and enable Chinese firms to regain market share from the foreign companies that had poured into the country over the previous decade. The biggest SOEs were reorganized under a central government agency with a mandate to turn them into global champions (see chapter 5). Infrastructure-intensive regional development plans such as "Develop the West" and "Revitalize the Northeast" aimed to spread the fruits of economic growth beyond the prosperous coastal provinces, which had reaped almost all the benefits from the FDI/export model.

These development efforts dovetailed with a construction surge set off by the privatization of the urban housing market under Zhu Rongji. As a result, demand for basic materials such as steel, cement, and glass soared, and China experienced perhaps the biggest heavy-industrial boom in world history. From 2000 to 2014, China's steel production rose nearly sevenfold, from 129 to 823 million tons, by which point China produced about half the world's steel and more than seven times as much as the second-biggest producer, Japan. During the same period cement production nearly quadrupled from around 600 million to over 2.2 billion tons a year, and again China was responsible for about half of world output.[8] The infrastructure and housing boom would probably have hit a natural peak around 2008–2009, but was extended for several years by the economic stimulus policies the government launched after the 2008 global financial crisis. The ultimate result was that China wound up with an oversupply of housing and excess capacity in many heavy industries (see chapter 4 for details).

An especially contentious element of Hu and Wen's industrial strategy was the effort to get Chinese companies to become more innovative, under the banner of an "Indigenous Innovation" policy launched in 2006. This policy included subsidies for research and development (R & D) in several priority high-tech industries, rewards for filing patents and creating technical standards, encouragement for domestic firms and government offices to buy Chinese-made products, and, most controversially, stronger requirements for foreign companies to transfer key technologies to local firms as a condition for being allowed to invest in China. Judged as an innovation policy, Indigenous Innovation produced few discernible gains, other than an upsurge in the filing of mainly worthless patents. As a quasi-protectionist effort to increase Chinese firms' market share in technology-intensive industries, it may have had some impact. Foreign firms' share of high-tech exports peaked at near 90 percent in 2005, and has since fallen to around 70 percent. It is hard to say, though, how much this shift owed to policy and how much simply to the maturation of China's privately owned technology companies.

How Will Chinese Industrial Policy Evolve over the Next Decade?

By 2013, when Xi Jinping took over the government, Chinese industry faced a number of problems. Heavy industry was bloated by excess capacity and too much production was still controlled by state firms, which were much less efficient and profitable than private firms. The ability to maintain fast economic growth by ramping up industrial production was pretty much exhausted. Most economists, both Chinese and foreign, agreed that the government needed to deemphasize heavy industry and do more to promote services, deregulate the prices of key inputs (notably energy, land, and capital) so that investment could become more market-driven and efficient, rationalize the sprawling SOEs, and create more space for private companies.

In November 2013, the party published a package of reform proposals that seemed to address most of these issues. Its core slogan was that market forces would play a "decisive" role in resource allocation, an upgrade from the "important" role assigned to the market in previous party documents. It also promised further deregulation, more room for private enterprises, and reform of SOEs through the introduction of private shareholders. (The reform program is discussed in depth in chapter 11.)

So far as industrial policy is concerned, this reform agenda appears to be a refinement of the general direction during the Hu years, rather than a decisive departure. The three main aims of Hu-era policy—state-sector consolidation, infrastructure development, and helping Chinese firms capture market share from foreign ones—remain in place. Market reforms such as deregulation and price liberalization are being introduced very slowly, and it seems clear that the role of centrally controlled SOEs in major sectors will remain essentially unchanged. Heavy industry will continue to be supported by infrastructure investment, partly within China but increasingly in other markets. Under the "One Belt, One Road" initiative, China seeks to spearhead hundreds of billions of dollars in new transport infrastructure (roads, rail lines, pipelines, and ports) along two routes: one overland route through Central Asia to Europe, and another maritime route through South and Southeast Asia to the Middle East.

One significant departure is the manufacturing strategy labeled "Made in China 2025," released in May 2015. Inspired in part by Germany's "Industry 4.0" plan of 2013 (which aims to upgrade industry through a systematic use of information technology), Made in China 2025 is a set of programs to improve the quality and technological level of Chinese manufacturing. It is both broader and more sophisticated than the Indigenous Innovation strategy, in that it sets goals for a range of traditional and advanced industries and addresses the whole chain of manufacturing processes (and related service industries), rather than narrowly focusing on innovation and a handful of high-tech industries as Indigenous Innovation did. Because of this broader scope, and a stronger call for use of market mechanisms, Made in China 2025 has a better chance of producing results than did Indigenous Innovation, and is seen as less threatening by foreign companies and governments. But it too has a nationalist component: one target is to raise the domestic content of important components and materials to 40 percent by 2020 and to 70 percent by 2025.[9]

Why Did Investment by Foreign Companies Play Such a Big Role?

A feature of China's industrial development that sets it apart from its East Asian peers is the large role of FDI. ("Direct" investment refers to money that is invested directly in factories, equipment, or real estate, as opposed to "portfolio" investment, which consists mainly of the purchase of minority shareholdings in companies.) From 1985 to 2005, annual FDI inflows averaged nearly 3 percent of GDP, a very large number (see Figure 3.3). For South Korea and Taiwan during their comparable high-growth eras (the early 1970s to the early 1990s), FDI inflows were only about 0.5 percent of GDP.

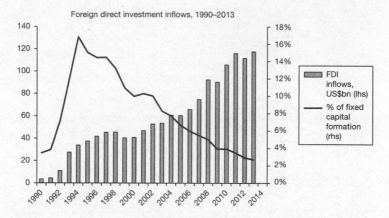

Figure 3.3 Foreign Direct Investment

Source: Author calculation from NBS data.

And in Japan from the mid-1950s to the mid-1970s, FDI was basically nonexistent, running at less than 0.1 percent of GDP.[10]

The role of foreign companies is particularly noticeable in China's export trade. The exports of Japan, South Korea, and Taiwan were almost exclusively booked by domestic firms. In China this has not been true at all; since the early 1990s a third or more of exports were produced by foreign-invested firms, and the foreign share peaked at 58 percent in 2005. For exports classified as high technology by the Chinese government, the foreign role is far larger: from the early 2000s until 2012, well over 80 percent of "high tech" exports from China were produced by foreign firms, and the foreign share is still around three-quarters (see Figure 3.4).

This extraordinary pattern results from a combination of circumstances and deliberate policy choices. The circumstances were that, when it decided to open up its economy around 1980, it was hard for China simply to replicate the strategy of Japan and South Korea of developing export-champion companies behind high protectionist walls. As we pointed out in chapter 1, a big reason for this was political. As affiliates of the US military alliance structure, Japan, South Korea, and Taiwan were tacitly allowed to run mercantilist economies, shutting out foreign companies from their markets even as their own companies enjoyed easy access to the US market. China was never going to get that deal; as the price of admission to the

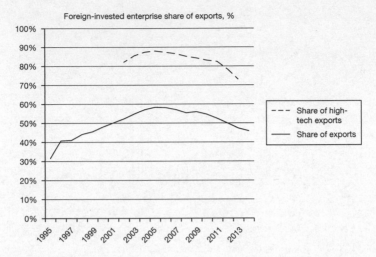

Figure 3.4 Foreign Enterprise Exports
Source: NBS/CEIC.

US-dominated world trading system, China would need to give foreign companies substantial market access.

The policy choices began pragmatically. China in the late 1970s was in dire economic straits, and had very few ways to raise foreign exchange to buy foreign technology. A quick way was to let export-oriented foreign companies set up factories inside China—at first through a handful of SEZs in southern China, and later throughout the country. The policy choices that led to the later surges in FDI—in the early 1990s and again in the early 2000s after China's WTO entry—were clearly more strategic in nature. Reformers knew they could accelerate reform of the domestic economy by introducing competition by big foreign firms.

Another facet of the FDI strategy was that much "foreign" investment was not really foreign. Nearly half of inbound direct investment has come from Hong Kong, and while much of that may simply reflect the activities of Hong Kong–based subsidiaries of American or European firms, it is clear that Hong Kong firms have been major investors in the mainland. In the 1980s and 1990s most of the city-state's manufacturing firms moved their production across the border to Shenzhen and neighboring cities in Guangdong. From the late 1990s onward Hong Kong property and infrastructure firms have poured many billions of dollars into toll roads, ports, and residential and commercial property developments. Although Hong Kong returned to rule by the mainland in 1997, its investments are still counted as "foreign" in Chinese statistics.

Moreover, as much as a third of China's reported FDI may in fact be "round-tripping"—investments by Chinese individuals and companies that are routed through companies in other jurisdictions, especially Hong Kong. Until about 2005, there was a strong incentive for round-tripping in order to capture tax breaks and other benefits reserved for foreign firms. Even as those preferences were phased out, other reasons for round-tripping remained. Some Chinese companies—such as Internet giants Alibaba and Tencent—are classified as "foreign" firms because they have set up offshore holding company structures in order to list on international stock markets. It may be that some investments of these firms wind up counted as "FDI."[11]

The peak of the FDI model came in 2002–2006, when the terms of China's WTO accession agreement required it to make a series of reforms giving foreign firms more access to its market. By the end of 2006, China had met all its WTO obligations, and an increasingly prosperous domestic economy was no longer in such desperate need of foreign capital. FDI in that year accounted for 6 percent of total investment in China, down from the peak of 17 percent in 1994. (By 2014 FDI accounted for less than 3 percent of investment.)

Reliance on FDI has brought China substantial benefits: the technology, production techniques, and management skills brought by foreign firms have been assimilated by domestic companies and helped them grow. Foreign firms also have little to complain about. Despite regulations that restrict their investments, affect certain industries, or force them into joint ventures with local firms, they enjoy greater market access and a more favorable regulatory environment than in many other large economies, including Brazil, India, Russia, and Japan.

But the relationship between the Chinese government and foreign firms is growing chillier. Since 2005 China's industrial policy has increasingly focused on building up domestic companies. There is nothing wrong with this; almost every country has some variant of a strategy favoring domestic producers over foreign ones. Given foreign firms' large existing footprint in China, however, and China's commitment to equal treatment under the WTO and other international agreements, it will be a tricky task to provide support for domestic firms without sparking increased criticism from foreign companies and governments.

Where Has "Industrial Policy" Succeeded, and Where Has It Failed?

The goals of China's industrial policy have been to create a broad set of industries, with Chinese companies progressively producing goods of greater technological sophistication and higher value, and gradually becoming more globally competitive. These aims have largely been achieved. China has moved from being a producer of low-end textiles and cheap consumer goods in the 1980s to a country with successful and large-scale automotive, shipbuilding, machinery, electronics, chemicals, and precision instruments industries. The global competitiveness of Chinese production has steadily risen, as shown by its growing share of global manufactured exports. Studies have documented that the research-and-development intensity of Chinese exports—that is, their technological sophistication—has risen as well.[12] Moreover, growing shares of exports and the trade surplus are generated by domestic firms. For most of the 2000s, foreign enterprises accounted for more than half of exports and as much as two-thirds of the trade surplus. By 2014 the foreign share of both was under half. The aggregate trade surplus of China's nonstate enterprises is now twice as big as the foreign-enterprise surplus. (This is partly offset by SOEs, which run a large trade deficit; see Figure 3.5.)

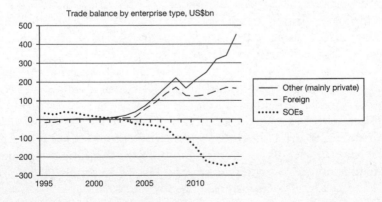

Figure 3.5 Trade Balance by Ownership
Source: Author calculations from NBS/CEIC data.

But China has not been equally successful in all industries, and in particular it has not always done well in ensuring that the production of higher-technology goods is controlled by Chinese-owned firms. The FDI model means that certain industries have been built mainly by foreign firms, and it has sometimes proved hard for Chinese companies to break in.

The two most prominent examples of this phenomenon are automobiles and electronics. Since 2010 China has been the world's biggest passenger car market, and virtually all the vehicles sold in China are built in China. There are essentially two types of producers: joint ventures between big global automakers and local firms (typically SOEs); and purely local private or SOE car firms. All of the globally important American, Japanese, and European car makers have joint ventures in China, and these joint ventures dominate the industry's revenues and profits. Chinese firms produce about half the cars sold in China, but these are mainly low-end vehicles with very thin profit margins. The foreign joint ventures control around 80 percent of the industry's revenues. Chinese firms are increasingly exporting their cars to low-income markets in the Middle East, Central Asia, and Latin America, but they have failed to make inroads in developed countries, and in general show no signs of being able to emulate the international success of Japanese and Korean automakers.[13]

The auto industry represents a failure of industrial policy in several dimensions. Since 1990, Beijing's stated aim has been to reduce the number of automakers and have three giant state-owned companies dominate the industry (similar to the triopoly of Toyota, Honda, and Nissan in Japan). In fact, the number of car assemblers has stayed constant at around 120 since the early 1990s. The "big three" SOE car makers make most of their money from joint ventures that are effectively controlled by foreign firms, and have proven unable to market their own independent brands. The success stories of the Chinese car industry have all been small, upstart companies, often sponsored by local governments—most notably the private firm Geely, which in 2010 acquired the Volvo passenger-car company.

The auto industry should be borne in mind when assessing claims about China's industrial and technological prowess. As it demonstrates, Chinese companies remain far from achieving the highest global standard in products that require multiple levels of technology, intricate production processes, and high degrees of precision. In addition to autos, examples include jet engines, airplanes (where China has tried for years, without much success so far, to develop homegrown commercial aircraft), and many consumer electronics sectors. International firms have been able to maintain a wide technological edge in these areas, despite having major production bases in China where concerns about theft of intellectual property are high. On the other hand, Chinese firms are highly competitive in technology-intensive industries of less complexity, and in particular those in which the customers are mainly businesses rather than consumers: auto components, power generation equipment, telecoms network equipment, and so on.

The electronics industry is another interesting case study. At one level, it is a spectacular success story: China now accounts for over 40 percent of global exports of electronics goods like computers and smartphones, up from 5 percent in the year 2000. But the vast majority of electronics activity in China remains final-stage assembly, where profit margins are extremely thin, and even this activity is largely controlled by foreign enterprises—especially Taiwanese firms, of which Foxconn (the main contract assembler of Apple products) is the best known. The highest-value components of the technology value chain—design and marketing of final products, design of integrated circuits, and original software development—remain firmly in the hands of global giants such as Apple, Samsung, Intel, and Microsoft.

Persistent efforts by the Chinese government to foster local challengers to these companies have failed. Today China has no globally significant software firms and only three prominent hardware companies: personal computer maker Lenovo, telecoms network equipment maker Huawei, and smartphone maker Xiaomi. (All three companies are privately owned, although the first two at least have enjoyed significant state support.)

Huawei and Xiaomi exemplify a business model that can be described as "80 percent of the quality for 60 percent of the price." Firms like this produce reliable equipment with functionality that is behind the leading edge, but still good enough for most buyers—and at an unbeatable price. This makes their products very attractive to a large number of customers that want to keep up with technological trends but cannot afford the latest and greatest: poor countries that want decent cell-phone networks, or lower-middle-income Chinese who want a smartphone but cannot shell out $700 for an iPhone. Most successful Chinese industrial firms employ a variant of this business model, exploiting China's low production costs and economies of scale to offer solid products at a low price. This enables them to generate large sales volumes; but their profit margins are low. They are essentially technology followers, not technology leaders.

Lenovo, now the world's biggest personal computer maker by volume, exemplifies how hard it is to get out of this trap. In 2005 it acquired IBM's legendary, but by then loss-making, personal computer division. It used that acquisition to turn itself into a true multinational firm, perhaps China's only one. It maintains two headquarters, in Beijing and in North Carolina; has its main design team (inherited from IBM) in Japan; and uses English as its company language. Yet it remains heavily dependent on its domestic market. Like many successful Chinese firms, it is caught at the bottom of what Taiwanese technology baron Stan Shih famously called the "smile." Shih observed that in the tech industry, high profits are earned at one end by companies that control the design of core technologies (such as Intel), and at the other by companies that control the design and distribution of products to consumers (such as Apple). In between are commodity firms that manufacture and assemble the products, in high volumes but for low profit margins. Taiwan is filled with such low-margin bottom-of-the-smile firms, such as Shih's own Acer, TSMC (the world's biggest contract maker of integrated circuits), and Foxconn (the world's biggest contract assembler of consumer electronics). For the most part, China's technology companies seem to be heading in the same direction.

Does China "Cheat"?

The charge is sometimes leveled—usually by manufacturing firms in the developed world, or their political allies—that China has achieved its industrial and export success by "cheating." That is, it showered its firms with subsidies; manipulated interest rates, the exchange rate, and energy prices; and created barriers to foreign competition in China, all for the purpose of creating an unfair advantage for Chinese firms. These claims are essentially political, not economic. Every country that has created a successful "catch-up" industrial economy has employed some or all of these tactics— including the United States, which was notorious for its disregard of other people's intellectual property for much of the nineteenth century, maintained high tariff barriers right up until World War II, and continues to subsidize politically important industries on a large scale.[14] These tactics may be "cheating" in some sense. But it is a type of cheating that every industrial country has indulged in, and generally diminishes in importance as the economy becomes more sophisticated—although all countries persistently try to bend trade and investment rules in their favor, and succeed to the degree that their market power enables them to do so. It is worth briefly considering the role that these factors have played in China's industrial development.

How Big a Role Did an Artificially Low Exchange Rate Play in China's Export Boom?

A low exchange rate played some role in China's export boom, but no more than a supporting one. From 2001 through 2010, when most experts agreed that China's exchange rate was undervalued, China's share of global manufactured exports rose by about 1.1 percentage points a year, from 5 percent to 15 percent. In 2010–2013, when China's exchange rate appreciated rapidly and other costs such as wages were also rising, China still gained about 0.9 percentage points of global market share each year, to nearly 18 percent in 2013. If a cheap currency were really the only secret to China's success, one would have expected its performance in 2010–2013 to be far worse.

Of course, as part of its East Asian developmental model, China has often had a bias to keep its currency slightly undervalued. But this bias has not been consistent, and more often than not the exchange rate has been set with an eye to regulating capital flows, not boosting exports (see chapter 7). And as we showed above, China enjoys many advantages that make it a powerful exporter: favorable geographical placement in the East Asian manufacturing hub, the combination of Third World labor cost and First World infrastructure, and so on. The exchange rate helped, but these other, more fundamental factors were more important.

Did Ultralow Interest Rates Subsidize Heavy Industrial Growth?

As with the exchange rate, cheap capital played a supporting role to other, more fundamental factors in China's heavy industrial growth. The main reason that China's heavy industry did so well in the 2000s was that the previous two decades of reform had set the stage for a surge of profitable investment in industry, infrastructure, and housing, and these investments created enormous new demand for heavy industrial products. The Hu/Wen government did set interest rates at a lower level, relative to inflation, than in the previous decade, and may have done so in part to reduce the funding cost for expensive infrastructure projects (see chapter 7). But once the boom got rolling, industrial firms financed their expansion largely by reinvesting their own profits, rather than taking out new bank loans. And private companies grew more rapidly than SOEs, even though they paid much higher interest rates.[15] Low interest rates certainly helped China's industrial surge, but they were not the primary cause.

Did China Keep Energy Prices Too Low?

There is also the question of energy prices: Did Beijing keep them artificially low to promote industrial growth? The answer is, not really. Energy prices are among the few that remained subject to a high degree of government control after the price reforms of the 1990s. But the idea that the main purpose of these controls is to keep energy prices at ultralow levels is wrong.

For most of the past two decades the central goal of energy pricing has been to reduce volatility. Policymakers want to ensure that businesses face a predictable environment, with relatively stable prices for electricity and fuels; in a more predictable environment, businesses are more likely to make large-scale capital investments. The government's main tools in achieving this stability are state-run firms that convert raw fuel into usable energy: power-generating firms and oil refiners. When fuel prices are high, these companies suffer depressed profits or even losses, because they cannot pass on the full cost increase to their customers. But when prices are low, their profits soar, because they are not required to pass on their full cost savings either. These industries can be thought of as "shock absorbers" that enable the economic car to drive relatively smoothly even when the road is full of potholes.

A quick glance shows that energy prices in China are not so low. Between 2011 and 2014, the average pump price of regular gasoline in China was about 27 percent higher than in the United States.[16] As the crude oil price fell by half in late 2014, the US gasoline price dropped by more than a third in four months. The Chinese pump price fell by less than 20 percent.[17]

More important for the economy is the price for electricity, of which about three-quarters is used by industry. (This contrasts with the United States and most developed countries, where most power is consumed by households.) The price of coal, which fuels about 80 percent of China's power plants, was essentially deregulated in 2003 and rose sixfold from $25 a ton in that year to $160 in 2008. Power prices however remained tightly regulated, and relatively little of the increase in the price of coal was passed on to end users. Instead, power-generation companies were asked to accept much lower profit margins. Despite this regulation, industrial power prices for most of the past decade were not notably cheap: generally speaking they were about the same as in Germany, and significantly higher than in other industrial countries such as South Korea, the United States, France, Brazil, and Russia. At the end of 2014, the average industrial power price in China was nearly 13 cents per kilowatt hour, about double the US average.[18]

How Big a Role Did Violation of Intellectual Property Rights Play in China's Industrial Development?

Protection of intellectual property rights (IPR) has been a contentious issue between China and its major trading partners— particularly the United States—since the early 1990s. Many firms from developed countries have long complained that their patents and trademarks were not safe in China, because local firms copied their products flagrantly, and the government did little to crack down on violators. The constant, high-profile battles about IPR violations contributed to a popular narrative that China only succeeded economically because of "unfair practices."[19]

Tolerance for copying and IPR theft is a tactic commonly used by technologically backward nations to catch up on the technological frontier. The development of the European porcelain industry in the early eighteenth century depended substantially on reports by Jesuit missionaries on Chinese ceramic techniques, which the Chinese state considered trade secrets. Theft of tea plants whose export was prohibited by China enabled the British to establish a tea industry in India. In the early nineteenth century, the United States was cavalier in its treatment of European intellectual property, and its first great textile complex in Lowell, Massachusetts, was founded essentially on industrial espionage.[20] After World War II, Japan, South Korea, and Taiwan relied in part on reverse engineering and copying of Western technologies, in violation of Western patent rules. Before China became the main target, the US government engaged in constant IPR skirmishes with Japanese and Taiwanese firms. The point is not that IPR violations are morally defensible, but simply that they are routine and last until a country has enough IPR of its own to decide that protection produces more benefit than stealing. This shift occurred in the United States in the mid-nineteenth century and in the East Asian states in the 1980s and 1990s. It has begun in China with the establishment of specialized IPR courts and the use of criminal penalties for some violations.

China is arguably a worse offender than many previous ones, both because its IPR violations are on an unusually large scale, and because its legal system is unusually weak and subject to political control, making it hard for the victims of IPR theft to obtain redress. On the other hand, the ultimate harm done to Western businesses is often hard to discern. Microsoft and other software companies have complained for years about high rates of software piracy in China; yet US software companies remain dominant in global markets and no Chinese competitors have arisen. For decades, Western consumer product firms have fought a losing battle against Chinese copycats of their trademarks, but most of these companies enjoy profitable and growing businesses in China. Most companies have built China's "Wild West" IPR environment into their business plans, and figured out how to prosper.

Another wrinkle is that the Chinese state has periodically tried to orchestrate IPR theft under the guise of "technology transfer," as for instance when the Indigenous Innovation policy made transfer of key technologies a condition for market access for some foreign firms. Though one might not approve of such tactics, it is more accurate to see them as business negotiations than as morality plays. China has a large market, and its firms are technologically backward. Foreign firms have the technology, and reckon they can make vast profits by selling it in China. The Chinese government is using market access as a bargaining chip in order to gain a greater share of the profits of technology development for Chinese firms. So far, however, foreign firms have successfully resisted these efforts.

Can Chinese Industry Become More Innovative?

A major preoccupation of Chinese policymakers, and of outside China-watchers, is whether China's economy can become more innovative. This is a tough question, because experts find it difficult to agree on what innovation is, how innovative China is right now, and what the ingredients are for an innovation-driven economy.[21] Without pretending to come up with a complete answer, we can make a few observations.

First, Chinese firms are broadly quite good at "adaptive" innovations—taking existing products, services, or processes and modifying them, often in substantial ways, to make them more responsive to the needs of the Chinese market. This is an important type of innovation. But Chinese companies have shown little ability to develop new products, services, or processes that are adopted or emulated in other countries. This is an important distinction between the China of today and, say, Japan in the 1960s and 1970s. Japan pioneered some important business-process innovations—notably "total quality management" or TQM in manufacturing (actually a Japanese development of ideas conceived by the American engineer W. Edwards Deming)—that were later studied and adopted by many firms in other countries. By the mid-1970s Japan had a long roster of companies that were beginning to set global quality and technology standards for a host of industries: firms like Toyota, Sony, Panasonic, Nikon, Canon, and Seiko. China has no such companies today, nor are any on the horizon. And no one is coming to China to figure out how to make factories in the United States or Europe run better.

Second, we can observe a confusion in Chinese innovation policy between the concepts of "innovation" and "autonomy." This is visible in the name of Hu Jintao's innovation policy, whose official

English name was "Indigenous Innovation." The Chinese term, *zizhu chuangxin*, could also be fairly translated as "autonomous innovation."[22] The aims of this and other Chinese innovation policies often seem less about creativity per se, and more about reducing reliance on imported products, services, and ideas. Autonomy and innovation are quite separate and perhaps even contradictory ideas. One can be "autonomous" or self-reliant by creating noninnovative domestic substitutes for foreign goods. In fact an entire school of economic development—the so-called import substitution strategy—was built around this idea in the 1950s, and implemented in Latin America and a few other places. This strategy ultimately failed to deliver sustained economic growth and had a miserable record in generating innovation. Instead, it created a class of inefficient local champion companies whose success depended on government patronage, rather than on constant improvement to meet global standards.

Industries and countries that are widely recognized as innovation leaders have no fear of importing ideas, people, and products from abroad, and in fact modern innovation processes increasingly depend on such cross-boundary movements. Japan made no bones about its debt to Deming as the originator of its TQM techniques: he was awarded a medal by the emperor, and the main Japanese engineering society named a prize after him. Hollywood, one of America's most creative industries, relies heavily on imported talent (it seems sometimes that more British than American actors work there) and on contract arrangements with animation studios in South Korea and, increasingly, China. And thanks to global production chains, the most iconic product of American innovation in the twenty-first century, the iPhone, shows up in the US trade accounts as a multibillion-dollar import item from China![23]

Finally, one must entertain severe doubts about the innovative potential of a society that has moved so aggressively in recent years to restrict the free exchange of ideas, which under any definition is surely an indispensable requirement for sustained innovative achievement. The Communist Party has always been relatively repressive of public information flows, but under Xi Jinping it has become much more so, by shutting down independent voices in social media, increasing censorship and blockage of both foreign and domestic websites, and harassing or closing civil society organizations that receive foreign funding or are suspected of propagating ideas from abroad. It has also launched a campaign to cleanse university textbooks of foreign ideas and to encourage university professors to promote "Chinese" ideas in their teaching. This oppressive and expanding hostility to ideas from other societies, and to domestically generated ideas not approved by Communist Party apparatchiks, is obviously inimical to innovation. For the time being, it is better to read Chinese "innovation" policies as efforts to increase the proportion of technology-intensive goods produced by Chinese-owned firms, regardless of their innovative content. And that is quite a different thing.[24]

4

URBANIZATION AND
INFRASTRUCTURE

How Fast Has China Urbanized?

Mass migration from country to city is a phenomenon that every country experiences as it industrializes. China is no exception to this rule, but has done it faster and on a far larger scale than most other nations. On the eve of the reform era in 1978, only 18 percent of the population lived in cities, a share that had been almost static since the late 1950s. Thirty-five years later, the urban population had swelled to 54 percent of the total. This roughly parallels what happened in the United States in the seven decades between 1860 and 1930, when the urban share of the population rose from 20 percent to 56 percent. In other words, China urbanized about twice as fast as the United States did.

Moreover, China's urbanization has involved vastly more people than any other country's. Between 1978 and 2013 the urban population rose from 172 million to 731 million—an increase of 559 million, or nearly double the average US population during that period. By contrast, between 1860 and 1930 the US urban population rose by just 63 million people. The only country that even comes close to China is India, which saw its urban population increase by 252 million in 1978–2013.

One way to make these large numbers easier to grasp is to imagine what China would have had to do if it decided to put each year's new urbanites in a brand-new city. To accommodate an urban population growing at 16 million annually, China would have had to build a new city, equal in size to greater New York City and greater Boston combined, every year for thirty-five years.

In absolute terms, the growth of China's cities is without peer. In proportional terms, it is rapid, but not completely unprecedented. The 36-percentage-point increase in China's urban population share between 1978 and 2013 was about double the average for other developing countries during the same period. But a few other places have made the shift from mostly rural to majority urban at least as fast as China. In its first three decades, the Soviet Union urbanized at about the same rate as China since 1978. And South Korea—a much smaller country—saw its population go from three-quarters rural to three-quarters urban between 1955 and 1990. This involved a total increase in the urban population of about 26 million people, less than China experiences in two years.

Despite the enormous increase in the city population, China today remains less urbanized than virtually any other country of its income level. The rural population kept growing until it peaked at 860 million in 1995; since then it has declined to 630 million (see Figure 4.1). If one assumes, as many demographers do, that the urban share of the population will level off at around three-quarters, China's urbanization process is only about two-thirds complete.[1]

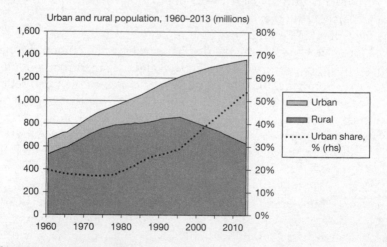

Figure 4.1 Urban and Rural Population
Source: NBS, China Statistical Yearbook 2014.

How Does Urbanization Relate to Economic Growth?

Urbanization interacts with economic growth in three ways, corresponding roughly to three stages of economic development. As an economy modernizes and industrializes, factories spring up in and around cities. These factories offer wages higher than the incomes available to people working in subsistence agriculture (which, at the beginning of industrialization, is most people). These wages pull people off the farm and into the modern economy, so we can call this stage of urbanization the "magnet" phase. Because a worker's productivity is much higher in a modern factory than in traditional agriculture, this transfer of population from the traditional to the modern economy is a major contributor to faster economic growth.

After a certain point, the urbanization process itself becomes a direct contributor to economic growth, not just a side effect of industrialization; we can call this the "building-binge" phase. The workers that have been brought in to staff the factories need housing, roads, sewers, water lines, electric hookups, telephone services, and so on. Construction of all this housing and infrastructure creates new employment opportunities, and it also stokes demand for basic materials like steel, cement, glass, aluminum, and copper. Urbanization becomes one of the processes that pushes economic growth. But it is important to note that this second type of urbanization-associated growth is of lower quality than the first, because it does not by itself create large productivity gains. For a period of time, construction of housing and infrastructure can push up the rate of investment and hence GDP growth. But once the building binge is over, the workers living in these cities are not necessarily a lot more productive than they were when living in company dormitories with minimal amenities.[2]

Once they are endowed with modern infrastructure, cities can become hubs of economic vitality. Their density of skilled workers enables the creation of knowledge networks, which generate specialization and productivity growth in particular industries. We can call this the "smart city" phase. Prominent examples of this sort of specialization include London and New York (finance), Los Angeles (entertainment), and the San Francisco–San Jose conurbation known as Silicon Valley (technology). A recent study by the Brookings Institution found that half of economic growth in the entire world now comes from the 300 biggest metropolitan areas, largely because of specialization in extremely high-value activities.[3]

China's urbanization in the first two decades of the reform era was mainly of the first or "magnet" type. Workers moved from the countryside to urban factories, but for the most part they did not bring their families. Their incomes were still low, and they tended to live in factory dormitories or other company-provided housing. The rapidly rising productivity of these workers as they moved from traditional agriculture to modern industry was the single most important contributor to economic growth, accounting for as much as one-fifth of the increase in GDP between 1979 and 1997.[4]

After 1998, urbanization moved into its second, building-binge, phase for several reasons. First, economic reforms and tacit relaxations of the rules governing migrant labor accelerated the pace of rural-to-urban migration, with the result that the average annual increase in the urban population leaped from 12 million people in 1978–1998 to 21 million in 1998–2013. Second, the urban housing market was privatized in the late 1990s, leading to perhaps the biggest housing boom in world history. Finally, government policy after 1998 increasingly supported the building of infrastructure. Some of this infrastructure—such as intercity highways and railroads—made it easier for people to move to cities in search of work. And some of it—such as urban roads, subways, and water treatment plants—directly contributed to the physical growth of cities.

The challenge for China today is that the building-binge stage of urbanization has reached a permanent plateau. Annual completion of new housing tripled between 1998 and 2013. Housing construction has now peaked, and while it might remain at the present high level for a few more years, it will almost certainly begin to decline after 2020 if not earlier (see Figure 4.2). Broadly the same story holds for urban infrastructure: much more needs to be built, but the annual amount of construction no longer needs to increase. So China is not going to get any more *growth* simply by building houses and infrastructure. Instead, it must enable its cities to move

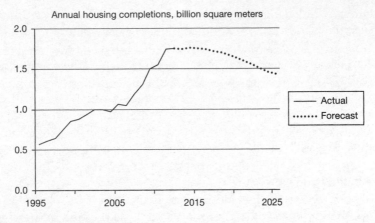

Annual housing completions, billion square meters

Figure 4.2 End of Building Binge
Source: Adapted from Yao 2014.

into the "smart city" phase, in which specialization and innovation become the main economic growth drivers.

Why Do the Chinese Often Say They Have Only "Partially" Urbanized?

China's urban population has grown very rapidly. But the raw figures we quoted up above are somewhat misleading. Just who counts as "urban" is a matter of definition, and China's urban population data are subject to various distortions. For one thing, the boundaries around Chinese cities keep expanding. As the city limits expand, large swaths of rural land are engulfed. According to the World Bank, the reclassification of previously rural land as urban accounted for 42 percent of the increase in the urban population in 2000–2010; migration contributed 43 percent and natural increase the remaining 15 percent.[5]

Because Chinese cities are officially defined by their administrative boundaries, their populations are often much larger than the number of people who actually live in recognizably urban areas. The most extreme example is the municipality of Chongqing, which is sometimes described as "the largest city in the world." In fact it is nothing of the kind: it is a territory the size of Austria (and almost as mountainous), carved out of the larger province of Sichuan in 1997, whose population of 29 million is about 70 percent rural. The urban core of Chongqing city has a population of about 7 million. The actual biggest city in China is Shanghai, with an urban population of 22 million. Under a broader definition, Guangdong's Pearl River Delta in 2014 overtook metropolitan Tokyo as the world's biggest urban area, with a population of 42 million.[6]

Urban geographers have carefully studied China's true urban population and have concluded that the total number is roughly the same as reported in official statistics, but the distribution is more scattered than it might appear at first. A large number of urban Chinese live in small "satellite towns" that orbit major metropolises like Beijing and Shanghai.[7]

The bigger problem—and the one that Chinese scholars mean when they refer to "partial urbanization"—is that the living conditions for Chinese urbanites are widely disparate. The lucky ones live in proper apartments and have full access to social services such as public schools for their children, medical care, and pension plans. The less lucky—who account for nearly 40 percent of China's urban population, or some 260 million people—live and work in the city but are not entitled to these social services, and in many cases live in substandard housing without their own kitchen or toilet.[8] Hundreds of millions of Chinese have physically moved into the cities over the past thirty-five years, but many of them are still waiting to be fully integrated into urban life. Put another way, China has done a good job of urbanizing *jobs*, but a poor job of urbanizing *people*. Turning these "incomplete urbanites" into full urban citizens is a major challenge for the next decade.

What Is the Hukou System and What Impact Does It Have?

One of the major reasons for this "partial urbanization" is the *hukou* or residence registration system. This system has its roots in the *baojia* household registration method established by the Song Dynasty in eleventh-century China, versions of which later appeared in other Asian countries including Vietnam, Korea, and Japan. The modern hukou, which dates from 1958, is far more restrictive than the traditional baojia, which was used mainly for census and taxation purposes. Hukou incorporates elements of the "internal passport" system used by the Soviet Union to limit the mobility of its citizens. In addition to assigning each person a place of registration that is difficult to change, the system sorts people into two categories: rural and urban. When it was strictly enforced during the Maoist era, hukou made it very difficult to obtain a job outside one's place of registration, and almost impossible for people to migrate from the country to the city. Between 1960 and 1978 the urban share of the national population actually fell, from 20 percent to 18 percent. This repression of city growth in the 1960s and 1970s is one of the main reasons why even today China's urban population is lower than is normal for a country of its income.[9]

Enforcement broke down in the 1980s as factories sprouted in coastal cities and began to suck up labor, at first from the surrounding countryside and later from provinces hundreds of miles away. Officials eager to promote economic growth allowed a free inflow of migrant labor. But migrant workers were not permitted to bring their dependent family members, because officials feared the emergence of uncontrollable slums. And if they did bring their dependents—as increasingly became the case in the 1990s and 2000s—migrant families remained shut off from social services. Migrant children could not legally attend local public schools, hospitals would not accept migrants for treatment, and migrants often had difficulty renting or buying formal housing. All these services were reserved for the people who held local, urban hukou.

In a strict sense, hukou has long ceased to be a barrier to labor mobility: workers are pretty much free to go wherever there are jobs for them. But it distorts labor flows in ways that impose some economic costs. The cities with the most vibrant economies and best job opportunities, like Beijing and Shanghai, also have the most restrictive immigration policies, so their populations and economies are smaller than they would be without hukou barriers. Many migrant workers are diverted from these hubs into smaller cities, where construction jobs have created a temporary demand for labor and more relaxed migration policies, but where the potential for long-term productivity growth is lower.[10]

Hukou is also a significant barrier to social mobility within cities: migrant workers persistently earn wages that are only about 60 percent of those earned by their urban, hukou-holding peers. And their families are locked into second-class status: unlike in

South Korea, where migrants from the countryside quickly became indistinguishable from longer-term city dwellers, even the children of China's migrant workers face discrimination in their access to housing and other channels of upward mobility.[11]

How Is the Hukou System Being Reformed?

The national government has very gingerly experimented with reforms to the hukou system over the past fifteen years. Key moves were a 2001 policy encouraging small cities and towns to grant urban hukou to migrants, a 2006 State Council decision that abolished arbitrary fees on migrants, national guidelines in 2011 for relaxing hukou restrictions, and a partial step toward implementing those guidelines in 2014. Policy announcements have proceeded at a slow creep; on-the-ground progress has been glacial. The central conundrum is figuring out a way (a) to give migrant workers equal access to social services in the cities where they live, without (b) subjecting those cities to unbearable fiscal pressures, and (c) ensuring that migrant workers flow more or less evenly to cities of all sizes throughout the country, rather than flocking to a small number of attractive cities mainly along the coast.

The third objective imposes a constraint on the ability to achieve the first two, and illustrates the tension between the policymakers' stated interest in market forces and their deeply engrained habits of top-level planning. The most straightforward way to equalize conditions for migrant workers would be to let them go without restriction to the biggest and richest cities. These cities already have the fiscal resources to begin making social services available to all; and, more importantly, their sophisticated and diverse economies ensure that the productivity of migrant workers can rise quickly. This would contribute to future economic growth, which in turn would boost these cities' fiscal resources and ability to expand social services.

It is clear, however, that this solution is not on the table. The 2014 relaxation of hukou restrictions explicitly stated that migration into cities with a population above five million (which already account for 20 percent of China's urban population) would be tightly controlled, while migration into the smallest cities with less than one million inhabitants will be actively encouraged.[12] This decision partly reflects the political power of elites in the big cities, who want to preserve their quality of life from the degradation they fear it would suffer from an influx of low-income migrants. It also reflects a long-standing bias among policymakers against permitting the emergence of sprawling, hard-to-control megacities. This bias is not irrational. The developing world offers plenty of examples, from Manila to Mumbai to Sao Paulo, of magnet cities that sometimes seem at risk of being engulfed by their own slums.

Yet East Asia also has successful megacities such as Tokyo and Seoul (whose metropolitan area houses about half of South Korea's population), which are well-ordered hubs of creativity and innovation. Chinese authorities may be right that a Chinese megacity would probably look more like Manila than like Seoul. But by deliberately restricting the growth of the country's most successful metropolises, they are probably slowing China's progress toward becoming a more innovative society and also making it harder to solve the inequities created by the hukou system.

Reform efforts now focus on the creation of a "residence permit" system, to operate in parallel with the hukou registration system. The idea is that social services would be delinked from hukou and tied instead to a residence permit, issued by the city or town in which a person actually works and lives. Since 2010 several cities, notably Guangzhou, Shenzhen, Chongqing, Shanghai, and Tianjin, have piloted residence permit programs. Most use points systems under which migrants earn credits for years of employment, taxes paid, educational qualifications, and other criteria; they get a permit once they accumulate a certain number of points. In theory, such a system could be implemented nationwide, in which case the primary remaining function of rural hukou would be to document rural land rights. In practice, residence permit reforms have remained stuck at the pilot stage, and will probably remain so until the central government issues national standards for such permits and also improves the fiscal transfer system, so that cities without the resources to provide social services to migrants can receive appropriate assistance.[13]

What Was the Impact of Urban Housing Privatization?

One of the great turning points in China's economic history was the decision to privatize the urban housing market. Until the late 1990s, most urban residents lived in apartments assigned to them by their work units, for which they paid a nominal rent. This legacy of the Maoist centrally planned economy meant there was little incentive for anyone to build new homes. As a result, housing was in short supply and most families lived in cramped quarters, with only about 150 square feet of living space per person.

Under Zhu Rongji's state-owned enterprise reform program, SOEs and government work units were ordered to sell off the housing they controlled to the occupants, at prices that represented a big discount to market value. How big a discount was difficult to judge, since there was at that time no real market for urban housing or land. Even at these low "insider" prices, many families had difficulty affording their apartments, so they received subsidies from the government or their employers, or mortgages at concessional rates. In return for these benefits, buyers were often prevented from selling their newly acquired apartments for a period of time, typically five years. In general terms, the program resembled Margaret Thatcher's privatization of state-owned housing in the United Kingdom in the early 1980s—but on a larger scale.

Housing privatization in China was one of the greatest wealth transfers in history, and it laid the foundations for the extraordinary housing boom of the following decade. Urban households got to buy valuable property for far less than its market value. The difference between what they paid their SOE landlords for this property, and the higher price they were ultimately able to sell it for, represented a transfer of wealth from the state to households. The total value of that wealth transfer was about $540 billion, or one-third of China's GDP in 2003, the year when housing privatization was largely complete.[14]

To understand its impact at an individual level, consider this simplified example. Imagine a family that buys a house in the center of a city for $100, using $50 of its own money and $50 borrowed interest-free from the family's work unit. After five years, when the family is finally permitted to sell, the market value of the house is $250. The family sells, and has $200 left over once it has repaid the loan to the work unit. The difference between the money the family put in and what it took out—$150—can be considered a transfer of wealth from the state to the family, since the individual is allowed to collect the capital gain that the work unit would have enjoyed if it had been allowed to sell the apartment on the open market.

As its next step, the family uses this money to buy two new apartments farther from the center of town, which cost only $100 each: one to live in and the other as an investment. After another few years the market value of each of these houses rises to $250. The family's original $50 investment has ballooned to $500, a tenfold increase. Meanwhile it has spawned demand for two new housing units, creating business for property developers.

Of course this example contains a number of assumptions, most importantly that house prices continue to rise at a rapid rate. House prices cannot simply rise forever—as homeowners in the United States discovered to their sorrow in 2007–2008. But China was able to sustain fast increases in house prices for over a decade, for a couple of reasons. First, the starting point for urban property prices was extraordinarily low. Because there was no active property market and most urban land before the late 1990s was controlled by state-owned work units, which in many cases had held the rights for decades, land values were far below what they would have been in a market system. Anyone who was able to get hold of urban property in the late 1990s or early 2000s—whether a homeowner buying at an insider price, or a property company gaining redevelopment rights—was almost guaranteed to reap spectacular gains as land prices adjusted up to their true market value. The second reason was that the starting point for housing supply was one of acute shortage. So again, once market conditions took hold, there was every reason for house prices to soar until supply and demand began to balance out.

Housing privatization undoubtedly created an enormous benefit for tens of millions of urban Chinese households, who were able to improve their living conditions and gain a valuable store of wealth. But these benefits came at enormous cost in the form of increased inequality and unfairness. Housing privatization was a great deal *if you already occupied a state-owned house.* (It was an even better deal if your family had the rights to several apartments, as sometimes occurred when both a husband and wife were assigned housing by their work units, or inherited housing units from their parents.)

If you did not happen to be sitting in a state-owned apartment in the late 1990s or early 2000s, or did not have the cash to get into the market in the early years, you were out of luck. Since you could no longer get a house from your work unit, you had to buy an apartment out of your own meager savings, in a market where prices (at least in some cities) were rising faster than incomes.

One consequence was that the great housing boom of 2000–2010 was driven principally by "upgrading demand" from urban hukou holders moving from an older home to a newer, better one. Relatively little demand came from new urban migrants, because they simply could not afford the high prices.[15] So even though China famously was experiencing a huge migration from countryside to city, the housing market was largely an insiders' game, where the housing needs of new migrants were given short shrift while some urban hukou holders enjoyed enormous financial gains. By 2012, a variety of studies suggested that the home ownership rate among urban hukou holders was 70–80 percent, well above the US rate that peaked at 69 percent in 2004. The rate for migrant families was 10 percent or less.[16] Instead, migrant workers lived in company dormitories, in underground apartments created in basements and air-raid shelters, or in rooms in converted farmhouses on the city outskirts.

A final point about housing privatization is that it is one of the starkest cases of urban bias in Chinese policymaking, and a major contributor to China's yawning inequality chasm. A group of urban households were given full property rights to their houses, including the rights to buy and sell, to keep most of the resulting capital gain (which remains untaxed), and to use their house as collateral for a mortgage. Urban residents now have an absolute right to private real property if they can afford to acquire it. By contrast, the property rights of rural farmers remain far more limited and a hot topic of debate. As we explained in chapter 2, farmers mainly just have use rights, and not the right to freely buy and sell their land on the open market. (They are, however, free to have their land seized by the government for infrastructure development, at prices that are unlikely to be fair.) The quality of those use rights varies widely by region, and in many cases title is not clear. The government remains deeply reluctant to give farmers the same level of property rights as urban households. So long as this disparity continues, high levels of income and wealth inequality between cities and the countryside will persist.

Is China in the Midst of a Housing Bubble Similar to What the United States Experienced?

Over the past fifteen years China has had one of the most extraordinary housing booms in history, with monumental increases in both the volume of housing construction and housing prices. Between 1996 and 2012, annual construction of new housing tripled, from 600 million to nearly 1.8 billion square meters. From 2003 to 2013, the average price of urban housing rose 167 percent. Average house prices in the most desirable cities, Beijing and Shanghai, nearly tripled.[17]

The mere fact of rising construction volumes and prices does not prove a bubble. Bubbles are notoriously hard to identify. The commonsense definition is a situation in which the prices of some asset (houses, shares on the stock market, tulips) rise far above their "fundamental value." But what is their "fundamental value"? There is no straightforward answer to this question, which is why bubbles are easier to see after they pop than before the fact. Usually, the approach is to look at how prices have behaved in the past, apply some normal range of variation, and then call it a bubble once prices move much beyond this normal range. Unfortunately this approach doesn't work for China's housing sector, since there was no private housing market before the early 2000s. Moreover, we know that at the start of the housing boom prices were far below their true market value, and there was also a severe shortage of housing. Under these conditions it would be natural for prices to rise quite a lot before reaching their market value.

For housing markets, a common approach is to look at the affordability of housing by comparing house prices (or average mortgage-servicing costs) with household incomes. But this approach has problems too. For one thing, affordability ratios vary widely by country. The US housing market flashes danger signs when the median house costs more than three times the median household income.[18] But the United States is a relatively sparsely populated country where land is cheap, the government provides enormous support to homebuyers, and investors have a wide range of other assets in which to store their wealth. In Asian countries like South Korea and Taiwan that are far more densely populated, that have little government support for homebuyers, and where property is considered the best store of wealth, house prices normally average six to eight times household income. China shares these characteristics and has another special one: as we showed above, a large proportion of housing in 2000–2010 was purchased not out of ordinary income, but out of the windfall gains urban households reaped from housing privatization. So for some years it was quite hard to establish what the "normal" ratio between house prices and income should be.

In sum, it is unhelpful to compare China's idiosyncratic housing market to that of the United States (or anywhere else for that matter) and try to predict when it will "crash." We can be reasonably confident that it will not crash, for a few simple reasons. First, buyers are not heavily indebted, and for the last decade incomes have generally risen faster than house prices. The minimum legal down payment for owner-occupied houses is 20 percent, and until recently most cities required a 60 to 70 percent down payment for investment properties.[19] Since the government started intervening to control rises in house prices in 2010, the average price of an ordinary flat has fallen from nine years of average household income to less than seven, a normal figure for East Asia.[20] This is a far cry from the United States in the early 2000s, where millions of people took on huge debt burdens to buy houses they could not really afford, often with down payments so low (5 percent or less) that even a small drop in house prices would wipe out their equity.

Second, the likely future increase in the urban population— around 200 million people over the next fifteen to twenty years— creates a large pipeline of demand. As long as developers and local governments can figure out ways to prevent inventories of unsold housing from coming to market too quickly, buyers are likely to emerge in a few years. And since there is an oversupply of high-end housing and a shortage of affordable housing for low-income people, some local governments are buying up empty housing developments to convert them into low-cost "social" housing, for which there is strong demand. Finally, the central government is aware of the importance of the property market and the economy-wide risks posed by a crash. For several years it has actively intervened in order to limit speculative price rises. These interventions are far from perfect, but they have succeeded in preventing a crash so far.

Rather than get caught up in an essentially metaphysical debate about whether the Chinese housing market is a "bubble" or not, it is more useful to describe the specific problems and distortions in the market, and how government policy is trying to address them (often, it must be said, by introducing new problems and distortions!).

What Problems Does China's Two-Tier Housing Market Create?

The fundamental issue is that China has a two-tier urban housing system. This is a legacy of housing privatization, which created a lucky class of homebuyers who could afford to purchase relatively expensive housing thanks to the benefit they got from privatization, and a second unlucky class who had to buy housing purely from their own hard-earned savings. The more market-driven tier of the housing system caters to the first class: upgraders and relatively high-income families. There is much evidence that this tier is now in chronic oversupply, because too many cities became too enthusiastic about promoting high-end housing developments—since city governments, which controlled the land on which those developments were built, stood to profit handsomely. The second tier of the system, which addresses the needs of migrants and families whose incomes are too low to enable them to buy housing on the open market, suffers from shortage.

The government began to identify this problem—too much supply of high-end housing, not enough supply of affordable housing—in 2007, and by 2010 it had a full set of policies to deal with it. On the one hand, sales of high-end properties were subject to severe restrictions, including higher down payment requirements, higher mortgage interest rates, and limits on how many properties a single person could buy. The idea was to dampen demand for high-end real estate, forcing down prices and discouraging developers from building more of this kind of housing.

The second part of the policy was a large-scale "social housing" program, which aimed to increase the supply of affordable housing for lower-income households through the use of various government incentives and subsidies. The initial target was to start construction of thirty-six million social housing units during the twelfth Five Year Plan period (2011–2015), or about seven million units a year. Since total housing completions were then running at about ten million units a year, this was an ambitious target.

These policies were somewhat effective in moderating the pace of increases in house prices, as well as in creating more housing options for low-income families. But the purchase restrictions did not achieve their intended effect of reducing excess supply of high-end housing. By early 2015, with the market segment of the housing sector under severe pressure because of the large inventories of unsold apartments, virtually all purchase restrictions were lifted.

As for the social housing program, it is best described as a mandate without a mechanism, and one that is inadequately financed. Localities were given quotas for the number of social housing units they were supposed to build, but little advice on how it should be done and, at least at first, minimal financial support. The result, unsurprisingly, was a wide divergence in outcomes. Richer cities such as Shanghai developed intelligent slum-upgrading programs, which renovated dilapidated units into modern housing at reasonable cost. Third- and fourth-tier cities often responded to the mandate by hastily erecting some buildings on cheap land far away from the town center and declaring "mission accomplished," even though shoddy construction and the lack of nearby shopping and transport rendered this housing literally unlivable.

Today social housing is a patchwork of a dozen different programs, financed by a hodgepodge of local resources, bonds, and bank loans (often backed by land assets at unrealistically high valuations), along with transfers from the central government that are often earmarked in ways unsuitable for the local governments that receive them. The emphasis has gradually moved from construction of new units that low-income people were expected to buy to the upgrading of existing low-quality housing that can be rented out. This is welcome: earlier expectations about the amount of money low-income people could present up front to buy housing proved wildly unrealistic.[21]

Meeting urban China's housing needs will continue to be a difficult challenge for the next couple of decades. For better or worse, the government will meet this challenge by increasing its role and reducing the role of the market. Between 2000 and 2010, about two-thirds of urban housing was provided by the market; the rest was social housing or subsidized apartments built by government agencies or SOEs for their workers. Over the next decade, a growing share of housing is likely to be either directly subsidized social housing or housing that is indirectly supported by the government through mortgage-guarantee programs, similar to those provided by the Federal Home Mortgage Association ("Fannie Mae") in the United States.[22] This may be a valid approach, but it creates a tension with the professed aim of Xi Jinping's government to let market forces play a larger role in the economy.

Why Does China Build So Much Infrastructure?

Related to the urbanization boom has been a boom in infrastructure spending. China made significant infrastructure investments in the first two decades of the reform era, notably in roads, ports, and telecommunications networks. Investment stepped up several notches in 1998, when in response to the Asian financial crisis the government launched a fiscal stimulus program whose main component was infrastructure spending, financed by special bonds. The main item was building a national expressway network, modeled on the US interstate highway system. This was achieved: the expressway system went from less than 5,000 kilometers in 1997 to 112,000 kilometers in 2014, half again as big as the US interstate system.

Other programs followed. Ports up and down the coast were expanded to accommodate the export surge of the 2000s. At the beginning of the decade, nearly half of Chinese exports went through Hong Kong, because domestic ports could not handle the load; and only one Chinese port, Shanghai, was among the world's top twenty container ports (it ranked nineteenth). By 2013 Chinese ports had expanded their volume sixfold, and they handled more container traffic than the next six countries combined. Shanghai had passed Singapore as the world's biggest container port, and five other Chinese ports ranked in the world's top ten.[23]

When Guangdong province, heart of the nation's export sector, started having occasional blackouts in 2003, investment in power plants exploded. Each year for the next decade China installed a Great Britain's worth of new power plants. Generation capacity quadrupled from 357 gigawatts in 2002 to over 1,300 gigawatts in 2014—20 percent more than in the United States. Large investments in telecoms and Internet network infrastructure enabled China to go from 68 million Internet users in 2003 to 650 million in 2014; the number of mobile phone users rose from 270 million to 1.3 billion during the same period. Most controversially, a massive program to blanket the country with 16,000 kilometers of high-speed passenger rail lines, modeled on Japan's bullet-train network, was launched in 2003. More recently, the emphasis has shifted to somewhat less sexy urban infrastructure projects such as subway networks (of which 3,000 kilometers have already been built in twenty-two cities) and sewage treatment plants.[24]

This building extravaganza had several causes. For sure, China had legitimate infrastructure needs that economic planners strove to meet. But other factors conspired to ramp up the scale and speed of construction—and also created problems such as redundant or wasteful projects, poor construction design and quality, and inadequate coordination. Local governments competing for investment felt pressure to install as much infrastructure as possible without careful cost-benefit analysis. The ultralow interest rates of 2002–2012, and rapidly rising revenues from land sales, made it cheap for them to do so. Bureaucratic incentives also played a role: in order for a small city to rise in the nation's administrative hierarchy (meaning promotion and higher status for the city's officials), it has to meet certain infrastructure standards. Local officials faced a strong temptation to build this infrastructure to advance their own careers, regardless of whether the projects were really necessary.

How Much of This Infrastructure Is Useful, and How Much Is Wasteful?

Most of the infrastructure China has installed in the past two decades is useful and productive, although there are some large exceptions. China's infrastructure mania is often criticized for wastefulness, mainly on the grounds that the volume of construction is so staggering as to beggar belief. These blanket criticisms ignore a number of factors, chief among them China's scale. China is a continent-sized country, as big as the United States including

Alaska, and with more than four times the US population. On a per capita basis, there are few infrastructure indicators on which China looks overbuilt relative to the United States or other developed economies.

China's infrastructure investment decisions are also driven by a complex set of factors often misunderstood by people coming from richer countries with slower growth rates, service-driven economies, and infrastructure built so long ago that it is now taken for granted. For one thing, China's 10 percent average growth rate for most of the past three decades meant that the economy doubled in size every seven years. All else being equal, this meant that for most of the reform era, you could reasonably assume that in seven years you would need twice as much infrastructure capacity as you had today. It often made sense to build first and ask questions later.

The complexities of investment decisions, and the inappropriateness of some international comparisons, is illustrated by the high-speed rail network. This project was criticized on the grounds that China had not yet reached the stage of development that justified such fancy kit, that it was too costly, that there was no way it could pay for itself, and that it was being built too fast. The first objection was simply patronizing nonsense: Japan opened the first line of its much-admired bullet-train network in 1964, when its per capita GDP was the same as China's in 2007.

The other objections, many of them raised by domestic critics, were reasonable. But there were counterarguments. High-speed rail lines are notoriously costly to build in rich countries with high labor and land costs. In China, lower costs for land, labor, and capital equipment meant per-mile construction costs were substantially less than in rich countries. Another factor was that China's existing rail network was bursting at the seams, with capacity utilization rates several times higher than in any other major economy: in 2008, China had 6 percent of the world's railroad-track miles, but carried one-quarter of the entire world's rail traffic. Building a separate dedicated passenger system would enable many passenger routes on the old network to shut down, freeing up much-needed space for freight shipments. Increased freight charges on these old lines, planners calculated, would ultimately pay for much of the capital cost of the new passenger lines.[25]

The high-speed rail network is a mixed bag, with some very profitable lines and others less so. On balance it will probably prove a worthwhile addition to China's transport mix. But the way it was built also illustrates a downside to China's approach to infrastructure, namely immense corruption. The high-speed rail project was originally designed as a seventeen-year program, but in the wake of the global financial crisis the powerful railways minister successfully argued for cutting back the timeline by five years. This provided economic stimulus, but also increased the scope for graft, since oversight was naturally laxer under the accelerated timetable. The minister and several colleagues ultimately wound up in prison for siphoning off billions of dollars. This, and many other Chinese infrastructure projects, could have been completed with more efficiency and less theft if the pace were simply slowed down.[26]

Another problem is needless duplication, caused by competition between cities. The prime example of this is airports: dozens of cities in China have built giant vanity airports in hopes of becoming the next major hub, only to see them stagger along with a handful of flights a day. This is genuinely wasteful spending and is made possible largely by the chaotic fiscal system that makes it hard to discipline profligate local officials (see chapter 6).

Even if we accept that most of China's infrastructure is useful, it is clear that the age of breakneck spending is drawing to a close. The return on investment in infrastructure and other capital-intensive projects has been falling since 2008, and with the economy slowing and shifting more to services, the requirement for new infrastructure will probably decline in the coming decade. Just as for housing, the building-binge phase of growth is almost over. This does not have to be a problem: all countries eventually reach the point where they have built most of the infrastructure they need, and start focusing on using it better. But adjusting to the post-infrastructure economy will be a challenge in a system where government officials have largely been rewarded for how much visible construction they could achieve.

What Is China's Plan for "New-Style Urbanization"?

As the above discussion makes clear, Chinese policymakers have long had conflicted views about urbanization. In the 1980s and

1990s, they tolerated the flow of migrant workers into urban factories, but did their best to prevent families from following the workers. This retarded the growth of cities and entrenched the pernicious class division between privileged urban hukou holders and second-class migrants. In the 2000s policymakers abandoned efforts to prevent rural families moving en masse and embraced rapid urbanization as a driver of economic growth. But they tried to steer migrant flows away from their natural course into big prosperous cities, and encouraged the proliferation of smaller cities whose economic rationale was much less clear. Poor budget controls and local fiscal systems overly dependent on land sales created sprawling cities and towns with abundant physical infrastructure but limited prospects for productivity-driven economic growth once the building binge ended.

Scholars and central government officials recognized these problems, and under the aegis of premier Li Keqiang the State Council in 2014 released a blueprint for "new style urbanization," meant to guide the development of China's cities over the next decade. The general idea is that future urbanization efforts will focus less on physical construction and more on developing cities' social services and human resources.

This reorientation is sensible, and it complements other elements of the Xi Jinping reform agenda, notably the fiscal package that seeks to harden local budget constraints, eliminate municipal reliance on land sales revenue (thereby reducing the incentives for sprawl), and strengthen the financing of social services. But the new-style urbanization plan offered few specifics, so it is hard to predict what impact it will have. Two aspects are worthy of comment.

One of the few hard targets in the plan is the aim of giving 100 million migrant workers—about a third of the total—full access to urban social services and housing by 2020, presumably via a residence-permit system. This would be a positive step toward eliminating the urban caste system that renders the lives of city hukou holders and migrants so unequal. The problem is that it is not at all clear where the money will come from for this broad expansion of social services.

The second noteworthy feature of the plan was that it specified a modest relaxation of migration restrictions. Unfortunately, it also specified that migration into the largest cities (with more than five million inhabitants) would remain tightly controlled, whereas migration into small cities of less than one million people would be actively encouraged. As we discussed above, this goes against economic logic and is likely to retard the progress of innovation and productivity in big cities. It is hard to escape the conclusion that urban policy is one area in which the desire to maintain social control has trumped the ambition of maximizing economic growth.

5

THE ENTERPRISE SYSTEM

Which Are More Important: State-Owned Enterprises or Private Firms?

One of the most contentious features of China's economy is its ownership. Two narratives are common, on the surface mutually exclusive. One is that the basic story of the reform era has been the steady retreat of state-owned enterprises in favor of the private sector, which now accounts for the majority of economic activity. The other is that China remains an extraordinarily state-dominated economy, in which state-owned enterprises (SOEs) command a far larger share of national assets than in other countries, and the vast majority of large firms in almost every economic sector are state-run.[1]

At first glance, these stories cannot both be true. Either the private sector or the state sector must be the dominant force in the economy. Yet both stories are true, and it is equally accurate to describe China as a private-led or a state-led economy. China has a large and fast-growing private sector, which in aggregate accounts for the majority of economic output and employment, and its share of both is rising. But private firms are, on average, small. The overwhelming majority of the largest companies in China are state-owned, and state firms dominate virtually all capital-intensive sectors. The state sector's share of national assets is far larger than in any other major economy. State enterprises command a share of resources (such as financial capital, land, and energy) much bigger than their contribution to economic output. The SOEs are also an integral part of the political power structure. They are often used as instruments of macroeconomic policy and industry regulation in place of relatively weak formal policy and regulatory instruments. So the power and importance of SOEs are much greater than implied by economic statistics alone.

A further complication is that much of China's private sector, and especially its biggest companies, is open to the charge of "crony capitalism." Many apparently private firms depend wholly or in part on investments or patronage by senior government officials. Others have large minority shareholdings by government agencies, making it questionable how independent these firms really are from state influence.

In order to understand how China arrived at this position—with a large, growing, but diffuse and perhaps cronyistic private sector, and a shrinking but concentrated and politically powerful state sector—we must first examine the historical development of what we may call the "enterprise system." This system is essentially a mechanism for organizing state ownership, but it has implications for the way in which the private sector has developed.[2]

What Are the Aims of SOE Reform?

When China began its reform process in the late 1970s, the vast majority of nonagricultural economic activity was controlled by the state, not through companies but through government ministries and bureaus at both central and local levels. The efficiency of this system was low, for several reasons.

First, the lack of market prices meant that it was impossible to know whether a "work unit" was really creating economic value. (There being no companies, economic activity was conducted by "work units," such as individual factories, under government agencies.) Second, this absence of knowledge about true economic value meant that work units did not face "hard budget constraints." In other words, if they ran out of cash to pay their suppliers or workers, they could usually find some other government agency to supply the money. Access to resources, such as working capital, thus depended on your political skills, not on how profitable you were.[3]

Third, the production of any given product was fragmented into dozens, hundreds, or even thousands of separate work units throughout China—a legacy of the autarkic Maoist ideology that emphasized local self-sufficiency. This made it impossible to achieve efficiencies from economies of scale. Finally, since the government directly controlled all production, there was no separation between producers and regulators. This worked—sort of—so long as the economy was organized around a centralized plan, in which the essential regulatory function of the state was simply to ensure that inputs were distributed so output targets could be achieved. Once the decision was taken to move in a more market-oriented direction, there was an obvious conflict of interest between the state's roles as owner of assets and as regulator of economic activity.

State-sector reform has addressed all these problems over the last thirty-five years and has made some progress on each, but none has been fully solved. By the late 1990s, most prices were marketized, but a handful of important input prices—notably for land, capital, and energy—remain subject to various kinds of state control. State firms were basically made responsible for their profits and losses in the 1990s, but their continued preferential access to resources at prices not fully set by the market means that their budget constraints are still softer than those of private firms.

The other two issues—excessive fragmentation and lack of clear distinction between the government's roles as regulator and owner of assets—proved thorny, and led to intricate maneuvers to create new forms of SOE organization. The desire of central officials to create larger SOEs fell afoul of local governments' determination to hang on to sources of patronage, tax revenues, and employment. And efforts to separate ownership and regulatory functions were complicated by the government's conflicting ambitions to make SOEs more efficient and profitable, and to ensure that they remained willing agents of state policy when needed.

The obvious solution to these problems would have been simply to privatize the SOEs. This has never been a serious option, because even the most reform-minded officials, from Deng Xiaoping on down, were committed to a strong state role in economic management. They further believed that this role had to be exercised, in part, through the direct ownership of assets, rather than merely through regulatory control of the distribution of resources, as was the case in Japan. Over time, officials became more comfortable with permitting the private sector to grow up and eventually overshadow the state sector—especially since many officials or their close family members held shares in these private firms. But the goal for the state sector itself has always been to make it a more effective instrument, not to dismantle it.

Do Chinese SOEs Resemble Japan's Keiretsu or Korea's Chaebol?

In the 1980s, Chinese scholars and officials searching for a better form of organization for state economic activity had two nearby models to choose from: Japan's *keiretsu* and South Korea's *chaebol*. Keiretsu are networks of firms linked by cross-shareholdings, typically with a bank (called the "main bank") at the center. The main advantage of the keiretsu system is that it promotes stable and collaborative relationships between industrial firms and their financiers, and between companies and their suppliers. This enabled big Japanese companies to engage in long-term planning and investment without having to worry about short-term fluctuations in their stock prices. The keiretsu system also made Japanese firms essentially invulnerable to takeover by foreign firms, and cozy supplier relationships enabled companies to rig domestic markets so that prices and profit margins stayed relatively high. Because of their secure positions, keiretsu firms were able to offer many employees guaranteed lifetime employment. This system worked quite well from the 1950s until the mid-1990s. It started to fall apart because of severe financial pressures on the main banks following the bursting of the Japanese stock-market bubble in 1990, as well as the increasing difficulty Japanese firms had in keeping up with the rapid pace of technological change in the Internet era, when commercial advantage shifted from companies good at organizing large production networks to those adept at quickly bringing new technology-based services to market.

Chaebol are diversified conglomerates, typically controlled by a founding family. Like keiretsu, they involve extensive use of cross-shareholdings among related companies. Unlike keiretsu, they are prohibited by law from owning banks. This prohibition on bank ownership was a deliberate choice made in the 1960s by the Korean government, which wanted to make the chaebol dependent on credit from state-owned banks and hence responsive to the government's policy objectives.

For Chinese policymakers, the keiretsu and chaebol models were broadly attractive because of the way in which they facilitated organization of complex economic activity at a large scale. This satisfied the demand for structures that would enable China to consolidate production in bigger units. But there was no obvious way to translate them into the Chinese context. For one thing, both keiretsu and chaebol had their origins in strong family-owned firms. China had destroyed all its large family businesses in the 1950s, so there was no obvious entrepreneurial basis for new conglomerates. And in any case, China's continued commitment at least in name to a Communist system dictated that the state maintain control of large-scale enterprises, rather than pushing them into private hands.

Two other concerns were important. First was a reluctance to permit business groups to have their own banks. Policymakers believed that direct government control over the banking system was crucial in order for macroeconomic policy to be effective, and they feared that too much control over their own funding would make state enterprises less responsive to government development objectives. The second was a preference for firms that focused on a single industry, which could eventually evolve into "national champions" in key sectors such as steel, petrochemicals, autos, and so on. Both chaebol and keiretsu systems, by contrast, tended to create sprawling empires spanning many different industries.

How Are SOEs Organized?

After much experimentation, the system that evolved in China was that of the "business group" (*qiye jituan*). The business group was first legally defined in 1987, and over the course of the next fifteen years the central government created about two hundred such groups by corporatizing various ministries and production bureaus. Provincial governments replicated this procedure, initially in a haphazard and incomplete way. Two further policy moves provided the next steps in the evolution of the business group system.

The first of these was the adoption in 1995 of a comprehensive SOE reform program, under the slogan *zhuada fangxiao* (grasp the big, release the small). This program had several aims. The immediate one was to clean up a morass of nonperforming loans that state enterprises had built up during the investment boom of the early 1990s, which threatened to bring down the whole economy. The longer-term one was to set state ownership on a more rational footing. The basic idea was that there was a host of industries, such as consumer goods manufacturing and services such as retail shops and restaurants, where state ownership was unnecessary. Small-scale SOEs in these sectors (most of which were controlled by local governments, not the center) could be privatized or bankrupted, and these economic areas could be handed off to the private sector. But state control of what is sometimes called the "commanding heights" of the economy needed to be strengthened. These commanding heights included:

- Important national networks including aviation, railways, telecoms, and power generation and distribution;
- Upstream production of oil, gas, and coal;
- Basic heavy industries such as steel, aluminum, and petrochemicals;
- Production of critical heavy machinery such as machine tools and power generation equipment;
- Infrastructure engineering for the construction of roads, dams, ports, and railways;
- "Pillar" consumer durables industries, notably automobiles;
- Military equipment.

Under the *zhuada fangxiao* reform, state ownership of these commanding-heights sectors was organized under large-scale business groups controlled directly, in most cases, by the central government. Formal rules governing the structure of business groups were published in 1998. With a few exceptions, notably the Ministry of Railways, ministries responsible for a specific industrial sector were broken up and corporatized. A key element of this procedure was that, in virtually every instance, the government set up not a single monopolistic state-owned corporation but several competing enterprises. The former electricity ministry was broken up into five large national power-generation companies and two regional grid companies, the telecoms ministry gave way to three telecoms firms, the aviation agency to three airlines, and so on. Provinces and cities were also permitted to retain control of state enterprises that they deemed strategic, but they were pressured to corporatize these firms, using the group-company structure, rather than continuing to run them simply as arms of the local government.

Another reform was the creation of subsidiaries suitable for listing on overseas stock markets. Typically this involved the packaging of an SOE's most commercially attractive assets in the listing vehicle, while lower-return investments in infrastructure, or politically sensitive projects, were retained in the unlisted parent company. So, for example, the principal oil company, China National Petroleum Corp (CNPC), created a subsidiary called PetroChina that listed in Hong Kong and New York. The listed vehicle included most of CNPC's oil and gas fields and refineries, but excluded some pipeline assets and investments in politically controversial regions such as Sudan.

These SOE stock-market listings were not privatizations, although stockbrokers and media reports often erroneously described them as such. In most cases, no more than 20 percent of shares were sold to the public, with the remaining 80 percent staying in the hands of the parent company—that is, in the hands of the Chinese government. The idea behind the listings was never to privatize these firms, even gradually. Instead, the purpose was to teach big Chinese firms how to tap international capital markets to fund some of their capital expansion plans, and to improve their commercial performance by exposing them to modest amounts of discipline from international shareholders.

The final move in SOE reform was the establishment of the State-Owned Assets Supervision and Administration Commission (SASAC) in 2003. The purpose of SASAC was in essence to act as the government shareholder in nearly two hundred centrally controlled SOE business groups. Instead of the State Council itself trying to figure out how to exercise its ownership interests in the sprawling business empire nominally under its aegis, SASAC took on the responsibility for appointing senior management and holding them accountable for meeting financial targets such as return on assets and market share, much as a controlling shareholder of a normal corporation would do. Local SASACs were also set up by provincial and city governments to oversee the smaller-scale SOEs.[4]

In addition to its job overseeing each company individually, SASAC was given two broad mandates: maximizing the aggregate value of state assets and gradually reducing the number of centrally controlled business groups to under one hundred. The logic of the latter target was that policymakers wanted the big SOEs to develop into globally competitive "national champion" companies, and felt that this could only be achieved by further consolidation. While SASAC's success in meeting its financial goals is debatable, it has achieved some consolidation. Over a decade it has boiled down the number of SOE groups under its control to 111, comprising about 23,000 individual companies.[5]

Yet SASAC's authority faces several important constraints. One is that its shareholding status is contested. Technically, the SOE groups that it supervises are supposed to be corporations, and SASAC owns their shares, but lack of information makes it impossible to know whether this is always the case. There are SOE groups that are not corporatized, have no shares, and whose relationship with SASAC is legally fuzzy.[6] In any case, several other agencies—notably the Ministry of Finance (MOF) and the Ministry of Industry and Information Technology (MIIT)—often assert shareholder-like rights over certain SOE groups. Second, about half of the central SOE groups are of the same bureaucratic rank as SASAC (ministry-level), and thus they are able to resist the demands of their shareholders. Finally, SASAC appoints the senior managers of only about half of the SOE groups it oversees; the other half are appointed by the Communist Party's Organization Department.[7]

How Are SOE Business Groups Structured?

The result of the process outlined above was the creation of a Chinese model of corporate organization as distinctive as the prior keiretsu and chaebol models in Japan and South Korea. The typical structure of a Chinese SOE business group is as follows:

- Top layer: unlisted parent group entity, controlled by the government via SASAC.
- Second layer: corporate subsidiaries wholly or majority-owned by the group entity. These may include subsidiaries listed on Chinese or overseas stock markets. In most cases, one of these controlled subsidiaries is a finance company.
- Third layer: minority-controlled subsidiaries and joint ventures, which usually enable the group to take an interest in peripheral activities. For instance, CNPC, one of whose core interests is the wholesale distribution of natural gas via pipelines, also has stakes in various city gas companies that deliver gas to households.

- Fourth layer: companies that have no equity relationship to the group entity or its subsidiaries, but are bound by various contractual relationships.

This structure is the same for centrally controlled SOE groups owned by the central SASAC, and for local SOEs owned by provincial and city SASACs.

Several features of this structure are worth noting. First, SOE business groups typically operate within a single industrial sector. This rule is somewhat elastic and most SOE groups have a cluster of investments in sectors unrelated to their core businesses, often in property, travel services, and restaurants. But these investments are generally modest relative to the core businesses. This single-industry focus distinguishes Chinese business groups from the highly diversified Japanese and Korean conglomerates. For example, before it broke itself up in a major corporate restructuring in the late 1990s, Korea's biggest chaebol, Hyundai Group, had significant interests in automobile manufacturing, shipbuilding, chemicals, semiconductors, personal computers, property development, and department stores. No major Chinese SOE has anything approaching such a spread of businesses, although a handful of private conglomerates have emerged with chaebol-like portfolios.

Second, most SOE groups have an in-house finance company. Enterprises registered as SOE groups are entitled to a finance company; enterprises that fail to meet the requirements for group registration—as is the case for many private enterprises—may not have a finance company. In-house finance companies are a bit like the "main banks" at the heart of Japanese keiretsu, but with a couple of important differences. For one thing, they are wholly owned by the parent company, and own no shares either in the parent or in any other group subsidiaries. For another, they are relatively small. Japanese main banks are among the biggest banks in the country; the biggest corporate finance companies in China are comparable in size to third-tier banks. The modest size and restricted role of corporate finance companies strikes a balance between objectives. On the one hand, the government wants its big SOEs to organize their finances flexibly—especially in the matter of moving money from one group company to another. But on the other hand, it does not want to lose control of the financial system by permitting the corporate finance companies to become full-fledged banks.

What Impact Did the SOE Reform Program of the 1990s Have?

The *zhuada fangxiao* ("grasp the big, release the small") SOE reform program, begun in 1995 and reinforced with additional measures in 1997, had two main aims. One was to refocus the SOEs in a smaller number of strategic sectors and make them more efficient. The second was to clean up a huge bad debt problem that had grown within the SOE sector in the mid-1990s. This was often referred to as the "triangular debt" problem (companies unable to pay their suppliers, and both kinds of firms unable to pay back their bank loans). Ultimately the debt problems were concentrated in the state-owned banks, whose nonperforming loans (NPLs) were estimated at an astonishing one-third of GDP in the late 1990s. Broadly speaking, the reforms were a success.

The basic idea of *zhuada fangxiao* was to shut down or privatize smaller SOEs in intrinsically competitive sectors (such as consumer goods manufacturing), while consolidating and corporatizing bigger SOEs in commanding heights sectors. The surviving SOEs were reorganized as joint stock or limited liability companies, under the big SOE groups described above, and made responsible for their profits and losses. Banks were relieved of their social responsibility to lend to nonviable SOEs simply to keep them afloat and maintain employment. Their main job was now to finance the expansion of viable SOEs in capital-intensive sectors.

Over the next decade, this reform program had three major impacts. First, the number of SOEs was slashed, from 262,000 in 1997 to 110,000 in 2008, by consolidation, privatization, and bankruptcy.[8] Second, employment in the SOE sector fell from 113 million, or nearly 60 percent of total urban employment in 1995, to 64 million (20 percent of urban jobs) in 2007. And finally, the financial performance of SOEs improved. The average return on assets in state firms soared from 0.2 percent in 1998 to 5 percent in 2007. The SOEs' profits rose from just 0.3 percent to 6.6 percent of GDP in the same period. This improvement resulted from a combination of reduced obligations to finance employee social welfare costs, increased competitive pressure, pressure from SASAC to hit financial targets, and subsidized access to land and capital.[9]

These gains were impressive. After the 2008 global financial crisis, however, many of these gains were partially reversed, as SOEs became more numerous, less strategically focused, and far less profitable. The implications of this shift, and the government's response to it, are discussed at the end of this chapter.

How Big Is the State Sector Today?

Despite the pruning of SOEs over the past three decades, China today still has by far the largest state sector, relative to GDP, of any major economy. According to the Ministry of Finance, in 2013 China had about 150,000 SOEs, with combined assets of around US$16.8 trillion, or 177 percent of GDP (see Figure 5.1). The SOEs controlled by the central government account for about one-third of the total number of state firms, and slightly less than half of SOE assets. The remaining two-thirds of SOEs, and a bit more than half of SOE assets, are controlled by provincial and other local governments.[10]

Cross-country comparisons are tricky, because there are no consistent standards for reporting data on state firms. But it is clear that China's state sector is unusually large (see Table 5.1). In 2011, researchers at the Organization for Economic Cooperation and Development (OECD) analyzed data on all SOEs appearing in the

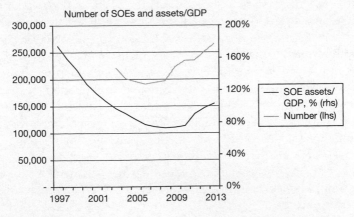

Figure 5.1 SOE Numbers and Assets

Source: Ministry of Finance.

Table 5.1 The World's Biggest State Sector: SOE Assets
and Revenues, percent of GDP, 2011

Country	Assets (%)	Revenues (%)
China	145	26
India	75	16
Russia	64	16
South Korea	48	7
Brazil	51	12
France	23	8
Indonesia	19	3

Source: OECD 2011.

Forbes Global 2000 list of the world's biggest companies. They found that China's major SOEs had assets equivalent to 145 percent of GDP, and revenues of 26 percent of GDP. Both figures were about double the numbers for the other big emerging economies—Brazil, Russia, and India. Among developed countries, the highest levels of SOE assets relative to GDP were in South Korea (48 percent) and France (23 percent).[11]

The biggest Chinese SOEs are very big indeed, and the vast majority of really large companies in China are state-owned. In 2014, 92 mainland Chinese firms appeared in the Fortune Global 500 list, which ranks the world's biggest firms by revenue. Of these, 59 were central SOEs and another 23 were local-government SOEs. Only 10 were private firms. Of the 40 largest Chinese companies on the Fortune list, 35 were central SOEs. These included three of the ten biggest companies in the entire world: Sinopec, CNPC, and State Grid.

So in terms of the assets and revenues they control, China's SOE sector is large. The picture looks different, however, when we turn to employment and contribution to GDP. Total employment by SOEs has been static at around 65 million people since 2005. Since the total number of jobs in the economy continues to rise, the SOE share of urban employment continues to fall, and in 2013 stood at an all-time low of 17 percent.

Contribution to GDP is harder to measure, because Chinese data do not always distinguish precisely between state and private firms.

But we can make an estimate based on information about the state role in three main production sectors: agriculture, industry, and services. In agriculture, most production is by private household farms. State firms do exist for scale production, especially in sectors like meat and dairy. A reasonable estimate of the state share of agricultural production is about 10 percent. Detailed data exists for industry, and the most careful studies show the state share of industrial production (on a value-added basis) is about 25 percent. For services, our information is spottier. In some services, such as telecoms, state firms are clearly dominant. In many others, such as retail, restaurants, and online commerce, private firms rule. Chinese scholars estimate that output in the service sector is about evenly divided between state and nonstate companies.[12] Adding up these contributions, and weighting each sector by its contribution to GDP, we conclude that SOEs account for about 35 percent of GDP. Roughly speaking, domestic private firms account for about 60 percent of GDP, and firms controlled by foreign investors account for the remaining 5 percent or so.

One observation that springs from these calculations is that SOEs' contribution to GDP is low relative to the vast swath of assets they control. This in turn implies that state firms extract a far lower return from their assets than do private firms—a conclusion that is strongly supported by industrial data. The low efficiency of SOE investment is an important problem for economic policymakers, and will be discussed at the end of the chapter.

Are SOEs Monopolies?

A common criticism of China's state-enterprise system is that it produces monopolies. This is not accurate. Indeed SOEs are pervasive, politically influential, and in command of resources disproportionate to their contribution to output. But with a handful of officially designated exceptions—the national railway system, the tobacco monopoly, and the salt monopoly (abolished in 2014)—SOEs do not occupy monopoly positions. As noted above, a deliberate feature of the SOE reforms of the 1990s was the creation of multiple, competing state firms even in sectors marked down for central control, such as aviation, telecoms, oil, and electricity generation. In less strategic industries the degree of state-sector fragmentation is even greater:

in 2011, for instance, there were 880 SOEs in coal mining, 312 in steel, and 264 in nonferrous metals processing. Detailed data on industrial enterprises fail to reveal any evidence either of an unusual concentration of industries in a small number of firms or of the excessive profits that one would expect from monopolists.[13]

The nonmonopolistic nature of the state sector helps explain why China has been able to sustain such high rates of economic growth despite its continued heavy reliance on state firms, which are clearly less efficient than private ones. One lesson from this experience is that, for countries making the transition from a socialist planned economy to a market economy, full privatization of state assets is not necessarily the critical step, as many economists believed in the 1990s. The indispensable feature of a market economy is not private property but competition. If state assets are privatized but competition mechanisms remain weak, the results will be poor: one just substitutes private monopolists or oligopolists for state-owned ones. (This was arguably the experience of Russia in the 1990s.)

If, on the other hand, competition is strengthened, it is possible to leave a large share of assets in state hands and see strong economic growth. This is because more productive private firms spring up to take advantage of market opportunities that state firms miss, and even state-owned firms are forced to up their game. Even if SOEs' productivity continues to lag the private sector, the *improvement* contributes to economic growth. The economist Barry Naughton coined the phrase "growing out of the plan" to describe China's strategy of relying on greater competition, rather than privatization, to manage its transition from plan to market.

This approach has limits, however, and China is now hitting them. For one thing, competition only works if the losing firms exit the market through bankruptcy or acquisition by stronger players. Since the conclusion of the *zhuada fangxiao* reforms in about 2005, state firms have rarely gone bankrupt or been taken over by more efficient private competitors. Local governments prop up their SOEs with preferential access to bank credit and other resources. Central SOEs are protected by formal or informal regulations that limit the entry of private firms into their sectors. The competition among central SOEs is vitiated by government interventions such as the rotation of senior executives: in the last decade Beijing has twice reshuffled the chief executives of the three big telecom firms, and also transferred the head of one state-owned oil company to the top job in another one. Such moves suggest that in the minds of Beijing's bureaucrats, SOE chiefs are not really the leaders of competing enterprises, but heads of different divisions within a single enterprise. Finally, competition law is weak and regulatory oversight poor. An antimonopoly law was passed in 2007, but enforcement was split among three agencies, and the law has mainly been used to limit the market power of foreign firms, rather than to break down anticompetitive behavior by SOEs or government agencies.[14]

In short, SOEs may not be monopolies, but they are certainly insulated from competitive pressures. This is now taking a toll on the economy. As we show below, since 2008 the financial performance of state enterprises has deteriorated, while that of private firms—which face intense competition—has continued to improve. In order to maintain rapid economic growth, the government will need to open up protected sectors—especially in service industries—to greater private competition, and it will need to force uncompetitive SOEs into bankruptcy.

Are Chinese Central SOEs Independent Actors, or Agents of a Government "Master Plan"?

This is a very thorny question. Our description of the "enterprise system" suggests that the activities of the big SOEs are coordinated by the central government through the shareholding agency SASAC; and by the Communist Party, which directly controls appointments of top managers of about half of the most "strategic" SOEs. There is also a very active "revolving door" that shuttles both SOE bosses into important government roles and government and party officials into the leadership of key SOEs.

Yet despite the density of ties binding together SOEs, the government, and the party, it is hard to show that SOEs simply follow orders from above. Like big firms in other countries, SOEs pursue their own commercial objectives, which may or may not be consistent with state aims. They lobby the government, with varying degrees of success, to change policies and regulations in their favor. Frequently the interests of different SOEs clash, and they lobby the government in opposing directions. A common example is in trade matters, where some SOEs may seek antidumping tariffs to be imposed on foreign competitors, while other SOEs that rely on imported materials oppose the duties and may team up with foreign firms to lobby against them.[15] The explicit mandate of SASAC to improve SOEs' financial performance means there is a bureaucratic check on political interference. The SOEs cannot simply execute politically driven tasks without regard to commercial considerations; if they did, they would fail to meet SASAC's financial benchmarks.

In practice, SOEs operate both as fairly autonomous fiefdoms, acting in ways that they believe will increase the size and power of their businesses, and as part of an elite network of institutions that includes the party and government. And many Chinese—including some within the government—increasingly believe that power flows not from the government to the SOEs but the other way round. A popular phrase in recent years was "there are no state-owned enterprises, only an enterprise-owned state." This is an exaggeration, but not a great one. Fear that the state was at risk of "regulatory capture" by its biggest business enterprises is likely a reason why Xi Jinping has made several big SOEs the target of his sweeping anticorruption campaign (see chapter 10 for more details).[16]

How Important Is the Private Sector?

The state sector has been a large part of China's growth model because, despite the steady erosion of its market share, this share is still quite high by international standards. The SOEs remain important tools for the government in managing macroeconomic policy, resource flows, and infrastructure development. But the rise of the private sector has been an even bigger contributor to China's sustained high growth rates over the past three decades.

Virtually all the gains in productivity and employment in the domestic economy since 1978 can be traced to the reallocation of resources from the state to the private sector. The private sector now accounts for a majority of GDP, employment, fixed investment, industrial production, new bank loans, and the trade surplus. Its share of all these indicators has steadily increased, even when media reports suggested that the state sector was regaining ground. In 2014, China had around 2,400 private-sector millionaires (putting it second behind the United States) and 324 billionaires. China's economy is largely a private-sector success story, and its ability to keep up fast growth in the future will depend mainly on private companies.[17]

How Has the Private Sector Evolved?

The rise of China's private sector since the beginning of reforms can be divided into three phases. In the first period (the late 1970s until the mid-1990s), private economic activity expanded very rapidly, but its legal basis was insecure. The dominant corporate form was the *getihu* (individual business enterprise), which by law could have no more than seven employees. Larger private firms existed, but because of the difficulty of registering a purely private company, many were often registered as "collective" enterprises, with significant shareholdings by local governments that acted as patrons and protectors—a practice known as "wearing the red hat."

The second era ran roughly from the beginning of the *zhuada fangxiao* SOE reform in 1995 until the global financial crisis year of 2008. During this phase, private property rights were strengthened, more flexible forms of corporate organization were opened up, and the state role in many sectors was radically reduced, offering private firms the chance to enter lucrative new markets and in some cases to buy up distressed SOEs or SOE assets. An important symbolic move was the decision in 2001 to permit private entrepreneurs to become Communist Party members, reversing a ban imposed following the Tiananmen demonstrations of 1989.

In this second period, the private sector boomed and rapidly increased its share of employment, output, and number of companies. This growth is hard to measure precisely because of technical problems in Chinese company statistics, which do not distinguish clearly between private and state firms.[18] The first comprehensive effort to measure the size of the private economy, a 2007 OECD study, found that the private-sector share of industrial value-added more than doubled between 1998 and 2003, from 15 percent to 33 percent.[19] More recent work by the economist Nicholas Lardy, which includes estimates for small-scale enterprises and nominally "foreign" firms that were really controlled by domestic private shareholders, suggests that the true private share of industrial value-added was higher: 56 percent in 2003 and 63 percent in 2007.[20]

In other words, in the first three decades of the economic reform process, private firms went from close to zero to controlling about two-thirds of China's industrial production. The SOEs saw their share shrivel from about three-quarters to just one-quarter. (The remaining 10 percent to 15 percent of industrial output came from locally controlled "collective" enterprises or from foreign-invested firms.)

Is It True That Now "the State Advances and the Private Sector Retreats"?

The third era of private-sector evolution dates from 2008, when the expression *guojin mintui* (the state advances and the private sector retreats) became common in Chinese media. This phrase reflected a belief that the government had launched a systematic effort to roll back private-sector gains and reassert the dominant role of the state. Evidence for this belief included the proliferation of industrial policies that seemed to benefit state firms; a few high-profile cases in which private firms were forced to sell out on unfavorable terms to state-owned competitors; and the consolidation of the coal industry in Shanxi province under a group of provincial SOEs, which bought up most of the privately owned mines.

Strictly speaking, the data do not really support this story. Even after 2008, the private sector's shares of industrial output, exports, employment, GDP, and market shares in most economic sectors continued to rise, as did its share of bank credit (see Table 5.2). By 2011 there were only 6 out of 40 major industrial sectors in which state firms accounted for more than 20 percent of output.[21] The phrase *guojin mintui* is clearly an exaggeration.

It is true, however, that the *rate* at which private firms displaced state firms slowed markedly from 2008. And the retreat of the state sector, which was extraordinarily rapid in 1997–2007, became much less pronounced. The number of SOEs stopped falling, stabilized, and began to rise again after 2010. Employment in SOEs stabilized. And the SOE share of fixed investment, which declined rapidly in the decade to 2007, started to decline much less swiftly, and in a

Table 5.2 Private Firms Gain Ground: Nonstate-Sector Share of Various Economic Indicators

	Registered companies (%)	Urban employment (%)	Exports (%)	Industrial output (%)	Fixed asset investment (%)	Bank loans (%)
2000	–	55	5	< 30	< 30	–
2005	55	77	20	–	47	–
2010	74	81	31	–	54	30
2013	93	83	42	> 60	60	39

Source: Author calculations from NBS/CEIC; Lardy 2014; and OECD 2007.

handful of sectors it began to increase.[22] In short, the retreat of the state sector became much slower after 2008. State firms continued to command a share of resources (land, capital, and energy) far larger than their contribution to economic growth.

Three factors lie behind this change in trajectory. One is that the Hu Jintao administration had in general a more statist bent than its predecessor and was more active in using SOEs as instruments of policy. The second is that Hu and his premier Wen Jiabao continued to promote some economic reforms that would benefit the private sector, but were ineffectual in doing so. Meanwhile, the newly profitable SOEs increased their lobbying efforts to prevent reforms that would erode their market power. Third, the government launched a massive economic stimulus program at the end of 2008 in response to the global financial crisis. Much of the stimulus spending went through SOEs and local governments into infrastructure projects. At the margin, the stimulus program gave SOEs a boost.

Is It True That Private Firms Can't Get Access to Bank Loans?

No. This is a frequently repeated, but out of date, assertion. According to the Ministry of Finance, 39 percent of bank loans outstanding in 2013 were to private firms, up from 30 percent in 2010. If one includes loans to farmers for the purchase of equipment, fertilizer, and seed, the 2013 figure rises to 48 percent. Of course it is true that private companies' share of bank credit does not match their much larger contribution to economic growth. But access to capital is no longer the most important thing holding back private firms. Discriminatory regulation, and barriers that limit private investment in potentially lucrative service sectors, are bigger problems.

How Is the Balance of Power between the State and the Private Sector Likely to Evolve in the Future?

To sum up, the picture we have painted is that state enterprises represent a large but steadily declining share of the economy, yet have a claim on resources and political influence that far exceeds their economic weight. The private sector in aggregate accounts for the majority of economic activity, but is fragmented and politically weak. Moreover, the private sector's gains have slowed markedly since 2008. How will the state-private balance of power evolve?

In answering this question, the crucial fact is the dramatically declining efficiency of SOEs. From 1997 through 2007, SOEs' financial performance improved, as measured by returns on assets and equity. Since the global financial crisis year of 2008, however, returns on assets and equity have both fallen by about one-third. The performance of private firms, meanwhile, has continued to strengthen. By 2014, private industrial companies generated a return on assets about double that of their state-owned counterparts (see Figure 5.2).

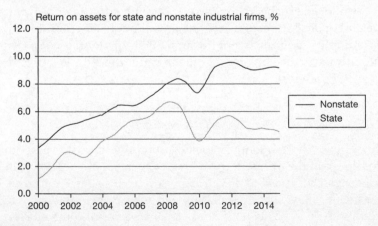

Figure 5.2 State vs Private ROA

Source: Gavekal Dragonomics.

The worsening performance by SOEs is both a reflection and a cause of China's recent economic slowdown. The SOEs tend to be concentrated in heavy industrial sectors that have been hit hardest by the end of the building-binge phase of growth we described in chapter 4. Private firms tend to be in consumer sectors that benefit from the spending power of the new middle class. So it is not surprising that, overall, SOEs have fared worse than private companies. But studies also consistently show that within a given sector, private firms outperform state firms. To stabilize economic growth, China needs to improve its overall return on investment. As in the past, this need not mean wholesale privatization of state firms. It will, however, require opening up service industries to private-sector competition, just as manufacturing was opened to private firms in the 1990s; a willingness to let smaller-scale SOEs (especially those controlled by local governments) go bankrupt if they cannot survive in a more competitive environment; and much stronger financial discipline on central SOEs.

In the reform outline released in November 2013, the Xi Jinping government identified state-enterprise reform as an important priority, but its actual policies so far are well short of what is needed. As in the past, large-scale privatization is not on the table. For local SOEs (those controlled by provincial or city governments), provincial governments have been required to develop "mixed ownership" plans. Under these plans, provincial and city governments will sell stakes in their SOEs to private investors. By the beginning of 2015, most provinces had published plans for mixed-ownership reform, typically aiming to have up to 80 percent of their SOEs achieve a diversified shareholding structure by 2020. But few share-sales have occurred.

This initiative is far more timid than the reforms of the 1990s, and it is hard to see what benefit it will bring. The financial performance of local SOEs is poor, much worse than that of central SOEs. Many of them have large debts, and stay afloat only because of local government support. Buying minority, noncontrolling stakes in such basket-case companies is unlikely to be an attractive proposition for private investors. The mixed-ownership reform only makes sense if it is really a code for outright privatization of many local SOEs. This may be the intention, but it is impossible to know for sure until we start to see some transactions.

For central SOEs, even mixed ownership is not an option. Instead, the plan under discussion is that shareholding rights will be transferred from SASAC to a set of "asset management companies"— one for each major industry sector—that will focus on improving the financial performance of the firms they own. Thus SASAC will cease to be a shareholding agent and will turn into a purely regulatory body. This system is modeled on Singapore's method of having all its state enterprises overseen by a quasi-independent holding company, Temasek. As with the mixed-ownership plan for smaller SOEs, it is hard to assess the impact of this program until it is put into practice.

The bottom line, though, is clear. For China's economy to keep growing at a rapid pace (say 6 percent a year for the next five to ten years), enterprise efficiency must be improved. Since private companies are already highly productive, these efficiency gains must come from both an expansion of the space in which private firms are allowed to operate and a rationalization of the state sector.

6

THE FISCAL SYSTEM
AND CENTRAL-LOCAL
GOVERNMENT RELATIONS

How Powerful Are Local Governments Compared to the Central Government?

As we observed in chapter 1, China is formally centralized but in practice highly decentralized. A recurrent theme throughout its history is the struggle between central and local governments, a struggle summed up in the Chinese expression *shang you zhengce, xia you duice*—"above there are policies; below there are counterpolicies."

Decentralization can be described either quantitatively or qualitatively. By the simplest quantitative measure—the proportion of fiscal revenue and expenditure handled by local governments—China is by a wide margin the most decentralized country on earth, with local governments' shares of revenue and expenditure more than twice those typical in developed OECD countries, which in turn tend to be more decentralized than developing nations (Table 6.1).

This extreme decentralization is worth bearing in mind when one hears people talking about China as an authoritarian country where the central government can just snap its fingers and make anything happen. One can also go too far in the direction of claiming that China is a fragmented country where local actors do whatever they want, regardless of what Beijing might say. Remember that "local governments" in the Chinese context includes the provinces, which have a median population of 46 million and are therefore essentially nation-sized units. If we consider provinces as part of the central government, then the "local" share of revenues falls from 40 percent

Table 6.1 The Most Decentralized Country: Local Government Shares of Fiscal Revenue and Expenditure, %

	Revenue (%)	Expenditure (%)
Developing countries	9	14
Transitional (post-Communist) countries	17	26
OECD	19	32
China	40	73

Source: Lou 2008.

to 34 percent, and the local share of expenditures falls from 73 percent to 51 percent—still high very high figures, but less extreme than the headline numbers.

Two other considerations mitigate the picture of a decentralized China. While it is true that local governments command a large share of revenue collections, they have little or no formal ability to set their own tax policies or tax rates. In the United States, every state and local government sets its own mix of taxes and tax rates based on local conditions. Some state governments (such as California) rely heavily on personal income taxes, while others (such as New Hampshire) have no income tax at all but depend mainly on sales taxes. In China, Beijing determines what kinds of taxes are allowed, sets their rates, and dictates how the revenues will be shared; localities have little leeway to adjust these parameters.

Furthermore, on a qualitative basis the central government's hold over localities is substantial. This is visible in the personnel system, substantially controlled by the party's Central Organization Department in Beijing, which systematically rotates senior officials between provinces in order to limit the authority of local networks. The party's Central Commission for Discipline Inspection, the anticorruption watchdog, is also frequently used to break up local power constellations.[1]

Still . . . *shang you zhengce, xia you duice.* For every mechanism the central authorities build to limit the autonomy of local officials, local officials are quick to build a workaround. As we shall see, a persistent issue in the fiscal system has been the rampant local practice of using extrabudgetary revenue sources (ranging from miscellaneous fees to land sales and leases) to finance extrabudgetary expenditures. And despite a formal ban on local government borrowing, China's local governments now have a gigantic debt burden.

A final point is that we should not uncritically accept stories about who the good guys and bad guys are in the central-local power struggle. Central officials moan that their wise policies are thwarted by short-sighted, greedy, and corrupt local functionaries. Local officials complain that their efforts to deal with pressing problems are undermined by senseless or contradictory edicts from arrogant, out-of-touch, and corrupt bureaucrats in Beijing. Both claims are often justified. Rather than assigning black hats and white hats, we should do our best to understand the forces that drive the power struggle: the conflicting demands for central control and local autonomy in a large country, and the incentives that drive officials at all levels to pursue ends that are sometimes in the public interest and sometimes not.

What Impact Does Decentralized Government Have on Economic Development?

From an economic standpoint, the high degree of effective decentralization brings both advantages and drawbacks. The main advantage is that decentralized authority permits policy experiments on a large scale. Sometimes the central government conducts these experiments deliberately, by designating certain cities or regions as "pilot areas" for specific policies. The largest experiments were of course the special economic zones or SEZs set up in the early 1980s, which had entirely different tax and business policies from the rest of the country. But sometimes Beijing's approach is more passive: it knows that practices in a certain locality diverge from national norms, but tolerates them either in recognition of inevitable local variation or in the hope that some interesting innovation will arise that can then be applied more broadly. This ability to experiment has been an important ingredient in China's success, and differentiates it from another large developing country, India, which can be considered China's inverse in that it is formally decentralized but in practice highly centralized.[2]

The drawbacks are that economic activity winds up being very fragmented, and local governments often lack accountability for their actions.[3] When we further consider the major incentive structures imposed on localities by the center since the early 1980s—rewarding officials for their ability to maximize GDP growth and maintain social stability—and the general tendency to focus more on capital accumulation than on economic efficiency, it is easy to see how undesirable consequences might arise.

These factors combine to produce the characteristic pathologies of Chinese local government: an obsession with large-scale, capital-intensive industrial and infrastructure projects, and a reluctance to permit loss-making enterprises to simply go bankrupt and exit the market. Capital-intensive projects are favored because they are highly visible; thus they are a good way to impress visiting officials from higher up in the bureaucracy, who can influence one's promotion prospects. They also contribute immediately to reported GDP while they are being built, because of all the investment dollars required during their construction.

If an operating factory runs into trouble, local officials have both the incentives and the means to keep it in business, even if doing so makes no economic sense. Reported GDP will suffer if the plant stops producing, and the laid-off workers could present a threat to social stability. Local governments control supplies of land and electric power and other utilities, have influence over the credit policies of local bank branches, are able to strong-arm local companies and government units to purchase goods from preferred local suppliers, and can set up trade barriers that make it hard for companies from other jurisdictions either to compete or to acquire local champions.

The power of localities to prevent the entry of new market players has substantially eroded, but their ability to keep terminally ill businesses on life support is as strong as ever. This helps explain the endurance of excess capacity and the proliferation of small players in many industries—why, for example (as we showed in chapter 3), there are still 120 automobile manufacturers in China, mostly sponsored by local governments, even though central policy for more than two decades has pushed hard for industry consolidation. When the economy's main job is to accumulate as much capital as possible—as it was in China until a few years ago—this sort of waste is manageable. But now that the economy's main job is to squeeze the highest possible return out of all its assets, the incentives of local governments need to be changed.[4]

What Was the Significance of the 1994 Tax Reform?

For a full understanding of central-local power dynamics, we need to understand the mechanics of fiscal arrangements. The history of the reform-era fiscal system divides neatly into two phases, separated by a major tax reform in 1994. A fiscal reform of comparable significance was initiated in 2014 and is supposed to be complete by the end of 2016.

The pre-1994 phase was one of rapid decentralization. During the planned-economy era, most revenue consisted of operating surpluses from state-owned enterprises (SOEs) rather than taxes, which were virtually nonexistent. This revenue was collected, mostly at the local level, and remitted to the central government. The center then sent money back down to the provinces each year to fund the next year's investment quota and to cover the administrative expenses of the local governments.[5]

Early in the reform era, policymakers made two major changes. First, they began to devolve the responsibility for investment decisions down to the enterprises. Second, to encourage local officials to promote market-driven economic activity, they allowed localities to retain any tax revenues they collected above a fixed annual quota that had to be sent to Beijing. These shifts were in keeping with the general move to reduce the roles of state planning and central control as well as to permit market forces greater play.

The effect on government budgets was dramatic. Total government revenues fell from over 30 percent of GDP in 1978 to less than 11 percent in 1994, as SOEs no longer sent their profits to the treasury. And as the free market began to take root in the late 1980s, the proportion of revenue controlled by the central government fell from a peak of 41 percent in 1984 to just 22 percent in 1993. By the early 1990s, policymakers in Beijing began to worry that the central government did not have enough revenue to finance its activities. Developing countries normally collect at least 20 percent of GDP in total government revenue, and for rich countries the figure is usually in excess of 30 percent. They also worried that with such a huge share of revenue controlled by local governments, Beijing did not have enough leverage to keep localities in line and enforce national policies.

The tax reform of 1994 aimed to solve these two problems by creating a system that would (a) increase total government revenues and (b) ensure that the central government directly controlled half or more of those revenues. Under the new arrangement, central and local governments were each given a fixed share of each tax. For the most important tax, value-added tax (VAT), the central share was 75 percent and the local share 25 percent. Localities were allowed to keep all the revenue from the "business tax"—a tax on enterprise revenues—and also the corporate income tax paid by locally controlled firms. (Centrally controlled SOEs paid corporate income tax to the central government, regardless of their physical location.) It was hoped that stronger central oversight, and improved mechanisms for collecting VAT and corporate taxes, would increase the overall revenue pie.

The 1994 reform had an immediate and permanent impact on the central-local revenue split (visible in Figure 6.1). The central share of revenues leapt from 22 percent in 1993 to 56 percent in 1994, and stayed above 50 percent through 2010. The impact on total revenue collection was slower to emerge, but impressive. After bottoming out at just over 10 percent of GDP in 1996, total government revenue inexorably rose to 23 percent of GDP in 2013.[6]

The 1994 reform had two lasting impacts. First, it enhanced Beijing's power by giving the central government greater control over the national budget, and much greater visibility on the true extent of the state's fiscal resources. Second, it imposed a structural operating deficit on local governments, since localities were

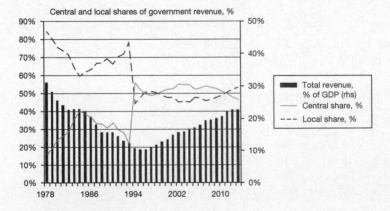

Figure 6.1 Government Revenue

Source: NBS/CEIC.

assigned a minority of revenues but a majority of expenditures—initially, about 70 percent. Technically, localities ran balanced budgets, because transfers from the central government covered their shortfalls. Only the central government was permitted to run a formal deficit and to issue bonds to finance that deficit. But in practice, the transfer system worked poorly, and localities felt immense pressure to raise extra revenues to cover their expenses. This pressure only mounted as their pretransfer deficits rose from about 3 percent of GDP in the mid-1990s to nearly 9 percent by 2013 (Figure 6.2).

In the 1990s, the favored tactic for raising extra funds was to impose ad hoc fees on whatever might occur to the imagination of the local bureaucrat. This produced a chaos of off-the-books tax collection (or extortion), and the burden fell heaviest on those who had the least ability to fight back—generally speaking, farmers. The central government responded with the "tax-for-fee" reform, which restored order by converting most of these fees to taxes, with published rates and assigned recipients. The tax-for-fee reform was completed by 2003.

But at the same time, Beijing was forcing local governments to take on an ever-wider array of responsibilities, and the central government did little to ensure that they had the tax base to fulfill these duties—a practice criticized in the United States in the 1980s with the phrase "unfunded mandates." The SOE reform in the late 1990s reduced or eliminated enterprises' requirement to

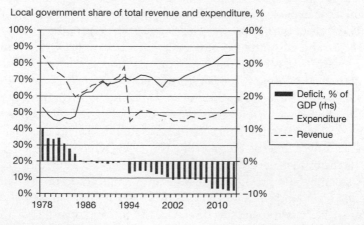

Local government share of total revenue and expenditure, %

Figure 6.2 Local Funding Gap
Source: NBS/CEIC.

cover education, healthcare, and pension benefits. Responsibility for funding these social services—and for providing welfare payments and retraining services for tens of millions of laid-off SOE workers—increasingly fell on local governments. Moreover, as the pace of urbanization increased, localities faced mounting pressure to build housing and urban infrastructure such as roads, power and water lines, and sewage systems. Between 2000 and 2011, local governments' share of total government expenditures rose from 69 percent to a staggering 85 percent. In absolute terms, it rose more than ninefold, from Rmb 1 trillion to Rmb 9.3 trillion. (During the same period, central government expenditures only tripled.) To fund these ballooning programs, localities turned to the biggest asset on their books: land.

How Does the Land-Based Local Financing System Work?

Starting in the early 2000s, city governments started to experiment with raising finance from the urban land they controlled. This was now possible because the housing privatization of 1998–2003 created a large-scale market for urban land, in which private developers were eager to get hold of city-center plots for redevelopment into modern housing, offices, and retail space. Because the price of urban land had been artificially suppressed, the difference between the current land price and its expected value after redevelopment was enormous. Local governments recognized this and began to borrow against the expected increase in land values.

The scale of the opportunity is illustrated by one of the first major deals, arranged by the China Development Bank (CDB) in Tianjin in 2003. In that year Tianjin's mayor announced a five-year infrastructure development project with a price tag of Rmb 170 billion (US$21 billion)—six times the city's combined infrastructure spending in the previous fourteen years, and more than five times the city's annual revenue. This seemingly outlandish plan was largely financed by a line of credit from the CDB, which reckoned that while the infrastructure projects themselves (roads, subways, parks, and so on) would produce little revenue, Tianjin could raise enough money from land sales to cover the Rmb 72 billion in principal and interest payments over the fifteen-year life of its loan. That forecast proved far too conservative. In the first six years of the project

Tianjin raised Rmb 95 billion from land sales, and in year seven it raised Rmb 73 billion—enough in a single year to pay off its loan.[7]

This experience, more or less, was replicated in hundreds of cities around China. To get around the formal prohibition on local government borrowing, cities usually transferred land assets into a special-purpose company; such companies later became known as "local government financing vehicles." This company would then use the land as collateral for a bank loan. Repayment of the loan was financed by sales or leases of the land. Since land values skyrocketed during the early 2000s, the collateral often wound up worth far more than was necessary to repay the loans, so at the end of the project whatever was left over could be used as collateral for a new loan. By 2010 or so, net revenues from land sales and leases accounted for about 20 percent of local government revenues.

In its early years, this model proved an effective way to finance rapid, large-scale urban improvements; it is one reason why most Chinese cities have better infrastructure than is usual in countries of similar income. The central government was fully aware of the technique, and most of the finance was supplied by the CDB, a centrally controlled policy bank.

But after 2008, the land-based finance model spiraled out of control. In response to the global financial crisis, Beijing approved a Rmb 4 trillion (US$590 billion) economic stimulus program, most of which went into infrastructure projects. To fund this activity, local governments borrowed heavily from commercial banks. These banks were less adept than the CDB and lent against land values that were unrealistically high, or sometimes did not ask for any collateral at all. The result was a tsunami of debt, much of which local governments had no hope of repaying. By the middle of 2013, the National Audit Office estimated that local governments had liabilities of almost Rmb 18 trillion, nearly double the figure for 2010. Local liabilities equated to one-third of GDP and were half again as much as the liabilities of the central government.[8]

How Big Is the Government Debt Problem?

This explosion of local government debt attracted a lot of attention, and rightly so. Unregulated borrowing by localities was at the heart of many previous emerging-market financial crises, notably the

Brazilian debt crisis of the 1980s. It was reasonable to worry that China might face a comparable problem. This was especially true since the central government statistics on local debt were opaque and sometimes contradictory, suggesting either that the central authorities were deliberately trying to obscure the magnitude of the problem or (perhaps worse) that they themselves did not really know how much debt was out there.

The general conclusion, however, is that the local debt problem is large but manageable. The IMF estimates the combined debt of central and local governments—including some local debt that the Chinese government does not count in its own estimates—at 54 percent of GDP. This is not especially high. Gross government debt in excess of 70 percent is common among OECD countries; the United States, the United Kingdom, Canada, and France have public debt loads above 90 percent of GDP. Moreover, the majority of China's public debt finances infrastructure that is likely to have a positive impact on economic growth eventually, whereas much rich-country government debt finances redistributive welfare spending. Provided it can be restructured to reduce the excessive reliance on rising land values, there is no reason why local government debt should prompt a fiscal crisis. China does have a serious debt problem, but this stems from inefficient SOEs borrowing ever more money to finance ever-less-profitable investments.[9] (See chapters 7 and 11 for details.)

The issue with local government debt is not that it risks sparking a crisis, but that it reflects a deeply flawed and unsustainable fiscal system that in turn springs from the tricky political relationship between central and local governments. Fixing this system is the aim of the fiscal reform package adopted by Xi Jinping's government in June 2014.

What Are the Biggest Problems of the Fiscal System Today?

As our discussion so far has shown, the fiscal system in place since 1994 created a number of problems:

- Local governments had expenditure responsibilities far in excess of their direct revenue resources, which encouraged them to seek ad hoc and unsustainable additional sources of revenue, such as land sales.

- Despite the formal prohibition on borrowing, localities incurred huge debts, which were often structured in an inappropriate way.
- Local governments resorted to ad hoc financing and borrowing because the central-local transfer system, which was supposed to balance their budgets, worked poorly.
- The structure of local government revenues encouraged excessive investment in capital-intensive industry and infrastructure.

The 2014–2016 fiscal reform program, overseen by finance minister Lou Jiwei (a veteran of the 1994 tax reform), aims to correct these problems—and also to increase the central government's power. But before we examine its details, it is worth looking a bit more closely at the defects of the present system.

The first is the transfer system. In theory, local governments are supposed to balance their budgets with transfers from the center. And in fact the center does transfer huge amounts of revenue to the local governments each year. But the way it does so is riddled with flaws. There are over 200 separate transfer programs with different rules, schedules, and formulas. The transfers go first from Beijing to provincial governments, which then distribute them on uncertain schedules and in highly variable ways to lower levels of government. (Transfers to the provinces are overseen by just four officials in the Ministry of Finance, so it is difficult for Beijing to track the distribution of transfers after the money goes to provincial capitals.) Many of the transfers are earmarked for specific purposes that may not suit the actual needs of the recipient agency. Some of the general-purpose transfer programs are based on formulas that deliver the most money to the richest localities, and the least to the poorest—exactly the opposite of what is needed to reduce China's stark regional income inequalities. The overall result is that local governments often do not know how much transfer money they will receive, when they will get it, and what they can use it for. This naturally gives them an incentive to hunt for other sources of revenue that they control and that are more predictable.[10]

Another issue is the inappropriate structure of borrowings. We have discussed one problem of the land finance model—that it relied on unsustainably optimistic forecasts of future increases in land values. Another is what bankers call "maturity mismatch." Localities often used three- to five-year bank loans to finance infrastructure projects whose economic benefits (and revenue streams, if any) would only materialize over two or three decades. The loans would come due long before the borrowers had enough revenue to repay them. In most countries, infrastructure projects are financed by long-term bonds, not short-term loans.

Last are the incentives created by the tax system. Generally speaking, the tax system encourages local officials—in their roles as promoters of economic development—to encourage overinvestment in infrastructure, heavy industry, mining, and property development and to give short shrift to service sectors. The basic reason is that local tax revenues historically have been dominated by production taxes on industry, volume taxes on mining, and transaction taxes on real estate.[11]

The fiscal reform package aims to address all of these problems. If successful—and that is a big if, given the size and intractability of the issues—it would be the most significant restructuring of China's fiscal relations since 1994 and would lay a solid foundation for a more durable economic-growth model based on a better balance between investment and consumption. If it fails, China will be stuck with a dysfunctional fiscal system and debt-ridden local governments.

How Does the Fiscal Reform Program Aim to Solve These Problems?

The government has not laid out all the specifics of the fiscal reform plan in a single document. But by piecing together various actions and public statements, we can see that the plan has four main elements: restructuring local government debt, reform of the tax system, improved central-local transfers, and clearer budget reporting. On the whole, it aims to strengthen the power of the central government. But it also will grant localities more discretion in organizing their budgets, in exchange for stricter accountability.

The first step has been to restructure localities' massive debts. In 2015, new borrowing by "local government financing vehicles" was banned, and Rmb 1 trillion in their debt was restructured into long-term bonds. Eventually, the aim is for all infrastructure-related local debt to be converted into either bonds or "public-private partnerships," in which private investors take over part of the debt in exchange for a share of project revenues.

The second component of the plan is to adjust both the level and the structure of local revenues. Local expenditures will be brought into closer line with the revenue base, by returning responsibility for some programs—in particular, education, healthcare, and some social welfare programs—to the central government. Even after this adjustment, localities will still rely on transfers from the center to balance their budgets. The structure of taxation will change to encourage local governments to deemphasize capital-intensive industries and promote services and consumer spending. These tax changes will include a reform of the VAT system so that it focuses more on consumption than on industrial production, switching mining taxes from a volume to a value basis (which should reduce localities' tendency to try to maximize production of raw materials like coal and iron ore regardless of market conditions) and stiffer environmental taxes.

Another tax advocated by the Ministry of Finance, but politically difficult to implement, is a tax on property values. At present China has neither a capital gains tax on property sales nor an annual assessment on property values, such as most American localities use to fund their school systems. As discussed in chapter 4, this encourages investors to buy as many properties as possible and hold them (vacant, if need be) for as long as possible until they can reap a capital gain. Imposing a property tax would make a lot of economic sense and would probably lead to a more sensible pattern of development in China's cities. But it has been vigorously opposed by property owners and by local governments, who would see a net revenue loss when they switch to a property tax from the current system of simply selling land outright.[12]

The other two important elements of the fiscal reform program are the central-local transfer system and budget accountability. The basic idea of transfer reform is to move away from the hodgepodge of earmarked transfers, and simply provide localities with general transfers or block grants that they can use to balance their budgets. At the same time, officials will be held more accountable for the way funds are used, under a revised Budget Law (passed in September 2014) that restricts the ability of officials to rely on off-budget funds and imposes stronger reporting requirements.[13]

How Will Fiscal Reform Affect Central-Local Relations and the Pattern of Economic Development?

The political aims of the fiscal reform are clear. Like the 1994 reform, it is a centralizing program whose intention is to strengthen the power of the central government and to subject the localities to greater discipline in various ways. Forcing localities to rely on bond issues for their borrowing needs, rather than on loans from compliant local bank branches, will impose market discipline. Localities that can build a good credit record will be able to go to the capital markets; more profligate governments may not be able to borrow at all. The new Budget Law strengthens discipline at higher levels of government by imposing tighter accounting standards and reducing the scope for raising and spending extrabudgetary revenue. And increased pressure on local governments to publish their budgets (a practice already piloted in Guangdong) could increase discipline by citizens, who may start to demand greater accountability in how public funds are spent. In exchange for accepting this greater oversight, local governments will gain relief from unfunded mandates, and will have greater flexibility in using transfer funds from the central government.

The economic aims are also clear. The intention is to change the incentives of local officials so that they are less inclined to promote infrastructure, capital-intensive industry, and land speculation. Instead, the hope is that they will shift their economic-development priorities to consumer-oriented service sectors. And perhaps more important, the idea is for local officials gradually to stop thinking of government as a glorified chamber of commerce, whose main aim is to make life easy for business, and to start focusing on the delivery of public goods and services—healthcare, welfare, education, a clean environment—as their main job.

These aims are part of the broader economic reform package introduced by president Xi Jinping in November 2013, which we will discuss in detail in chapter 11. And it is no accident that Beijing has moved more speedily on fixing the fiscal system than it has in other important areas, for instance, the reform of state-owned enterprises. The high priority put on fiscal reform reflects a belief that it is essential to change the incentives of the government officials who play such a large role in shaping economic activity. If those incentives are changed, the other reforms in the financial system and the corporate sector stand a decent chance of success. If the incentives are not changed, the other reforms are likely to fail no matter how ingenious they are. This logic is sound and the fiscal reforms are well designed. But it is as yet far too early to judge whether they will be successful.

Moreover, one obvious difficulty with the first part of fiscal reform—the local government bond program—is that there is no procedure for handling defaults, and indeed the authorities have made clear that they do not intend to permit defaults.[14] Localities that are unable to service their bond obligations will be able to borrow money from the central government or the People's Bank of China to cover their repayments. In the short run, the no-default rule may be helpful in creating a market for local government debt. But in the longer term it is hard to see how this market can function properly, or impose the desired discipline on local governments, without real default risk. The first issues of local bonds, in 2015, all carried virtually the same interest rate, very close to the rate on central government treasury bonds. This showed that investors saw these bonds as central-government guaranteed securities. If all local governments can borrow at the same low interest rate regardless of their individual circumstances, safe in the knowledge that Beijing will bail them out if they fail to make a payment, there is no incentive for localities to tighten up their fiscal management.

Why Doesn't Personal Income Tax Play a Bigger Role in Tax Reform?

Alert readers will have noticed that we have managed to devote nearly an entire chapter to the fiscal system without once mentioning the personal income tax, which is a crucial part of the tax systems of advanced countries. There are good reasons for this omission, which are worth touching on.

One characteristic of the Chinese tax system is that virtually all taxes are paid by companies, and the direct tax burden on individuals is very light. Personal income taxes account for only 5 percent of government revenue, a share that has remained virtually unchanged for more than a decade. Excise taxes on personal consumption items account for another 6 percent. The three main corporate taxes—VAT, business tax, and corporate income tax—account for 55 percent of government revenues, with customs tariffs, excise duties, and various other charges, many of which are paid by enterprises, accounting for the rest. There is no tax on the value of property, or on capital gains from financial assets (although transaction taxes are levied when people sell their house or their stock-market holdings).

This makes the structure of China's tax system quite different from that of most other countries, and in particular developed countries, which rely primarily on personal income taxes, real estate taxes, and consumption taxes. In the United States, for instance, nearly half of federal government revenues come from personal income taxes, and state and local governments rely heavily on real estate and sales taxes.[15]

The main reason for China's enterprise-focused tax structure is that it is a lot easier to collect taxes from a relatively small number of companies than from hundreds of millions of wage earners. This is especially true for VAT, which has built-in incentives for compliance. When a company pays its VAT, it can deduct the VAT it paid when buying goods and materials from its suppliers. Since it is relatively easy for tax officials to force the biggest enterprises to pay their full tax bill (because there are so few of them), those enterprises have a strong incentive to force their suppliers to charge VAT and provide them with proper tax receipts. Those suppliers in turn have the same incentive for their suppliers, and so on down the chain. Taxes on corporate revenues and profits are easier to evade through accounting tricks that enable firms to understate their sales and earnings.

It is interesting to speculate whether a subconscious political motive is also at play. Tom Paine's famous slogan, "no taxation without representation" has enduring relevance: a government that directly taxes its citizens gives those citizens a strong incentive to demand greater accountability for how their money is spent. It is a short step from that demand to the desire for more representative government. By essentially exempting the majority of wage earners from income tax, and by not taxing the vast earnings on the capital invested in the nation's booming property and stock markets, the government—whether intentionally or not—defuses a potential source of political activism.

Whatever the reasons, widening the base of the personal income tax has played no visible role in the government's fiscal reform program so far. And given that Xi Jinping's political agenda is to tighten top-down control by an authoritarian Communist Party, it seems unlikely that the income tax will rise in importance any time soon.

7

THE FINANCIAL SYSTEM

What Role Do China's Banks Play in Financing Growth, and How Has This Changed?

China has a bank-dominated financial system. About 80 percent of finance is provided either by banks or by other lenders that act like banks (see Figure 7.1). Only about 20 percent comes from the capital markets (issuance of stocks and bonds). In this respect China lies squarely in the tradition of East Asian developmental states, all of which mainly used banks to finance their growth. This pattern is also found in many continental European economies, such as Germany and France, although those countries also have better-developed corporate bond and stock markets than Asian countries. China's system differs most sharply from those of the United States and the United Kingdom, both of which have unusually large capital markets and banking systems with an unusually low share of total financial assets.

That said, the nature of Chinese banks, and the financial system in China more generally, have changed enormously in the thirty-five years of the reform era.[1] At the beginning of reforms, banks were simply the distribution agents for investment funds that came out of the state budget. In the 1980s and 1990s, more banks were established. They began to issue real loans, but these loans were driven more by central and local policy directives than by commercial considerations. In the late 1990s banks were restructured along more commercial lines, and they began to diversify into household mortgages, credit cards, and other forms of consumer lending. And starting in 2010, the bank share of financial activity began to decline as nonbank lending companies, and the bond and stock markets, began to play a larger role in a more diverse financial ecosystem. Even so, banks remain the core of the financial system, and their

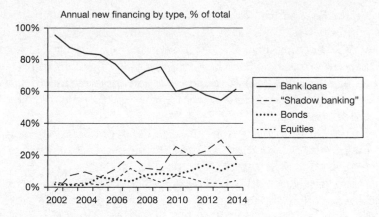

Figure 7.1 Structure of Financing Flows
Source: Author calculaons from PBOC data.

lending remains subject to much political influence from central and local governments.

During the planned economy period, China effectively had one bank, the People's Bank of China (PBOC), which was both the central bank and the sole commercial bank. Technically, two other banks existed, but the Bank of China was in essence the unit of the PBOC that handled foreign exchange transactions, and the China Construction Bank was a unit of the Ministry of Finance (MOF) that distributed funds for investment projects. A network of rural credit cooperatives enabled collection of deposits from farm families and the distribution of credit to small-scale rural enterprises. Under the Communist system, the PBOC "monobank" was simply the fiscal agent of the state, moving funds into state enterprises to enable them to buy their supplies and pay their workers, and transmitting enterprise surpluses back to the central treasury.

In the early 1980s, the PBOC was gradually turned into a regular central bank, and commercial lending functions were gradually separated out into the "Big Four" commercial banks directly controlled by the MOF—the Bank of China, the China Construction Bank, the Industrial and Commercial Bank of China, and the Agricultural Bank of China. The Big Four dominated China's financial system from the mid-1980s until the early 2000s, for most of that period accounting for two-thirds or more of total bank credit. Until the late

1990s, the Big Four continued to act more as state fiscal agents than as proper banks. Their main job was to collect deposits from individuals and companies and to extend working-capital loans to state-owned enterprises (SOEs). They made virtually no loans to private firms or households. Basic elements of consumer finance that we take for granted, such as personal checking accounts and credit cards, did not exist.

This model hit a crisis in the late 1990s. Following Deng Xiaoping's southern tour of 1992 (see chapter 1), the nation went on an investment spree, and SOEs—especially those controlled by local governments—invested heavily in new capacity to produce goods for which there were often no markets. Inventories piled up in warehouses. Much of the SOE sector was engulfed in an abyss of unpayable "triangular debt": producers of final goods could not pay their suppliers, and companies could not repay their bank loans. Government data was murky, but subsequent research suggests that bad loans in the Big Four reached a staggering one-third of GDP in 1998.[2] A leading international analyst concluded that "China's four major banks as a group have a negative net worth and are thus insolvent."[3] The economy risked suffocating under the weight of dead capital.

Premier Zhu Rongji organized a restructuring plan that solved the problem. First, most bad loans were extracted from the banks and placed in specialized asset management companies. The banks got fresh capital from the MOF and were told they no longer had to lend to zombie SOEs; instead, their job was to finance viable businesses and give mortgages to families buying homes in the freshly privatized housing market. Next, in 2001–2006, the Big Four were reorganized as shareholding companies, found "strategic shareholders" (mainly foreign commercial and investment banks) that gave them infusions of capital and bolstered their international credibility, and were listed on international stock markets.[4]

While it restructured the banks, the government made other moves to create a more diversified and better regulated financial system. In 1994, it set up three "policy" banks to finance government-directed projects that would likely not generate a commercial rate of return.[5] In the late 1990s, a dozen or so smaller "second-tier" or "shareholding" banks were encouraged to expand their operations. These banks were also state-owned, but their shareholders were a congeries of local governments and other SOEs, rather than the MOF. At least in theory, they were nimbler than the Big Four because they were not subservient to the central government and operated only in the most vibrant regions. Urban credit cooperatives were organized into about a hundred city-level banks, and rural credit cooperatives were restructured into rural banks. Thanks to this proliferation of new lenders, by 2014 the Big Four's share of total bank loans shrank to about 40 percent. Finally, regulation was made more professional by the creation of the China Banking Regulatory Commission (CBRC). Led for its first decade by an experienced reform-oriented banker, Liu Mingkang, the CBRC did a good job of ensuring that banks adopted modern risk-management practices and stayed well capitalized.

As a result of all these factors—a stronger capital structure, increased competition, a healthier universe of borrowers, discipline from domestic and international stockholders, and a vigilant regulator—the quality of China's banks has improved, and they finance a much wider array of activities at present than in the 1990s. Consumer lending, virtually nonexistent in 2000, now accounts for 19 percent of bank loans and consists mainly of home mortgages. Contrary to a widespread view that the banks are just ATM machines for SOEs, a large and rising share of new corporate lending goes to private firms.

What Is "Financial Repression" and How Has It Affected China's Growth?

The term "financial repression" refers to a set of policies designed to channel funds away from household and corporate savers and toward the government. A common method is to cap bank-deposit interest rates at or below the rate of inflation. If, for instance, the interest rate on a one-year bank deposit is 2 percent, and the annual inflation rate is 3 percent, then the $100 I put into a bank account today will be worth $102 a year from now in nominal terms, but only $99 in real, inflation-adjusted terms. Such ultralow interest rates are a hidden tax on depositors, whose benefit is that it keeps interest costs low for the people who borrow money.

China and other East Asian developmental states used a broader set of financial repression tools to maximize the government's control over money flows. These include:

- Tightly regulated interest rates;
- Rules to prevent banks or nonbank financial institutions from skirting the deposit-rate caps by offering other, higher-yielding financial products;
- An undervalued exchange rate (encouraging investment in export industries and discouraging purchases of imported consumer goods or borrowing in foreign currencies);
- Capital controls (to prevent savers from escaping the low yields at home by investing their money abroad).

The main aim of such policies is to increase the availability of funds for investment in infrastructure, basic industries such as steel and petrochemicals, and export manufacturing. China only slowly groped its way to a financial repression package in the 1980s and 1990s. At the beginning, the exchange rate was gradually depreciated in order to promote exports, and capital movements were strictly controlled. But domestic interest rates were not held especially low. Zhu Rongji hiked interest rates sharply in 1994 to tame double-digit inflation. Even after he got inflation under control, Zhu kept deposit interest rates relatively high. From 1997 through 2003—roughly the period of Zhu's premiership—the average real (inflation-adjusted) interest rate for one-year deposits was almost 3 percent. But this changed in 2004, under the government of Hu Jintao and Wen Jiabao, which adopted a classic financial repression strategy. In 2004–2013, the average real deposit rate was *negative* 0.3 percent (see Figure 7.2).[6]

The main reason for the adoption of this implicit tax on depositors probably had to do with the bank bailout of the late 1990s. This bailout was in essence a series of accounting tricks, and to rebuild their true capital base the banks needed to have abnormally high profits for an extended period of time. One way to guarantee such profits was to hold banks' funding cost (deposit rates) at very low levels, while letting them lend out funds at whatever rate the market would bear.[7] It is also likely that Hu and Wen kept interest rates low in order to ensure cheap funding for their ambitious infrastructure programs.

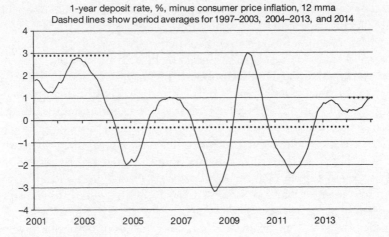

1-year deposit rate, %, minus consumer price inflation, 12 mma
Dashed lines show period averages for 1997–2003, 2004–2013, and 2014

Figure 7.2 Real Interest Rates

Source: Author calculations from NBS/CEIC.

Ultralow interest rates did indeed help the banks get back on their feet. And they also facilitated the extraordinary construction boom of the 2000s, which gave China first-class infrastructure and provided modern housing for tens of millions of urban Chinese households. But financial repression also incurred large costs. By subsidizing energy-intensive and polluting heavy industry, it accelerated the pace of environmental degradation and helped turn China into the world's biggest emitter of carbon dioxide. And, just like the ultralow interest rate policy in the United States in the early 2000s, it ultimately led to an oversupply of housing and other excesses, creating the worry that China was heading for a financial crisis.

What Is the Risk That China Will Hit a Financial Crisis?

One of the most common worries about China is that it will encounter a severe financial crisis. This worry arises partly from the track record of emerging markets in general and partly from problems specific to China's financial sector.

Fast-growth emerging economies are prone to financial crisis. The litany of the last three decades includes Brazil and other Latin American countries (1982–1984), Mexico (1994), South Korea and several Southeast Asian countries (1997), Russia (1998), and Argentina

(1998–2002). Why should China prove immune to the financial shocks that beset other big emerging economies?

Moreover, China has recently experienced two phenomena that often presage financial crisis: a housing bubble and a rapid increase in overall debt. The housing bubble is of particular concern, because on the surface it looks as though China is repeating the errors of the United States in the early 2000s. Between 1998 and 2012 China's annual completions of urban housing tripled, and the average house price rose fourfold. Most Chinese cities have a temporary oversupply of housing; both new construction and prices must fall while this excess supply is absorbed. It was precisely such a fall in construction activity and prices in late 2006 that triggered the US subprime mortgage crisis.

Look below the surface, though, and the resemblances between the Chinese and US housing markets melt away. We discussed the differences in detail in chapter 4; here it is enough to note that the financial condition of homebuyers is far less fragile in China than it was in the United States. The average down payment for a home purchase in China is well over 30 percent and the legal minimum is 20 percent. On average, urban households carry debt that is less than 50 percent of their annual disposable income. This is a far cry from the United States, where down payments of 5 percent or less were common, and household debt peaked at nearly 130 percent of disposable income. This means that even if house prices fall quite a bit, Chinese homeowners will still have positive equity in their homes and will be able to continue paying off their mortgages. China is unlikely to suffer a housing-related financial crisis.

A more serious worry is the rapid increase in national "leverage"—that is, the ratio of debt to GDP. The combined gross debt of households, corporations, and the government was relatively stable at around 140 percent of GDP for several years until 2008. By the end of 2015 this figure had risen to around 230 percent, thanks mainly to greatly increased borrowing by local governments and SOEs during economic stimulus programs in 2009 and 2012.

The *level* of debt is not itself worrisome. A debt-to-GDP ratio of 230 percent may sound scary, but many advanced economies, including the United States and Japan, have higher ones. With its faster-trending economic growth rate, China will have more income to service its debts than slow-growth countries with higher debt levels. It also has plenty of assets that could be sold to pay down debts, such as land controlled by local governments or plant and equipment owned by SOEs.

Whatever the level, however, a large and rapid *increase* in debt, such as we have seen in China since 2008, often does lead to financial crisis. But not necessarily. To have a crisis, you need two things: fast-rising debt, and a *trigger event* that forces shaky borrowers to pay up or go bankrupt. China has the debt, but not the trigger.

The classic trigger for an emerging-market debt crisis is an inability to pay back foreign lenders. The usual consequence is a collapse in the country's currency, which then causes the local-currency value of all foreign debts to skyrocket. This brings down borrowers who previously thought they were fine—including, sometimes, banks who may have raised funds on foreign debt markets. Inability to repay large foreign debts was the basic problem for Latin America in the early 1980s; for Russia and the Asian crisis countries of the late 1990s; and for Ireland, Iceland, and Greece in Europe more recently.

This is obviously not China's problem. Its foreign borrowings are small—about 10 percent of GDP—and its gigantic foreign reserves of US$3.5 trillion (nearly 40 percent of GDP) give it plenty of ammunition to ward off a speculative attack and preserve the value of its currency. It runs an annual current account surplus of 2 to 3 percent of GDP, meaning that it has more than enough current income to cover its short-term foreign debts.

It is, of course, perfectly possible for a financial system to run into trouble even if it has little foreign exposure. This can happen if banks lend to a lot of borrowers who cannot repay their loans—as Chinese banks did in the 1990s and US subprime mortgage lenders did in the 2000s—*and* if banks start to experience a lack of liquid funds, which causes them to put pressure on shaky borrowers to repay. This can create a downward spiral in which borrowers are forced to sell assets at fire-sale prices to meet their creditors' demands. The fall in asset prices turns previously safe borrowers into shaky ones, and they too must start selling assets. Banks face mounting losses because the market value of the collateral backing on their loans is suddenly far less than they thought it was. This is what happened in the United States in 2008.

The crucial point is that the immediate cause of the crisis is not the bad loans: it is the *lack of liquid funds*, which triggers the demand that a lot of assets be sold at once, often for prices far below their true value. If funds are abundant, lenders can be more patient about calling in their loans, asset prices adjust slowly rather than all at once, and crisis is averted. No liquidity trigger, no crisis. And in China, there is no obvious liquidity trigger. Virtually all the credit in China is backed one-for-one by deposits, the safest and most stable kind of funding. By contrast, in the United States in 2008, nearly three-quarters of credit was funded not by bank deposits, but by funds raised on wholesale financial markets. When those markets froze up after the Lehman Brothers bankruptcy, liquidity dried up and financial panic ensued.[8]

Evidence that a financial system can be riddled with bad loans but still avoid an obvious crisis is provided by Japan in the early 1990s and China itself later in the decade. In the late 1980s Japanese banks lent vast amounts to commercial real estate projects, based on land values that proved to be several times higher than could be sustained. In 1991 land prices collapsed, as did prices on the overextended Tokyo stock market. But the financial system did not crumble. Regulators encouraged banks not to call in their bad loans, but to keep them on their books as if they were still normal; and the central bank printed enough money to keep the banks from being dragged down by their unprofitable portfolios.

The long-run consequences of this approach, of course, were not so good. Since there was no mechanism for restructuring or cleaning up the bad debts, Japanese banks spent years weighed down by unprofitable loans, unable to increase lending to productive enterprises. And companies spent years devoting all their spare cash to paying down debt, rather than investing in new projects. Japan did not suffer a financial crisis, but it did endure a "lost decade" during which economic growth virtually ground to a halt.[9]

China's own experience after 1997 provides a more inspiring example. Zhu Rongji and other senior leaders did not want a financial crisis, but they didn't want a lost decade either. So they fixed the banks' balance sheets by hiving off the bad loans into asset management companies and by pumping in fresh capital from the treasury and later from foreign investors. Then they undertook big structural reforms—closing down zombie SOEs, deregulating manufacturing, and privatizing the housing market—all of which made it possible for the banks to find profitable new projects to lend to. As a result, the economy took off again, and the mountain of bad loans that seemed so daunting was whittled down to a rather unprepossessing molehill by a decade of fast growth. In 1999, the bad loans transferred from banks to asset management companies amounted to 15 percent of GDP, and more than a year's worth of government revenue. Ten years later, they were less than 4 percent of GDP, and one-fifth of annual government revenue.[10]

Is China today more likely to repeat its own post-1997 experience, or fall into a Japan-style "lost decade"? The answer is, probably somewhere in between. On the plus side, the stresses on China's financial system are lower than they were in the 1990s. The official ratio of bad loans to banks' total assets (the nonperforming loan or NPL ratio) is just over 1 percent; many bank analysts believe the true figure could be 5 percent or even higher. This is bad, but a lot better than the 30 percent bad loan rate in the late 1990s. Furthermore—and contrary to the popular belief in Western financial circles that Chinese banks do nothing but shovel money into unproductive SOEs or local governments—the quality of bank lending is gradually improving, with more of it going to the dynamic private sector. The private-sector share of outstanding bank loans has gone from virtually zero in the late 1990s to nearly 40 percent in 2014 (see Figure 7.3).[11]

China's financial sector is somewhat healthier than many pessimistic reports suggest. That is the good news. The bad news is that

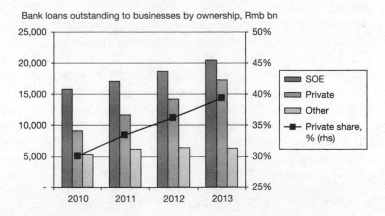

Figure 7.3 Private vs State Credit Share

Source: Ministry of Finance.

China escaped from its financial bind of the 1990s mainly through fast growth, and such growth is no longer available. Today, potential GDP growth is probably around 6 to 7 percent at best, compared to 10 to 11 percent in the early 2000s. Another bit of bad news is that in the late 1990s, China's overall debt level wasn't very high, even if the quality of lending was poor. So China did not have to slow down the growth of debt; it just had to make sure that debt was used for more productive purposes. China today does not have that luxury. Debt is high and growing fast, and over the next several years the debt-to-GDP ratio must be stabilized. To do this, the growth rate of credit must be cut approximately in half from the present level, so that it matches the GDP growth rate.[12] But it is very difficult to cut back credit growth without slowing down the economy. This risks creating a vicious cycle: as you cut credit growth, the economy slows. So you have to cut back credit even more in order to meet the target of stabilizing the debt-to-GDP ratio, and this slows growth even more. Eventually you wind up with no growth at all.

The way to avoid this trap is to focus on efficiency. Instead of cutting back the growth in credit, make sure that each dollar of credit generates more GDP growth. Once greater efficiency is achieved, you don't need as much growth in credit to achieve a given level of GDP growth, and credit and GDP can gradually converge, stabilizing the debt-to-GDP ratio. Achieving such efficiency gains, however, is difficult: deep-rooted reforms in both the financial system (the lenders) and the real economy (the borrowers) are necessary. Private firms are getting more credit than in the past, but still far less than their contribution to the economy warrants; there is still too much low-return, politically driven lending to SOEs and local governments. The government is targeting reforms to cut back credit to SOEs and governments, and to deregulate industries so private firms have more profitable investment opportunities. It is hard to judge whether these reforms are bold enough or will occur fast enough to ward off a severe economic slowdown (see chapter 11).

How Worried Should We Be about the Rise of "Shadow Banking"?

After the 2008 global financial crisis, regulators and financial sector analysts started to pay attention to so-called shadow banking, which the IMF defines as "financial intermediaries or activities involved in credit intermediation outside the regular banking system, and therefore lacking a formal safety net"—or in simpler language, banking done off the balance sheets of regular banks. In some countries with highly developed financial systems, notably the United States and the United Kingdom, these lightly regulated "shadow banking" activities were bigger than the formal banking systems, and many believed that they contributed to the financial crisis.[13]

By 2010, shadow banking began to emerge in China, through two channels. Banks and trust companies started offering "wealth management products," which gave investors higher rates of interest than bank deposits. And an increasing number of loans began to be made outside the traditional bank channels—mainly through trust companies. (Trusts are lightly regulated institutions that collect funds from wealthy individuals and companies and invest in a range of credit instruments. They are not banks but sometimes work closely with bank partners.) The expansion of nonbank loan activity was dramatic: from 2010 through 2014 annual growth in bank lending stayed fairly stable at around 14 percent, but a massive increase in shadow lending drove total credit growth to a peak of 23 percent in early 2013.

Chinese shadow banking differs greatly from shadow finance in advanced countries, particularly in the United States. First, Chinese shadow banking is fairly small. The Financial Stability Board, an international group that monitors shadow banking around the world, found that for the entire world in 2013, nonbank assets accounted for 25 percent of all financial system assets, and were equivalent to 120 percent of world GDP. In the United States, nonbank assets accounted for nearly 60 percent of all financial assets, and equated to 150 percent of GDP. In China, nonbank assets were just 9 percent of financial assets, and a relatively modest 31 percent of GDP.[14]

Second, China's shadow finance is boring. Almost all of it consists of ordinary bank loans that are routed through nonbank institutions. Virtually all of the exotic features that make shadow banking both difficult to measure and potentially destabilizing in advanced countries are absent in China. China has basically no securitized loans, no derivatives, no collateralized debt obligations, no credit default swaps, few hedge funds and real estate investment trusts, and no structured finance vehicles.

Despite its small size and dull nature, China's shadow finance is important: its emergence sounded the death knell for China's system of regulated interest rates. Wealth management products emerged because depositors were tired of getting a measly 2 to 3 percent return on their money, especially when inflation rose to around 5 percent in 2010. The rise of these products in China parallels the rise of money market funds in the United States in the 1970s, which was also a response to regulated deposit rates falling behind inflation. Within a decade after the creation of the first money market funds, US deposit interest rates were fully deregulated.[15]

Shadow lending is also a revolt against outdated regulation. Until early 2015, Chinese banks were required by law to maintain a loan-to-deposit ratio of less than 75 percent—that is, the total value of loans on their books must not exceed 75 percent of the value of their deposits. (The other 25 percent of deposits must be used to buy liquid securities, such as government bonds.)[16] In a fast-growing developing economy, this is a sensible rule. It makes it almost impossible for banks to run into a liquidity shortage, which as we have seen is a trigger for financial crisis. But in a more mature, slower-growing economy, this regulation becomes a straitjacket that makes it difficult for many worthy borrowers— especially higher-risk small and medium enterprises—to get loans. Shadow lending arose as a way to satisfy legitimate credit demand that banks could not meet because of their loan-to-deposit ratio requirement.

China's financial regulators, the CBRC and PBOC, at first took a positive view of shadow banking, believing that its benefits in giving more choice to depositors and borrowers outweighed the risks. But by 2014, they began to focus on reining in the rapid growth of shadow lending and on deregulating the banks so that the need for shadow finance would become less acute. The most important deregulatory step is the liberalization of interest rates.

How Did China Liberalize Its Interest Rates?

China abolished the ceiling on bank loan interest rates in 2004 but, as we have discussed, the more important control is on deposit rates, which for most of 2004–2013 were set at or below the inflation rate, enabling a classic financial repression strategy. The rise of shadow finance, however, made clear that artificially low deposit rates could not be enforced forever. Recently, regulators have taken steps that should lead to the full deregulation of deposit interest rates. Banks have been given more leeway to offer deposit rates higher than the benchmark rates set by the PBOC. And in 2015 China established a long-awaited deposit insurance system, which like the FDIC system in the United States provides security for most household bank deposits. The last restrictions on deposit interest rates were lifted in July 2015.

Deposit insurance means that guaranteed bank deposits will carry relatively low interest rates, while other financial products—deposits above a certain size, money market funds, wealth management products, and so on—will offer higher rates to compensate investors for the risk that they might lose some or all of their principal. As investors move more and more money into higher-yielding products, banks will face pressure to lend more money at higher rates to riskier, mainly private-sector borrowers. This is already happening in the "shadow banking" sector, where high-yielding wealth-management products finance high-yield loans. So long as the interest rates on these new loans are high enough to compensate for the risks, the process can be beneficial. The price of money will increasingly be set by the market supply and demand for credit, rather than by government fiat. In theory, this more market-based pricing will make credit more efficient. More loans can go to private companies, generating a high return on their invested capital and less need to go to SOEs and local governments making low-return investments. Over time, this greater efficiency could solve the problem of debt growing faster than the economy as a whole.

Why Has China Controlled Its Exchange Rate So Tightly?

China has a managed exchange rate, not a free-floating one. Contrary to a widespread view in the financial media and US Congress, China has never really had a policy of deliberate under-valuation to ramp up its exports. For most of the reform era, the main aims of exchange-rate policy have been to ensure that (a) prices in China were reasonably comparable to those in the rest of the world; (b) China's exports stayed competitive (but exporters also faced pressure to keep moving up the value chain); and (c) businesses had a stable and predictable investment environment, and didn't have to worry that wild swings in the currency might suddenly destroy their profits or raise their operating costs. In general, the last goal—stability for investors—has been the most important.

The balance of these different aims has shifted over time, along with changes in China's economy. From 1979 to 1994, the renminbi steadily devalued, from 1.5 to the dollar to 8.7. This was because during the 1980s, the main task of the exchange rate was to enable a move from a Communist-style import-substitution economy to an East Asian export-oriented one. In the planned economy period, China—like virtually every other Communist country—had a severely overvalued exchange rate, reflecting the Communist economic principle that domestic investment in heavy industry, rather than international trade, was the route to wealth. In this set-up, a high exchange rate was useful because it made imports of capital goods and raw materials cheap.

The new export-driven growth model required an exchange rate that was, if anything, a little undervalued, so that China's exports would be competitive on global markets. Over the first fifteen years of reform, China let its exchange rate gradually fall to a more realistic level. It also maintained two exchange rates: a high official rate, used, for example, when foreign tourists converted their money into renminbi; and a second, market-oriented rate that was available only to licensed foreign trade organizations.

In 1994 the two exchange rates were combined (at the lower market rate), and over the next couple of years the authorities let the exchange rate float fairly freely, in an effort to figure out the renminbi's true international market value.[17] By the end of 1996 the rate had settled at 8.3 to the dollar, and this was adopted as the fixed rate for the next nine years, with only a small daily trading range permitted.

Why did China shift from steady devaluation to a fixed rate against the dollar? The reason is that the main job had changed: from making the renminbi safe for Chinese exporters, to making the renminbi safe for foreign investors. Foreign companies were pouring into China at a high rate in the 1990s and building huge numbers of export-oriented factories. Such investors wanted reassurance that their big investments would not be rendered worthless by dramatic swings in the exchange rate. China's exchange rate thus needed to meet two conditions: it had to be low enough to ensure that China's exports would remain competitive, but it also had to be close enough to the true market level that it could be maintained for a long time with little variation.

Almost immediately after its adoption, the fixed exchange rate faced a challenge. During the Asian financial crisis of 1997–1998, several neighboring Asian countries, many of whom had export baskets that competed directly with China's, were forced to devalue their currencies massively. Most observers assumed that China would devalue the renminbi as well in order to keep its exporters in business.

They were wrong. China did not devalue: in fact, it tightened the peg to the US dollar by reducing the permitted daily trading band to a minuscule 0.1 percent. Instead of succumbing to the temptation to devalue, it doubled down on its fixed currency bet. Why? Basically, because the principle of long-run stability for investors trumped the expedient of short-term support for exporters. For a couple of years, the costs were high: export growth ground nearly to a halt, and the trade surplus shrank. But foreign investors were heartened by Beijing's commitment to a stable exchange rate, and FDI continued to pour in. By 2001 China had established a clear reputation as one of the best places in Asia to do business, and exports were growing again at double-digit rates.

By 2004, China's trade surplus was exploding, and critics in the United States began to argue that an undervalued currency was helping Chinese factories steal market share from American firms. Note that China's currency in 2004 had exactly the same value against the US dollar as in 1998. China had not devalued its currency to gain exports. But two things had happened. First, Chinese workers had become far more productive, because industrial reforms made them move from inefficient SOEs to better-managed private and foreign firms. And second, the US dollar weakened sharply after 2000. The renminbi, pegged to the dollar, got cheaper against many other currencies (such as the euro), and this helped Chinese exporters.

In 2005, China abandoned the fixed-dollar peg and let the renminbi "crawl up" against the dollar. The initial pace of appreciation was slow, but after China's current account surplus hit $400 billion, or 10 percent of GDP, in 2007, the renminbi's rise accelerated. By the end of 2013, after eight years of gradual appreciation, the renminbi touched a rate of 6 to the dollar, making it nearly

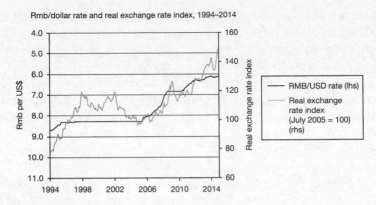

Rmb/dollar rate and real exchange rate index, 1994–2014

Figure 7.4 Exchange Rate
Source: NBS/CEIC.

40 percent more valuable than in 2005 (see Figure 7.4). Thanks in large part to this shift, the current account had shrunk to a much less scary 2 percent of GDP.

A new stage in Beijing's currency management appears to have begun in August 2015, when the PBOC announced that its daily fixing of the "central parity rate" (the rate around which the currency may trade up or down by up to 2 percent in a single day) would be based on the previous day's market close. Previously, the PBOC set the daily fixing without reference to recent market activity. This was a step toward a more freely floating currency. Even so, the authorities will probably continue to intervene to prevent the currency moving too far in one direction or another. One reason is that maintaining a stable environment for investors—and keeping the trade surplus and the pace of capital flows stable as well—remain important policy goals. A second reason is that Beijing now wants the renminbi to evolve into an important international currency, like the dollar, euro, or yen. And for this purpose, a stable value is also useful.

Why Is China Trying to Make the Renminbi an International Currency?

Beginning in 2009, China began a concerted push to increase the international use of the renminbi, which until then had been minimal. Key features of the program were increasing the ability of

Hong Kong residents to open renminbi bank accounts, boosting the use of renminbi in the invoicing of China's huge trade flows, and the opening of a renminbi bond market in Hong Kong. (Renminbi bonds issued outside of the Chinese mainland are colloquially known as "dim sum" bonds.)

Results of this program were in many respects impressive. By the end of 2014 outstanding dim sum bonds totaled Rmb 400 billion ($65 billion); renminbi deposits in Hong Kong totaled Rmb 1 trillion, or 12 percent of total deposits in the territory; and 22 percent of China's trade was settled in renminbi. Renminbi bond issuance expanded beyond Hong Kong to other financial centers, notably Singapore and London. From a standing start only five years earlier, this was a large increase in the renminbi's international presence, comparable in many ways to the internationalization of the Japanese yen in the 1980s.[18]

That said, the renminbi is still very far from being a major international currency. In 2013, the last year for which we have firm data, the renminbi ranked ninth on the list of the most frequently traded currencies on foreign exchange markets and was involved in 2 percent of global currency trades by value. The shares of the three main global currencies—the US dollar, the euro, and the yen—were respectively 87 percent, 33 percent, and 23 percent. (Because every trade involves two currencies, the total for all currencies is 200 percent.) Even secondary currencies like the British pound, the Australian dollar, and the Swiss franc traded three to five times more frequently than the renminbi. The dim sum bond market has grown rapidly, but it is still a tiny fraction of the US$22 trillion of international bonds outstanding.[19]

One reason that the renminbi began to internationalize was simply that it was quite odd for the currency of a trading nation of China's size *not* to be internationally traded. After nearly two decades of double-digit growth in its total trade, China became the world's biggest exporter in 2009 and overtook the United States as the world's biggest trading nation (imports plus exports) in 2013. With so many countries and companies shipping goods to and from China, it is natural that more of them would want to conduct that trade in China's currency—just as international use of the deutschemark and yen soared in the 1970s, when West Germany and Japan became major trading powers.

There were also policy reasons behind the renminbi's abrupt takeoff. One has to do with the 2008 global financial crisis. China's closed financial system was not damaged by the crisis, but its trade flows were: exports fell by nearly 20 percent in the year after the crisis, the worst decline ever. Many people, including Chinese officials, believed one reason for this was a freezing up of the market for letters of credit, the most important instrument of trade finance. Most letters of credit were denominated in US dollars. Chinese officials believed that increasing the proportion of its trade financed in renminbi, rather than dollars, would strengthen its ability to weather any future international financial storm.

Another factor was the desire by the PBOC to force the pace of China's *domestic* financial liberalization. China's closed and repressed financial system made sense so long as the main economic task was mobilizing resources to maximize investment in infrastructure and basic industry. But by 2009 it was apparent to many policymakers, including the leaders of the PBOC, that this mobilization phase was nearing its end, and that future economic growth would have to come more from efficiency gains. For this to happen, the financial system had to become more competitive and efficient, and the cost of money (interest rates) had to be driven more by the market and less by government planners. But many financial institutions, and the SOEs that benefited from cheap capital and a closed system, opposed financial liberalization. To get around this resistance, the PBOC started building up the renminbi market in Hong Kong. The idea was to create a place outside of mainland China where renminbi interest rates could be set by the market. Once that small-scale, controlled experiment succeeded, it would be easier to make the case that liberalizing interest rates on the mainland was both beneficial and relatively low-risk.[20]

What Is the Likelihood of the Renminbi Becoming an Important Global Reserve Currency and Even Supplanting the US Dollar?

The question of the renminbi's reserve-currency potential gained new relevance in November 2015, when the currency became the fifth to join the IMF's special drawing rights (SDR), an artificial reserve currency. This was important symbolic recognition of China's growing importance in the global economy, but says little about the currency's future role.[21] The renminbi could become a secondary reserve currency, like the yen or the Swiss franc, within the next decade. Its chances of replacing the US dollar are close to zero. The financial press frequently carries stories about how China plans to turn the renminbi into an alternative to the dollar, which since the end of World War II has been the world's principal currency for trade and investment. This plan might exist—we have no way to know—but we can be sure that it will be many decades before the renminbi rivals the dollar, and there is a good chance that it never will.

First, international use of the renminbi is still microscopic compared to that of the dollar. The dollar is over forty times more frequently traded than the renminbi on foreign exchange markets. The dollar accounts for about 60 percent of the reserve holdings of the world's central banks, a share that it has maintained, with some variation, since the late 1940s. Virtually all the rest of central bank holdings are in euros or yen; the renminbi's share is probably less than 1 percent. Even if the renminbi continues its current rapid pace of internationalization, it will be many years before it comes close to rivaling the dollar's influence.

Moreover, there are reasons to think that renminbi internationalization will slow down. Here the precedent of Japan is interesting. In the 1980s, many people talked about Japan in much the same way they talk about China today, as a rising financial superpower. By 1990, the yen accounted for 14 percent of international foreign exchange trading (seven times China's level in 2013) and 9 percent of global central bank reserves. Backed by Japan's seemingly unstoppable economic juggernaut, the yen seemed poised to join or perhaps even replace the dollar at the top of the international currency rankings.

It never happened: 1990 turned out to be the peak of the yen's importance. By 2010 its shares of foreign exchange trading and global reserves fell to 9 percent and 3 percent, respectively. This was partly because Japan's economic growth slowed to almost zero for nearly a decade. But it was also because its leaders refused to open up the financial system, and clung to an economic growth model that depended on large trade surpluses. For a nation's currency to be truly global on a sustained basis, it must have deep, open, and trustworthy financial markets that foreigners can easily move money in and out of. In the absence of such markets, foreigners will be inclined to look elsewhere for places to park their liquid funds. Willingness to run a trade deficit also helps. When the United States runs a trade deficit, as it has virtually every year since the early 1970s, it sends more dollars abroad than it collects. That means the world has an abundance of dollars. People are always hungry for safe places to invest these extra dollars, and America's deep, open, and trustworthy bond market is a good place to do so.

Japan proved unwilling to open up its financial markets or to run trade deficits—which meant that its own demand for yen exceeded the supply it was able to pump out to the rest of the world, making it difficult for foreigners to maintain large yen balances. Will China prove any different? Perhaps. For now, it seems committed to keeping its financial markets relatively closed and to running trade surpluses. According to the standard indices of financial openness, China has the least open financial sector of any major economy. It is opening up (for instance, by letting foreign investors buy stocks on the Shanghai market through brokers in Hong Kong), but at a sluggish pace.[22] So long as those conditions hold, the ability of the renminbi to become a major international currency will be constrained.

8

ENERGY AND THE ENVIRONMENT

In the preceding chapters we have examined three of the systems that support China's economic structure: the financial, fiscal, and enterprise systems. In this chapter we will look at the fourth major system, energy. This is in some ways the most complex, because China's energy use is tied up in two other major issues: the nation's air pollution problem and global climate change. Securing diverse, stable supplies of energy to fuel its future growth is also a big factor in China's emerging geopolitical strategy.

How Much Energy Does China Use?

China is the world's biggest consumer of energy; its energy use accounts for close to a quarter of global consumption. China burns 30 percent more energy than the United States and nearly twice as much as the European Union. It is by far the world's biggest user of coal, accounting for about half of global consumption. Consequently, China is also the world's biggest contributor to carbon dioxide (CO_2) emissions that are the main driver of global warming.

Of course, China has a lot of people and a very large industrial economy, so it is not surprising that it would use a lot of energy. The more important question is, does China use a lot or a little energy *relative to its population and economic weight*? To answer this question we have to convert all of China's energy consumption—whether from oil, coal, gas, nuclear, or renewables—into standard units and then divide by its population and GDP. The results, which convert all energy use into their equivalents in barrels of oil, are shown in Table 8.1.

On a per capita basis, China does not look so bad. It consumed the equivalent of sixteen barrels of oil per person in 2014, only

Table 8.1   China's Energy Use in Global Context (2014)

	World	China	United States	European Union
A: Total energy consumption *Billion barrels of oil equivalent*				
Oil	31	4	6	4
Natural gas	22	1	5	3
Coal	28	14	3	2
Other	13	2	2	3
Total	95	22	17	12
B: Energy per capita and per unit GDP *Barrels of oil equivalent*				
Energy use per capita	13	16	53	23
Energy use per US$m of GDP	1,217	2,103	967	640

Source: BP Statistical Review of World Energy 2015, World Bank, author calculations.

slightly above the world average, and less than a third of the fifty-three barrels consumed by the average American. But when we turn to the economic comparison, China's numbers are dismal. It needs to burn the equivalent of 2,000 barrels of oil to generate a million dollars' worth of economic output, more than twice the figure of the United States and three times that of the European Union. China is by a sizable margin the world's most energy-intensive major economy.[1]

Why Is China's Energy Intensity So High?

There are three reasons for China's high energy intensity: its economic structure, the structure of its energy demand, and inefficiencies. The structural factor is that China's economy relies far more on manufacturing, and industry generally, than that of any other major country. The industrial sector uses a lot more energy for each dollar of output than the service or agriculture sectors, so an economy that relies mainly on industry will consume more energy than an economy of equal size that is based mainly on services.

Until very recently, nearly half of China's economic output came from industry, compared to less than a quarter for the United States. Moreover, an unusually high proportion of China's industry is *heavy* industry: manufacturing steel; smelting aluminum and other metals; refining petrochemicals; and making cement, glass, and so on. These industries are especially energy-intensive. Given a structure of production so reliant on energy-hogging industries, rather than the energy-light services that dominate advanced economies, it is not surprising that China's energy intensity is very high.

The second factor is the structure of China's energy supply, specifically its reliance on coal, which accounts for nearly three-quarters of its electric power generation. (By contrast, coal fuels only a quarter of power production in Europe and 40 percent in the United States.) This leads to relatively high energy intensity because coal is a less efficient fuel for power production than the main alternative, natural gas: it takes about 25 percent more coal than gas to produce a unit of electricity.[2] Economically, China's heavy reliance on coal makes sense, because it has abundant domestic supplies, whereas natural gas must for the most part be imported at a high cost (China has 13 percent of global coal reserves, but less than 1 percent of world oil and gas reserves).[3] Unfortunately, the heavy use of coal imposes great environmental costs, as we shall see below.

The third factor, efficiency, is less straightforward, because China's use of energy is not inefficient across the board. Its coal-fired power plants, for instance, are on average about 10 percent more efficient in their conversion of coal into electricity than are US coal power plants. This is because American plants are typically forty to fifty years old, whereas the majority of Chinese plants were installed in the last decade, thus taking advantage of newer and more effective technology. Similarly, China's fuel efficiency standards for vehicles, first adopted in 2004 and then strengthened in 2008, are stricter than those in the United States and all developing countries, ranking only behind Japan's and Europe's in toughness.[4]

There are, however, numerous ways in which China's use of energy—and natural resources more generally—is quite inefficient. One of the most significant of these is in buildings. During the construction boom of the past fifteen years, Chinese houses and office buildings went up at a frantic pace, and little attention was paid to sealing or insulating them to minimize heating and air conditioning costs. Another major source of inefficiency is in industry, which accounts for about three-quarters of the nation's electricity consumption and is also a major user of other types of energy (for example, burning coal to heat industrial boilers). In some cases, these inefficiencies arise because firms use outdated equipment. But this is less and less the case due to government campaigns to shut down obsolete production lines. The bigger issue is the way in which local governments support unprofitable local industries. Local governments will sometimes set artificially low prices for inputs like coal and electricity to keep plants humming, thereby maintaining employment and tax revenues. This results in a lot of energy being used for relatively little contribution to economic value added. From an energy efficiency perspective, it would be better to shut down these plants and, if need be, import the products they used to make from locations that can produce them more efficiently.[5]

What Kinds of Energy Does China Use, and How Is the Mix Changing?

The first word that comes to mind when examining China's energy system is "coal," on which China relies far more heavily than any other major country. Coal accounts for 66 percent of total primary energy demand—more than double the world average of 30 percent—while oil takes up 18 percent, natural gas uses 6 percent, and 11 percent comes from other sources (mainly hydroelectric power but also nuclear, wind, and solar). Half of all coal consumed in China goes into power plants. Most of the rest is used in industry for things like cement production and the heating of boilers.

Coal is abundant in China and relatively cheap, but it is also a major source of air pollution and climate-warming emissions of CO_2. Consequently, the government has spent most of the last decade trying to diversify its sources of energy by ramping up the use of natural gas, nuclear power, and renewables. These efforts have had some success: in the past decade annual output of both nuclear power and hydropower has more than doubled, and electricity from renewable sources has risen almost twentyfold. Yet this has barely made a dent in coal's dominance: its share of primary energy consumption and electricity output has fallen by only six and eight percentage points respectively since 2005. Some projections suggest that coal may continue to account for around half of China's energy mix as late as 2050.[6]

The most recent data suggest that coal use is close to peaking and its share of China's energy consumption will decline more rapidly than previously expected. According to official Chinese data, coal use flatlined in 2014 and declined further in early 2015. But caution is advisable. Weaker coal demand is largely a function of the severe slowdown in heavy industrial production in 2012–2014; if heavy industry stabilizes and picks up again, then coal demand will rise once more. In addition, China reported a similar decline in coal use in the late 1990s, but it was later discovered that many small coal producers were deliberately not reporting their production in order to evade government controls on small-scale mines. A similar crackdown on small-scale production has been underway for the past few years, and this might be creating analogous reporting problems.[7]

How Much Does China Rely on Imported Energy?

Despite its enormous energy use, China has traditionally satisfied most of its demand from domestic sources. This is gradually changing, however, as China's energy mix diversifies. It still sources more than 90 percent of its principal fuel, coal, at home, and its gigantic reserves mean that imports of coal will always be relatively modest compared to total demand.

The story for oil is different. China was self-sufficient in oil until 1993, when it became a net importer. Since then import reliance has steadily grown to over 60 percent. In 2013 China surpassed the United States as the world's biggest oil importer, and it now brings in about seven million barrels a day. A similar story is taking place in natural gas, where imports rose from almost nothing in 2002 to about 30 percent of demand in 2014. In theory, China could greatly increase its gas production, as the United States has, by unlocking its reserves of shale gas, which by some estimates are bigger than those of the United States. But doing so will be very difficult because the geology of China's shale formations is very different than that of the United States, and new and expensive extraction technologies may be required. It is likely that China will continue to be a big buyer of liquefied natural gas from Australia and Indonesia and also of gas brought in by pipeline from Central and Southeast Asia.

China's increasing reliance on imported oil has strategic consequences. Despite efforts to diversify its sources of supply, China continues to rely on the Middle East for more than half of its oil imports, and this creates two risks. First, oil supplies from this politically volatile region could be disrupted by war or social unrest. Second, most of this oil reaches China by tankers that must travel through the narrow Strait of Malacca between Malaysia and Sumatra. In the event of conflict with the United States, it would be easy for the US Navy to severely crimp China's oil supply by blockading this passage.

Because of these risks, the Chinese government believes it has a strong interest in continuing to develop new and less vulnerable sources of oil supply and transport. This interest means that China will probably continue to be an active investor in new oil and gas fields and pipelines in Central and Southeast Asia.

What Impact Does China's Energy Use Have on Climate Change?

In 2007, China became the world's biggest emitter of the greenhouse gases that cause climate change. By 2012, the last year for which fully comparable international data are available, China accounted for 24 percent of global greenhouse gas emissions, more than the United States and European Union combined. About 85 percent of China's total emissions are CO_2. And again, the main culprit is extreme reliance on coal, which releases far more CO_2 when it is burned than other fossil fuels: twice as much as natural gas, and about 40 percent more than oil. So the single most important variable determining China's future impact on global warming is its rate of coal consumption.[8]

China's leaders have been concerned about the nation's impact on global warming for over a decade, but until recently their stance on international climate negotiations was defensive. They argued, first, that China's per capita emissions were much lower than in most rich countries; and second, that early industrializers such as the United Kingdom and the United States should shoulder a much larger share of the burden of reducing carbon emissions because of their long history of pumping CO_2 into the atmosphere. Countries like China that came late to the development game should have a chance to get rich first before working hard to reduce their emissions. Finally, they claimed that part of China's emissions are in effect really the responsibility of rich countries, insofar as multinational companies moved much of their production to China and hence also "exported" their pollution.

In recent years China has quietly retreated from these positions. The first argument is now untenable, because China's greenhouse gas emissions are now well above the global per capita average. The second may have some moral justice to it, but is essentially irrelevant because the emissions reductions required to stabilize the global temperature are so large that they cannot possibly be achieved if the world's single biggest emitter opts out. The third made little sense to begin with, since most of China's CO_2 emissions came from heavy industries like steel and cement that cater to domestic construction demand, not from export-oriented consumer goods factories that foreign companies established.

China has now committed to a target of capping its CO_2 emissions by 2030, through a combination of (a) shifts in the structure of the economy to make it less energy-intensive; (b) changes in the energy mix to rely less on coal and more on cleaner fossil fuels (such as natural gas) and renewables; and (c) promotion of energy efficiency. There are strong incentives for the government to make these reforms. For one thing, it is clear that sustained and balanced long-run economic growth depends on reducing the country's energy intensity. For another, the policies needed to reduce China's contribution to climate change are the same policies required to bring under control the country's terrible air pollution problem, which is a matter of increasing social concern.

How Bad Are China's Environmental Problems?

China's environmental damage has attracted worldwide notice, and with good reason. Rapid industrialization has exacted a toll in extreme degradation of the country's air, water, and soil. In January 2013, Chinese and global news media focused the world's attention on an especially terrible smog episode in Beijing—the so-called Airpocalypse—when the skies darkened under a load of particulates measured at nearly 800 micrograms per cubic meter, more than thirty times the maximum level considered safe by the World Health

Organization. This dreadful event became a catalyst for more serious governmental action to combat pollution.[9]

It is, however, worth putting China's environmental challenges in international and historical perspective. Every country that has grown rich has gotten quite dirty along the way. Today the headlines are filled with stories about toxic smog in Chinese cities and chemical spills in Chinese rivers. It is easy to forget that four decades ago, almost identical headlines were being written about Japan; and that in the 1960s the United States faced severe air pollution problems in big cities like Pittsburgh and Los Angeles, rivers in industrial regions caught on fire, and localities were rendered unfit to inhabit because of chemical pollution. These environmental disasters took decades to clean up, and much work still needs to be done. Even "Airpocalypse" was, unfortunately, far from unprecedented. Estimates suggest that particulate concentrations during London's deadly Great Smog of December 1952, which resulted in over 4,000 identifiable deaths in five days and as many as 8,000 more in subsequent months, may have been as much as five times higher than those registered in Beijing in January 2013.[10]

The point is not to gloss over China's environmental problems, which are extraordinarily bad. Rather, it is to suggest that we resist the tempting assumption that these problems are uniquely attributable to shortcomings in China's economic growth model or political system. It is more accurate to see them as severe variants of a syndrome that has afflicted every industrializing country.

How severe? Figure 8.1 tries to answer that question. It compares the score on Yale University's comprehensive Environmental Performance Index (EPI) with per capita income (adjusted for purchasing power) for thirty of the world's most important economies. The list includes all the major developed economies; all of the industrializing nations of Asia (including aspirants such as Vietnam and Bangladesh); and most other large emerging economies, such as Russia, Brazil, South Africa, Mexico, and Turkey. It excludes city-states and countries with small or sparse populations or no significant industry (for instance Singapore, Saudi Arabia, and New Zealand).

Two things jump out. First, there is a tight correlation between a country's income level and its environmental performance. This supports the common intuition that nations care little about pollution when they are poor and then grow markedly cleaner as they

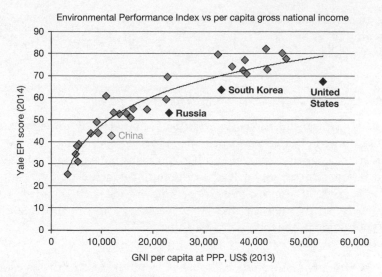

Figure 8.1 Environmental Index vs GDP

Source: Yale Environmental Performance Index, World Bank.

get richer. The improvement in environmental performance seems to be especially sharp for countries entering middle-income territory (roughly US$10,000 to $20,000 according to this measure)—again, supporting the idea that environmental protection rises higher on the national agenda when an enlarged middle class starts demanding safer air and water.[11]

Second, China's performance is quite bad: its EPI score is about 14 percent lower than predicted by its income level. Three other countries have EPI scores at least 10 percent lower than suggested by income levels: Russia, South Korea, and the United States. These observations suggest a framework for thinking about China's environmental issues. Some of its pollution problems can be considered "normal" attributes of its recent rapid industrialization and relatively low income, but not all. As a relative "environmental underperformer," it shares important characteristics with the other members of that club. Like Russia, China is a post-Communist "transitional" economy with an authoritarian state, weak legal institutions, and a feeble civil society. Like South Korea, it is an "East Asian developmental state" that puts an unusually high premium on maximizing economic growth through forced-march industrialization. And like the United States, it aspires to be a superpower and so has a natural tendency to subordinate "soft" concerns, such as the environment, to ambitions for industrial and technological development that lay the foundations for global power.

How Likely Is China to Address Its Environmental Problems?

The above considerations suggest that China is likely to remain an environmental underperformer for many years to come. A review of the mechanisms by which other countries have addressed their environmental problems leads to a similar conclusion. Successful environmental improvement programs in the rich countries of Europe, North America, and Japan have typically included some combination of the following elements:

- Stricter environmental laws combined with stronger enforcement
- Market mechanisms such as pollution-permit trading schemes
- Legal redress via class action lawsuits against major polluting companies or industries
- Activism by environmental nongovernmental organizations (NGOs)
- Media exposés

The nature of China's political system means that it will rely almost exclusively on the first instrument, with modest support at best from the other four. Media exposure of pollution problems is to some extent tolerated: in this as in other areas, the central government is happy for the press to unearth problems that local officials would rather keep buried. But once the authorities in Beijing think they know enough, they tend to clamp down on reporting. A classic example of this pattern came in March 2015, when veteran CCTV investigative reporter Chai Jing distributed a scathing documentary about air pollution, *Under the Dome*, over the Internet. Within days, the video was watched by over a hundred million people. Then the censors stepped in, forced the video to be removed from all websites, and closed off social media discussions. In a freer country, this documentary could have prompted a large-scale, long-running national debate on how to balance the imperatives of environmental protection and economic growth. In China, this conversation was strangled in the cradle.

Similarly, the central authorities keep environmental NGOs and legal activism on a tight leash. A significant reform announced in late 2014 was a set of guidelines under which approved environmental NGOs would be permitted to file lawsuits against polluting companies in specialized environmental courts. This is a step forward, but the impact is likely to be limited so long as the central government vets in advance the organizations that are allowed to bring suit. Furthermore, many judges remain susceptible to bribery or influence by powerful economic interests, and the ability of environmental courts to enforce their judgments is unproven.

The authorities have shown enthusiasm for emissions trading schemes, especially for CO_2 emissions. In principle this is a good thing: a permit trading system was a key component of the United States' successful drive to reduce emissions of sulfur dioxide (the main cause of acid rain) following the passage of the Clean Air Act of 1990. In practice, however, these systems are difficult to implement and require both robust market infrastructure and a vigilant and powerful regulator. It is not obvious that China is close to satisfying the basic conditions needed for a successful emissions-trading system.

Can Top-Down Pollution Control Work?

China's environmental protection drive will depend largely on top-down administrative action. The effectiveness of these administrative measures in turn depends on the quality of their design and—perhaps more important—on the political will of the central government to address the problems.

Because of the depth of the problems and the government's demonstrated obsession with economic growth (not to mention scary events like "Airpocalypse"), it is easy to be cynical about Beijing's commitment to an environmental agenda. But the truth is that the fight against air pollution has made progress over the past decade, is now a declared priority of the national government, and is likely to see an acceleration of gains in the near future. Progress on water and soil pollution, however, has been much slower.

China's air pollution derives overwhelmingly from the burning of coal. Estimates vary, but typically find that coal combustion accounts for at least 50 percent of air-polluting emissions, mainly thanks to the electric power, cement, glass, and metals-smelting industries. The contribution from automobile emissions is much lower, probably 15 to 20 percent. This distribution of pollution culprits has several implications. On the downside, the heavily polluting industries are politically powerful and resist efforts to clean them up. On the other hand, the relatively concentrated nature of the problem makes it simpler to attack. Moreover, reduced reliance on coal is an aim not just of environmentalists but also of the bureaucrats managing China's energy strategy and industrial policy. This convergence of interests makes it more likely that coal use will be reined in and made cleaner.[12]

Energy efficiency and reduced coal reliance became important policy objectives in 2005, when the government started fretting that China's highly energy-intensive growth model was unsustainable. An important but clearly secondary worry was that excessive reliance on coal (which then accounted for 70 percent of primary energy use and over 80 percent of power generation) would worsen local air pollution and increase China's already enormous contribution to the emissions of greenhouse gases that cause climate change. Beijing therefore set a target of reducing energy intensity—the amount of energy needed to generate one yuan of GDP—by 20 percent by 2010. It also began to focus on reducing the nation's reliance on coal by pushing large investments in cleaner-burning natural gas, hydropower, nuclear power, and renewable sources such as wind and solar power.

These efforts had measurable impact. The centerpiece of the energy efficiency drive was the "1,000 Enterprises Program," which set individual efficiency targets for the country's biggest firms in heavy industry; after a few years this system was adopted by most provinces as well. Energy intensity fell by 19 percent in 2005–2010, just shy of the target, and the goal of a further reduction of 16 percent in 2011–2015 has also been met. Coal's share of primary energy, which peaked at around 73 percent in 2005, dropped to 66 percent in 2014. It is likely that China's coal demand has peaked, and will decline further from here (although remember the caution offered above about the reliability of coal use statistics).[13]

In addition to policy, structural economic changes played a large role in these gains. Most energy is used by industry; services require far less energy to generate a unit of GDP. Until 2013, industry was a larger part of the economy in services, but services are now a larger sector and growing faster. Construction of housing—which as we saw in chapter 5 tripled between 1996 and 2010—was the biggest single source of demand for the materials whose production drives energy use and air pollution: steel, cement, and glass. But housing construction seems to have peaked as well.

A final component in reducing energy intensity is gradual reform of prices. For the most part, China's energy prices are not especially low: electricity prices for industrial users are slightly higher than the global average; pump prices for gasoline and diesel fuel since 2008 have ranged from 20 to 40 percent above US levels and are about the same as in Canada and Australia; and the contract price for coal used by power plants, which began to be deregulated in the early 2000s, tripled between 2005 and 2014 and is now basically the same as the global spot price.[14]

But it is also true that China's energy prices remain subject to various controls by the government and do not respond fully to changes in supply and demand. Electricity prices, for instance, remain tightly regulated and have not risen nearly as much as the price of the main power-plant fuel, coal. Under price reforms that began in 2009, gasoline and diesel prices fluctuate with crude oil prices, with a short lag; but the government's pricing formula prevents a full pass-through to consumers of very high crude oil prices. This means that when crude oil prices are high (as they were from 2010 to 2014), there is less incentive than in a full market system for users to make energy-saving investments in more fuel-efficient cars or industrial equipment. For controlling air pollution, the electricity price is most important, since electricity demand largely determines the demand for coal. Tentative steps toward more market-based electricity pricing began in 2014, but it will be several years before the benefits are fully realized.

All in all, progress on reducing air pollution has been decidedly mixed. Emissions of sulfur dioxide (which creates acid rain) have fallen significantly, thanks to cleaner and more efficient coal-fired power plants. But concentrations of other pollutants, notably the small $PM_{2.5}$ particulates that are the major source of smog in northern China's cities, kept on rising even after several years of energy efficiency and pollution control campaigns. Beijing's "Airpocalypse" moment spurred the new government of Xi Jinping into stronger action. In September 2013 it rolled out a national air pollution action plan, which requires rich coastal provinces to cut their $PM_{2.5}$ emissions by 15 to 25 percent by 2017 and sets more relaxed targets for interior provinces to cut their output of larger PM_{10} particles. Premier Li Keqiang also began listing environmental protection as one of the government's top priorities in his annual reports to the legislature, something no previous premier had done.

It appears that the government has finally made a priority of environmental protection—or at least controlling air pollution in China's richer regions—in part because of citizen pressure. Over the past decade China has demonstrated an ability to change patterns of energy use through top-down measures. The extension of those techniques to air pollution targets, along with the natural restructuring of the economy to a less polluting path, should cause the air pollution problem to abate slowly, beginning in the next few years. But emissions levels remain extremely high, and even optimistic officials believe it will be fifteen to twenty years before the air in Chinese cities approaches levels that would be considered acceptable in the developed world. Work on other critical environmental issues, such as cleaning up contaminated rivers, lakes, and soil, has barely begun. Environmental damage will continue to be a huge problem for years to come.

9

DEMOGRAPHICS AND
THE LABOR MARKET

What Is the "Demographic Dividend"?

The "demographic dividend" refers to a period during which the proportion of nonworking, dependent people in a population falls substantially. This usually occurs in a traditional agricultural society in which birth rates start out very high, because many children die in infancy: for a family to be sure it will have several surviving children, it needs to have a lot of births. Then, as better sanitation and health care become available, child and infant mortality drop. Eventually, families respond to this increased survival rate by having fewer children. In many cases, this tendency is encouraged by the government's birth control policies.

The result of these shifts is a two-stage evolution of the population age structure. In the first stage, the number of people of working age rises rapidly, due to the population boom that occurred while child mortality rates were falling but fertility rates were still high. Meanwhile, the rate at which people have babies slows. In consequence the country winds up having a relatively large number of productive, working-age people, and a shrinking proportion of dependent children. Put another way, the "dependency ratio"—the ratio between the number of young and old people on the one hand, and the number of working-age people on the other—falls.

This age-structure shift does not guarantee faster economic growth, but it certainly can help. With more productive workers, and relatively few dependent mouths to feed, families can save more of their income. If the country has an effective mechanism for capturing those savings and recycling them into investments in infrastructure and manufacturing, a virtuous cycle can be created in which higher saving leads to greater opportunities for income growth. Faster income growth in turn encourages people to put off having children while they pursue economic opportunities; and this in turn leads to further falls in the fertility rate, higher savings, and so on.

Unfortunately, after a few decades this process starts to go into reverse. The "bulge" of productive workers turns into a bulge of retirees, who make increasing demands on the nation's healthcare and pension systems. Meanwhile, the next generation of workers is much smaller. So instead of having a large number of workers supporting a small number of (mainly young) dependents, the country now has a small number of workers supporting a large number of (mainly old) dependents. This stage, when the population ages rapidly, is called the "demographic transition" and tends to be associated with slower economic growth rates.

How Has the Demographic Dividend Worked in China?

Most of China's East Asian peers (Japan, South Korea, Taiwan) enjoyed a solid demographic dividend, and this was a contributing factor in their high-growth eras. China's demographic dividend was unusually large and long-lasting.

To understand why, we need to go back to the late 1950s and early 1960s. For around three years, from 1959 through 1962, large parts of China suffered near-famine conditions, thanks to disastrous economic policies during the 1958–1959 "Great Leap Forward," when millions of farmers were pulled off the land to engage in ill-advised rural industries such as small-scale steel plants. Although this great famine has never been officially acknowledged by the Chinese government, demographers have shown that it probably caused around 30 to 40 million deaths.[1]

After this catastrophe, fertility soared, and in the decade 1963–1973 China had a tremendous baby boom, during which the population rose from 680 million to 880 million. Contributing factors included the natural tendency toward fast population growth after wars or natural disasters, government policies that encouraged large families (largely based on Mao Zedong's belief that a more populous country was a more powerful one), and improvements in sanitation and healthcare that dramatically decreased infant, childhood, and maternal mortality.

By the early 1970s government officials became worried that the population was expanding too rapidly, and that it would become difficult for the nation to feed itself or provide enough jobs. In 1973 it introduced the "later, longer, fewer" campaign, which encouraged couples to marry later, space children more widely, and limit their offspring to two in cities and three in the countryside.[2] In the 1970s, the fertility rate plunged from 5.8 to 2.4, partly due to these policies and partly thanks to the normal impact of lower childhood mortality. Despite this impressive drop, which brought China's fertility close to the "replacement rate" of 2.1, which enables a stable population size, the government in 1980 introduced the draconian "one-child" policy, which contributed to a further fall in the birth rate in the 1980s and 1990s.

The combination of excessive deaths during the famine years (which reduced the number of people entering retirement in the 1980s), the big baby boom of the 1960s, and the large fertility drop that began in the 1970s produced a deep and long-lasting demographic dividend (see Figure 9.1). Between 1975 and 2010, the dependency ratio—the number of young (under 15) and old (over 65) people for every 100 working-age people—fell from 80 to 36. During the same period, the national savings rate rose from

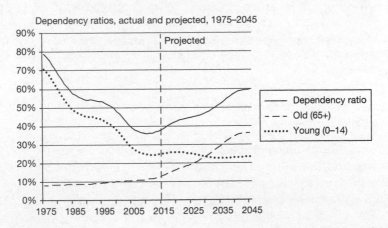

Figure 9.1 Dependency Ratio

Source: United Nations Ageing and Development Database.

33 percent of GDP to over 50 percent, real annual growth in investment spending averaged 12 percent, and the economy grew at an average rate of about 10 percent a year. The relationship between demographics and economic growth is far from straightforward, and it would be wrong to say that this big demographic dividend *caused* China's fast economic growth. But it was clearly an important favorable condition. Probably the best way to sum it up is that the demographic dividend helped create the opportunity for fast economic growth, and the reforms that began in 1978 enabled that opportunity to be realized.

What about China's "Demographic Transition" to an Older Population?

Unfortunately, China is now coming out on the other side of the demographic dividend, and in the coming years the dependency ratio will rise. As the chart above shows, the fall in dependency occurred entirely because the young people of the 1960s–1970s baby boom became workers. The rise in dependency over the next few decades will occur entirely because those baby-boom workers are turning into retirees. Now, about one in six Chinese is over the age of 60; that figure will rise to one in four by 2030, and one in three by 2050. The burden on the pension, healthcare, and social services systems will grow enormously. Today there are about seven people of working age for every person of retirement age (65 or older). By 2030 there will be only about three-and-a-half workers per retiree, and by 2050 there will be only two—about the same figure as in present-day Japan, a famously "old" society (see Figure 9.2).

What Does the Aging Population Mean for the Labor Force and Economic Growth?

China's future demographic trajectory is certainly one of rapid aging, and this will put downward pressure on economic growth and push up the fiscal burden of the social security system. A common phrase describing this situation is that China risks "getting old before it gets rich." But contrary to the common saying, demography is not destiny when it comes to economic growth. Demographic trends are an important constraint, in part because once established

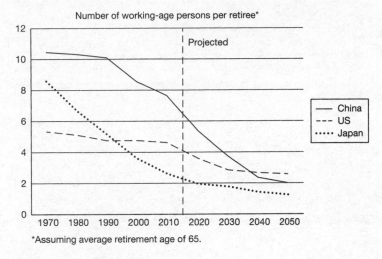

*Assuming average retirement age of 65.

Figure 9.2 Workers per Retiree
Source: UN World Population Prospects (2008).

they can take decades to reverse. But economies have a lot of room to maneuver within the limits set by demography.

For China, the immediate problem for the next decade or so is that the working-age population, which grew rapidly for many years, is starting to shrink. But the *working-age population* is not necessarily the same as the *labor force*. The labor force consists only of people who are either working or actively seeking work. The share of people in any age cohort who are working or actively seeking work is called the *labor force participation rate*. A striking fact in China is that the urban labor force participation rate is very high until people hit their mid-forties and then declines precipitously (see Figure 9.3). At age forty, 82 percent of urban residents are active in the workforce. By age fifty that share drops to 64 percent; and by age sixty only 30 percent of urban residents are active in the workforce. And somewhat surprisingly, participation rates in 2005 were consistently lower than they were in 1990. This probably relates to the fact that in 1990, many people had essentially useless, make-work jobs at SOEs. By 2005 most of these jobs were gone, and people could only stay active in the workforce if they had reasonably high level of skills and education.

The conclusion from this is that China still has the ability to increase its *labor force*, even though the *working-age population* has

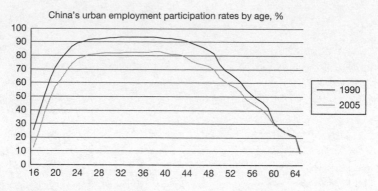

China's urban employment participation rates by age, %

Figure 9.3 Labor Force Participation
Source: Judith Banister, NBS.

started to decline. To do this it must increase the participation rate, especially among older workers in the 45–65 age range, who will constitute nearly half of the working-age population by 2030. There are many ways to do this. One is to increase statutory retirement ages, which are quite low in many government agencies and SOEs (60 for men and 55 for women). Another is to improve access to education—not only traditional schooling but also adult education and on-the-job training. Increasing workers' ability to get training at different stages of their careers will improve their chances of adapting to changes in the economy and staying employed for longer. Finally, shifting the emphasis of the economy away from industry and toward services will help because services are more labor-intensive than industry, and it will create a larger number of physically undemanding jobs that people can keep doing through their sixties.

A final consideration is that the economic impact of labor is partly a function of the number of workers, but more importantly of the productivity of those workers. The importance of labor productivity is illustrated by the fact that China's economy is still only about two-thirds the size of the US economy, even though China's labor force is nearly five times bigger. This implies that, on average, a Chinese worker produces only about one-eighth of what her US counterpart does. So to offset the economic impact of a shrinking working-age population, the government should focus not just on increasing participation but also on boosting productivity. Improved efficiency and productivity are indeed key goals in the government's economic reform agenda, which we will consider in more detail in chapter 11.[3]

There is, unfortunately, a bit of a problem here. As we saw above, one of the most effective ways to increase the participation rate is to shift the economy to a focus on services, which is more labor-intensive than industry. But labor productivity in services tends to be lower, and enjoy lower growth rates, than in industry. (This is because it is harder to boost a service worker's output by simply linking her up with a machine.) So as the economy inexorably shifts toward services, productivity growth will trend lower. The good news is that there is almost certainly a lot of "low-hanging fruit" in the form of service industries—including logistics, finance, manufacturing-related services, and healthcare—that are heavily dominated by inefficient SOEs. Simply by opening up these sectors to increased competition from the private sector, there is potential to unlock productivity gains that are more rapid than one would normally expect in services.[4]

What Is the Importance of the "One-Child Policy"?

As a population control measure, the significance of the "one-child policy" is far less than is generally believed. The major decline in China's fertility rate occurred in the 1970s—before the "one-child policy" was adopted in 1980. During the 1980s enforcement of the new policy was chaotic and fluctuating: sometimes savage, with widespread reports of forced abortions and forced sterilizations; and sometimes relaxed, leading to surges of births in the countryside. By the late 1980s the policy was codified in a more pragmatic way, with a blanket exception for rural families (who were permitted to have a second child if their first was a girl) and more relaxed quotas for ethnic minorities. It might more accurately be called the "one-and-a-half-child policy," since under perfect enforcement, only 60 percent of families would be limited to one child, and the fertility rate would be about 1.5.[5] This policy remained in full effect for a quarter-century, until a slight easing in late 2013. In late 2015, policy was changed to allow all couples to have two children.

The impact of the policy is far from clear. In 1980 the fertility rate was 2.4; by 1990 it was around 2.1, which is the replacement level. By

2000 it was down to 1.4, and since then it has fluctuated between 1.4 and 1.5. It is impossible to know how much of this reduction came from the policy, and how much resulted from factors such as the migration of vast numbers of country dwellers to the city (migrant worker families have fewer children than families that stay on the farm). Other East Asian countries without similarly restrictive birth control policies have seen even more rapid reductions in their fertility rates, to about China's level, in recent decades. In South Korea, fertility fell from 2.8 in 1980 to 1.6 in 1990 and reached 1.2 in 2010; in Thailand during the same 1980–2010 period, the rate fell from 3.4 to 1.4.[6]

It is hard to avoid the conclusion that the one-child policy was one of the worst major policies of the reform era. It was unnecessary when it was introduced; savage at times, and consistently intrusive and demeaning to the women who had to endure annual birth-control examinations even if they were not forced into abortions or sterilization; and far more long-lasting than it should have been. The main reason it endured is bureaucratic inertia: the State Family Planning Commission (SPFC) that enforced it has 500,000 employees and six million part-time workers, and it collects millions of dollars in fines every year. It had every incentive to keep the policy in place simply to protect all these jobs and revenues, and it did so by constantly overstating the fertility rate and claiming that its services were still urgently needed.[7] Only after the 2010 census conclusively proved that the fertility rate was far lower than the SFPC had claimed, and after the SFPC was deprived of its separate status and put under the Ministry of Health, could the policy finally start relaxing.

In November 2013 the government announced that urban couples in which either the husband or the wife was an only child could have a second child. (Previously, only couples where *both* people were only children could have a second child.) This was a timid reform, but even on its own limited terms it had far less impact than the government hoped. In the first year, only 1.1 million couples applied for permission to have a second child, far below the 12 million eligible, and below the two million officials had hoped for. The policy was further relaxed in November 2015 to permit all couples to have two children. But the evidence so far is that urban China is not immune to the low birthrate dynamics now common in most other East Asian countries, which are driven by the high cost of raising children, cramped living spaces, and limited availability of affordable childcare. Just as the one-child policy probably contributed little to China's falling birthrate, ending the policy will do little to encourage Chinese to start having more babies. Removing the hand of the state from family child-bearing decisions will be a great improvement in personal liberty. But the direct economic benefit of eliminating the one-child policy will be negligible.

Why Did Chinese Workers Start Moving from the Countryside to the City?

The story of China's labor market in the reform era has been one of steady movement of workers out of agriculture and into urban employment in industry and services, and out of the state sector into the private sector. At the outset of the reform era in 1978, 70 percent of workers were engaged in agriculture in the country-side, and nearly all city workers worked either for state-owned or "collective" enterprises. By 2013, only 31 percent of workers were in agriculture and only 18 percent of urban workers were employed by SOEs and collectives. A careful study of China's messy and incomplete employment data by the scholar Nicholas Lardy concluded that two-thirds of China's urban labor force in 2011 worked in privately controlled companies—and more impressively, that 95 percent of net urban job creation since 1978 has been generated by private firms.[8]

The first wave of off-farm employment growth came in the 1980s, with the creation of township and village enterprises (TVEs), or small-scale rural industrial firms, which we discussed in chapter 2. Employment by TVEs grew rapidly after agriculture was liberalized in the late 1980s, and exploded in the aftermath of reforms in 1983–84 that let farmers engage in marketing their own produce and permitted them freely to seek work off the farm. From 28 million in 1978, TVE employment rose to 70 million in 1985 and surged to an astonishing 123 million in 1993—nearly 20 percent of the entire nation's active workforce.[9]

At first, the great majority of TVE employment was in "collective" enterprises controlled by local governments.[10] In some cases, these firms were really run by private entrepreneurs, who thought it wise given the ambiguous status of private business in those days to seek political cover by enlisting government shareholders. (These companies were often described as "wearing a red hat.") In other cases, TVEs were sponsored by local governments eager to generate sources of economic growth and fiscal revenue, and whose officials were also interested in getting some off-the-books income for themselves. Whether these hybrid companies were "really" private or "really" state-owned is a moot point. In order for startup companies to succeed in the political environment of the time, a combination of entrepreneurial energy and political patronage was required, and TVEs provided the necessary structure. Today, however, the vast majority of TVE employment is clearly in private firms. This is because privately owned TVEs grew much faster than collectively owned ones, and many ostensibly "collective" or state-owned TVEs threw off their "red hats."

What Was the Impact of SOE Reform on the Labor Market?

After the employment boom of the late 1980s and early 1990s, the next major turning point came in the late 1990s, when the government embarked on a massive reorganization of state-owned enterprises, which in 1995 still employed about 60 percent of urban workers but were increasingly plagued by inefficiency and financial losses (see chapter 5). Between 1995 and 2005 employment in urban SOEs fell by nearly 50 million people, from 113 million to 64 million, and around 30 million people were officially laid off. Most of the job losses occurred in industrial firms. Other SOE workforce reductions were achieved by early retirement schemes or privatization of the companies. The SOE share of urban employment plummeted to 23 percent in 2005. Total job losses in the state sector over the decade equated to 20 percent of the average urban workforce during that period.[11]

To put this in perspective, in its decade of retrenchment China's total state-sector job losses were more than five times the number of jobs the US economy shed between 2008 and 2010 in the Great Recession (9 million). And the 30 million industrial layoffs were more than four times the total number of jobs lost in the US manufacturing sector from 1979 to 2009 (8 million).[12] In some ways, the slashing of China's state sector was comparable to the Great Depression, when the US employment rate soared to 25 percent.

But in fact China did not go through a great depression. During the decade of these massive layoffs, total urban employment actually increased by 90 million people, a gain of nearly 50 percent. There were four reasons for this extraordinary result. First, the government effectively deregulated manufacturing, allowing a surge of more efficient private companies to take over the production gaps left by the shrinking state sector. Second, trade liberalization, culminating in China's WTO entry in 2001, enabled many of these new manufacturing companies to tap into booming global demand. Third, a host of new service businesses (such as transport firms and restaurants) grew up to cater to the needs of the manufacturing firms and their employees. Finally, increased government spending on infrastructure, and the real estate boom unleashed by housing privatization, boosted the demand for construction workers.

How Big an Unemployment Problem Does China Have, and Are Wages Rising?

This generally positive picture glosses over some problems. First, plenty of people got left out of the party. China does not publish reliable unemployment statistics, but estimates by labor scholars suggest that the urban unemployment rate rose from under 7 percent in 1996 to over 11 percent by 2002. In the subsequent economic boom the unemployment rate fell, and it remained at a relatively low level even after the 2008 global financial crisis. A government survey reported an urban unemployment rate of just 5 percent in the first half of 2013; various scholars have estimated rates of 6 to 9 percent in recent years. The general conclusion is that while China has created lots of jobs, maintaining full employment for its huge working-age population remains a challenge.[13]

A second problem is that the labor force participation rate declined substantially between 1995 and 2010 (from 79 percent to 71 percent), as discouraged workers gave up and stopped seeking work. More than half of the workers laid off during the SOE restructuring never found another job. China's overall labor force participation rate remains higher than the global average of 64 percent. As we noted above, though, this high overall rate conceals the fact that participation in the workforce plummets for people over the age of fifty.[14]

Finally, because of the enormous glut of labor—caused not only by the state-sector layoffs but by a swelling in the working-age population of nearly 200 million between 1995 and 2005—wages for ordinary workers did not rise fast enough to prevent the emergence of serious income and wealth inequality. As with so much else in China, the story is complicated. Manufacturing wages rose far more rapidly in China than in other low-income countries in the 1990s and 2000s. In 1994, for instance, a Chinese factory worker made US$500 a year, only a quarter of the wage of her counterpart in Thailand. By 2008, the Chinese worker was earning $3,500 a year, nearly 25 percent more than the Thai worker. This is an impressive gain.

But manufacturing accounts for only one-quarter to one-third of urban employment. Most of the rest consists of relatively low-wage jobs in construction and services. Wages in these sectors also rose, but not nearly as fast as in manufacturing. And in general, wages did not rise nearly as fast as the income of the owners of capital. So in aggregate, labor's share of national income fell from 54 percent in 1995 to 47 percent by 2008, while the corporate profit share rose. And the Gini coefficient, a standard measure of income inequality, rose from a fairly unexceptional level of around 0.35 in the mid-1990s to an uncomfortably high 0.49 by 2010.[15]

What Is the "Lewis Turning Point" and What Does It Mean for China?

This term derives from the work of Sir W. Arthur Lewis, a West Indian economist who won a Nobel Prize in 1979. In the 1950s, Lewis developed a simple model for a developing economy, which, though subject to criticism on various grounds, is useful for a stylistic understanding of the stages that a country like China goes through on its route to industrialization.[16]

Lewis imagined an economy with two sectors: a subsistence agricultural sector and a modern industrial sector. Higher wages in modern industry draw labor out of the countryside, but because the supply of surplus agricultural labor is so large, companies can get away with raising wages at a slower pace than the rate of productivity growth. In this first stage, the economy sees rapid accumulation of capital, a rise in the corporate profit share of national income, and a fall in the labor share.

At a certain point, however, the supply of surplus rural labor begins to dry up, and then companies have to start raising wages much more aggressively. In this second stage, a reallocation of national income away from the capitalists and toward the workers can occur, so long as the capitalists do not keep wages low by importing workers from abroad, or moving their investments to low-wage countries. The transition from the first to the second stage is called the "Lewis turning point."[17]

The Lewis model is helpful in understanding developments in China's economy and labor market over the last quarter-century. In the 1990s and early 2000s, China had a virtually unlimited supply of labor, thanks to the demographic dividend and mass layoffs in the SOE sector. This enabled a large expansion of industry and the building of huge amounts of infrastructure. A greater share of the financial gain from this economic activity flowed to the capitalists through rising profits than to workers through rising wages— although as we noted above, wages also increased quite rapidly. Consequently the investment share of GDP (financed by corporate profits) rose, and the consumption share of GDP (funded by worker wages) fell.

Beginning in about 2005, however, the labor supply began to top out. This was first visible in the supply of young workers (ages 15–24), which peaked in 2005 and began to fall in 2010. By 2023, the supply of these young workers will have fallen by one-third from its peak level.[18] The overall working-age population (ages 15–64) will peak around 2015 and will then decline steadily.

The impact of a gradually more restricted labor supply has been evident both in wages and in patterns of migration. Soon after the supply of young workers stopped growing in 2005, export-oriented factories in Guangdong that depended heavily on migrant labor started reporting labor shortages. Since the young worker population started to decline in 2010, wage growth for migrant workers and for relatively low-skilled jobs in general has accelerated; these wages are now growing faster than those for white-collar jobs.[19] This trend was exacerbated by the central government's decision in the late 1990s to dramatically increase university enrollments. That decision was taken in part because of a desire to upgrade the quality of the workforce, but more importantly to keep young people *out* of a labor force that the government rightly saw was already glutted. Between 2000 and 2013 annual graduations from tertiary institutions rose from less than one million to more than six million. These graduates were not interested in factory work, but a paucity of white-collar jobs awaited them.

There is thus little doubt that China has begun to enter its "Lewis turning point"—although it will be a rather extended "point," lasting a decade or two. One consequence—faster growth in wages relative to corporate profits—is already evident both in the wage data we just cited and in the fact that the investment/GDP ratio has leveled off and the consumption/GDP ratio is starting to climb. (The deeper implications of this shift are examined in more detail in chapter 11.) Another subtler consequence is a likely change in migration patterns. Young workers are quite happy to move to wherever the jobs are; but after the age of thirty, their willingness to move decreases, because they have stronger family ties that hold them in place. This means either that the rate of rural-urban migration will slow down, or that employers will have to offer even higher wages to attract the workers they need—or most likely, a combination of both.

How Many More Workers Can Move from the Countryside to the Cities?

Migration from countryside to city has been one of the great facts of China over the past three decades. In 1982, only 7 million people in all of China worked outside their native county. By 2012, that figure was 163 million. Another 99 million migrated within their own county to find work (usually moving from the country to the main county town), bringing the total number of migrants to 262 million, or a bit more than a quarter of the working-age population. Eighty-five percent of these migrant workers started out in rural areas.

There is a common perception that China's great migration consists mainly of workers moving from the poor interior of the country to the rich coast. This is only partly true. About 40 percent of migrants work in the central and western provinces, and 43 percent originate in the coastal provinces. Only about one-third of migrants work outside their home province. The main story of China's great labor migration is not movement from hinterland to coast. Rather it is one of people moving from rural areas to urban areas—mostly nearby towns, but sometimes distant cities—to pursue higher wages.[20]

How much longer will this migratory pattern endure, and how many more people will make the move? Here we enter the realm of educated guesswork. Broadly speaking it appears that China's rural-to-urban migration is about two-thirds complete. The World Bank estimates that the excess rural labor supply (i.e., workers not needed to maintain the present level of agricultural production) is somewhere around 100 million people. Accounting for future increases in agricultural productivity, somewhere around 120 to 135 million workers are likely to move from country to city between 2012 and 2030—in other words, about half as many as have already made the move. Migration will continue on a large scale, but the wave is past its peak.

An important footnote is that while worker migration to the cities will slow down, movement of nonworking family members to the city will probably pick up, as immigration restrictions are relaxed. This could add as many as 100 million more people to the migrant flow by 2030. At that point, China's total urban population will be about 1 billion, or roughly 70 percent of the total population.[21]

How Bad Are Conditions for Chinese Workers, and Is There Hope That They Will Get Better?

The answer to this question depends entirely on the point of comparison. Conditions for Chinese workers are worse than for those in rich countries today, but arguably better than those in many other developing countries, and definitely better than conditions in China two or three decades ago.

There is little doubt that working conditions for many Chinese are harsh. Long hours and compulsory overtime are routine in many factories; safety conditions in factories, mines, and other hazardous workplaces fall well short of Western standards; and employers have wide latitude to fire workers, dock their pay, or impose other arbitrary punishments. Workers have little recourse, and no ability to organize independent labor unions. (There is a single nationwide union organized by the Communist Party, but it does little to advance worker rights and often acts as an agent for management.)

It is also true that certain types of labor abuse common in other developing countries are much less common in China, and that the government has made efforts to strengthen worker protections in some areas. Child labor, for instance, remains common in India and other South Asian nations, but is a minor issue in China, where the government has successfully imposed near-universal education through age fifteen.[22] A major campaign on mine safety beginning in the late 1990s brought the number of coal-mine deaths down from a horrific 7,000 in 1997 to 1,000 in 2013. A labor contract law effective in 2008 makes it far more difficult for employers in the formal sector to fire employees without cause, and sets generous standards for maternity leave, sick leave, and compensation for the early abrogation of a contract.

Market forces are also strengthening labor's hand. When labor was superabundant, as it was up until 2005 or so, employers could get away with a lot. But under the increasingly constrained labor-market conditions that have taken hold in the past decade, workers' bargaining power has increased substantially. This is visible first and foremost in rising wages (see Figure 9.4). As noted above, manufacturing wages have risen faster in China than in most other Asian developing economies. This pattern was already well established even in the 1990s, but has become more pronounced now that China's labor supply has stopped growing. Workers have taken

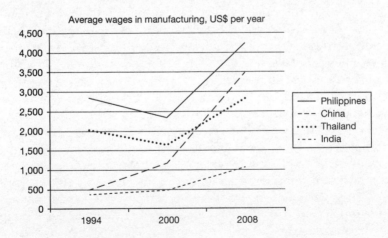

Figure 9.4 Manufacturing Wages

Source: World Bank/DRC 2013.

advantage of their stronger position to agitate not just for higher wages but also for better conditions and fairer treatment.

In short, the picture of Chinese workers as virtual slaves toiling in concentration-camp conditions is a caricature—and a patronizing one at that, since it implicitly denies any agency to the workers, who constantly make active decisions not only to leave the torpor of subsistence agriculture for a more materially rewarding life but also to move from bad employers to better ones.[23] Both the current state of Chinese working conditions, and their upward trajectory, echo the earlier experience of Japan, South Korea, and Taiwan. Establishing a consistently humane working environment will take longer in China because of the vast numbers of people involved. But there is progress in that direction.

10

THE EMERGING CONSUMER ECONOMY

Is China's Growth "Unbalanced," and How Much Does It Matter?

There is little doubt that China for the last three decades has been mainly an investment-driven economy. Growth was powered by capital spending on basic industries, export-oriented factories, infrastructure, and housing. In the "expenditure" accounting that economists use to break down gross domestic product (GDP), the share of investment (technically, "gross fixed capital formation") steadily rose, while consumption's share steadily fell.[1] In 1981, capital formation accounted for 27 percent of the economy and spending by households for 52 percent. Three decades later, the investment share had soared to 46 percent—the highest figure ever recorded for a major economy—while consumer spending had fallen to just 35 percent.[2] About two-thirds of the increase in investment, and the decline in consumption, occurred between 2000 and 2010 (see Table 10.1).

These data have caused much confusion. Some commentary suggests that there is something wrong with China's economic model because growth has been "unbalanced," with investment growing much faster than consumption. A corollary is that Chinese consumer spending is unusually weak, and that therefore government policy should seek to boost it.

There is some truth in both these propositions, but they should not be accepted uncritically. The first one, that unbalanced growth is intrinsically undesirable, goes against the experience of post–World War II East Asia, whose growth model China has largely copied. All the countries in this region that grew rich—Japan,

Table 10.1 Investment Overtakes Consumption: Share of GDP, %

Year	Gross fixed capital formation (%)	Household consumption (%)
1981	27	53
1990	25	49
2000	34	46
2010	46	35

Source: NBS.

South Korea, and Taiwan—went through a period of "unbalanced" growth during which investment grew much faster than consumption. Because of these different growth rates, the investment share of GDP grows substantially in such periods, and the consumption share naturally falls.[3]

The reason for this is quite simple. To make the transition from a mainly agricultural to a mainly industrial economy, countries must install a huge amount of fixed capital: factories, infrastructure, and modern housing. During this installation process, investment spending grows very rapidly. Household incomes and spending also enjoy strong gains, as workers move from low-wage agricultural jobs to higher-paying industrial ones. But for a while, these gains do not keep up with the breakneck pace of investment. Once the "installation" phase is over, investment spending slows down, household spending becomes the main engine of the economy, and the consumption share of GDP begins to rise again. In other words, a period of "unbalanced" growth can be a perfectly natural stage for a country moving from low-income to high-income status.

Has China's "Unbalanced" Growth Been Bad for Consumers?

A simple stylized example can clarify why a period of "unbalanced" capital-intensive growth is not necessarily bad for household welfare. Imagine a poor country with a per capita GDP of US$1,000, in which 80 percent of national income ($800 on average) comes from farmers selling their crops. The farmers, who constitute almost the entire population, spend seven dollars out of every eight they earn buying clothing and other necessities they cannot make for themselves. Thus in this economy, each person spends about $700 a year, and consumption's share of GDP is 70 percent.

Then suppose this country undergoes a successful industrialization drive. During this period capitalists build factories and infrastructure, and farmers start to move to higher-wage jobs in the cities. By the end of this period about half of national income goes to the capitalists, who mostly reinvest these profits in new factories. So the household income share of the economy falls from 80 percent to 50 percent. Moreover, families now have to save one dollar out of every three they earn, because they must buy expensive urban housing, provide against medical emergencies, and have a nest egg for their old age. This means the household consumption share of GDP has fallen in half, from 70 percent to 33 percent. Per capita GDP, though, has risen to US$10,000.

Is the average household better or worse off as a result of this process? If you look at the aggregate ratios, they seem to be worse off. The household share of national income has fallen by 30 percentage points; the average consumer only feels safe spending two of every three dollars she earns, instead of seven out of eight; and consumption's share of GDP has fallen in half.

Yet if you look instead at how much money the average consumer has to spend, it is clear that her life has improved a lot. In the old agricultural economy, each consumer spent $700 a year. In the new industrial economy, average spending is $3,350 a year—a nearly fivefold increase.[4] The fact that the household consumption share of GDP has fallen by half is dwarfed by the fact that GDP has grown by a factor of ten. The reason the income pie grew so much was that intensive investment—"unbalanced growth"—created large numbers of new jobs in high-wage manufacturing sectors.

This imaginary example actually describes pretty well what has happened in China (see Figure 10.1). Between 1990 and 2013, average per capita consumer spending rose fivefold in terms of real, inflation-adjusted US dollars—an average annual growth rate of 7 percent. This was nearly double the rate of increase in the next-fastest-growing big economy (India), and far above the rates experienced by the rich economies and by middle-income countries in Latin America. This explosive growth in consumer spending occurred even as the consumption *share* of the economy fell by about

Index of per capita consumption in 2005 US$, 1990 = 100

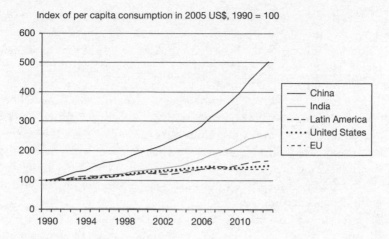

Figure 10.1 Rise of the Chinese Consumer
Source: World Bank.

15 percentage points, and as the household saving rate rose from about 20 cents of every dollar of income to 30 cents. The spending power of consumers in China's "unbalanced" economy grew much faster than that of consumers living in more "balanced" economies.

The new spending power of Chinese consumers is visible in a wealth of particular examples. Here are two. First, China became the world's biggest passenger-car market in 2010, and annual sales of nearly 20 million units are now about 30 percent higher than in the United States. Second, Chinese consumers are increasingly taking their money abroad. China surpassed Germany as the world's leading source of international tourist trips in 2012, and by 2014 it recorded over 100 million such trips, five times the number a decade earlier. Spending by Chinese international tourists was $165 billion—eight times the figure in 2004.

Of course this does not mean that the only way for a country to grow rich is through intensive investment, or that all investment is a good thing. China's pre-1980 period, and the history of the Soviet Union, provide examples of investment-intensive economies that did not lead to vibrant consumer spending. This was because those economies invested mainly in heavy industries like steel and petrochemicals, deliberately suppressed production of consumer goods, and failed to achieve the productivity gains needed for sustained wage growth.

Nor does it mean that China's situation today is without flaws. Far from it. The capital spending share of GDP is extraordinarily high, even for an East Asian economy; returns on investment have been falling since 2008; and evidence of wasted investment is everywhere in "ghost cities," empty shopping malls, and factories churning out more steel, cement, and glass than the nation can absorb. Perhaps more important, China's capital-intensive stage of growth created far more income inequality than was the case in Japan, South Korea, and Taiwan. The society China has created is quite a bit less fair than its East Asian models.

It is clear the investment-heavy phase of growth is nearing its end, and in the future the economy will have to be driven by consumer spending and by more selective, high-return investments. We will explore this future "rebalancing" from an investment-led to a consumer-led economy further in chapter 12. For the moment, it is enough to observe that China's consumer spending has in fact grown very rapidly for many years. From a policy perspective, the task of "rebalancing" has less to do with boosting consumer spending—which is already doing fine on its own—than with increasing the efficiency and productivity of investment, and ensuring that the profits from capital are properly taxed and redistributed into appropriate social goods.

Why Is the Consumption Share of China's Economy So Low?

This unfortunately is a technical question to which there is no definitive answer. According to official data, household spending in 2013 was just 36 percent of GDP. Virtually every other major economy in the world has a household consumption rate of 50 to 65 percent of GDP.[5] As we have just argued, China's low figure does not indicate that consumption is weak; in fact it is quite strong. What it mainly shows is that China's investment boom was unusually large: consumer spending grew very fast over the last quarter-century, but investment spending grew even faster.

A couple of other factors are at work. One is that consumer spending is almost certainly undercounted. This reflects the bias of the Chinese statistical system. Because economic policymakers are mainly concerned with promoting investment and industry, the data on investment and industry are detailed and accurate. The data on consumer spending, wages, and services are of much lower quality, and almost certainly miss a lot of activity. It is increasingly accepted that Chinese consumption data understate the true value of housing services, and probably miss much spending on transport and leisure as well.[6] Plausible upward revisions of these sectors produce a consumption ratio of 40 percent—still low, but not as dire as the official figure. Some Chinese economists have argued, with weaker evidence, that the true consumption ratio may be as high as 45 to 50 percent, or at the low end of the normal range for a country at China's stage of development.[7]

Another point often overlooked by analysts is that China's present low consumption rate is in part an artifact of its unusually low consumption rate at the beginning of economic reforms. When Japan started its most investment-intensive stage of growth, in 1955, household spending was 66 percent of GDP; the comparable figures for Taiwan and South Korea were 62 percent and 71 percent. After a decade or more of heavy investment, these ratios all fell into the low 50s before gradually recovering. But at the beginning of China's reform process in 1980, the consumption ratio was *already* barely above 50 percent. Most likely this reflects the structure of the planned-economy period, when consumption was deliberately suppressed in favor of large-scale state investments in heavy industry. Although that economic structure gradually disappeared, influential vestiges remain, such as the tendency of some urban consumer spending to come in the form of in-kind benefits from work units (gifts of food at the Lunar New Year, all-expenses-paid company outings, etc.). This again supports the notion that true consumer spending is likely to be higher than is shown in official statistics.

What Is China's "Middle Class"?

When we talk about Consumption with a capital "C" in China, we mainly refer to the spending of the urban middle class. About half of Chinese still live in the countryside, working mainly in farm-related activities, and of course they account for a large share of purchases of basic necessities. But their incomes are low: the average rural household has the same income as one in the poorest 10 percent of urban households. So the bulk of consumer spending in the "modern economy"—purchases of branded consumer goods, and of transport, leisure, finance, education, and healthcare services—is done by urban households.

Before trying to pin down how many people are in this urban consuming class and how much money they have to spend, it is worth clarifying the term "middle class." Although the words imply a group of people in the middle of a country's income distribution, the term is generally used in a much fuzzier way. It refers to the group who share certain characteristics broadly considered typical of the mainstream of people in a modern urbanized economy. They work for a living, in jobs that pay them enough so that they can buy their own house, a car, and other consumer durables like televisions, computers, and air conditioners. They invest significantly in education, and usually hope their children will work at white-collar jobs rather than on a factory floor. And because they typically own property, they pay a lot of attention to ensuring that their property rights are secure.

China has many such people, but we should bear in mind two characteristics that distinguish the Chinese "middle class" from the "middle class" in developed countries. First, the Chinese middle class is neither the middle nor the majority of society. Below we will offer a generous estimate that the middle class comprises about one-quarter of the national population, enjoying incomes in the upper third of China's income distribution. In other words, the people with a middle-class lifestyle in China constitute an elite, rather than a majority "middle class" in the American or European sense. This has an important political implication: the Chinese middle class is unlikely to become an advocate for political change anytime soon, since it is a privileged minority that benefits disproportionately from the present system.

The second characteristic is that one can qualify as a member of the Chinese middle class with an income far lower than that required for middle-class status in the United States, Western Europe, or Japan. So when we start looking at the size of China's middle class, it is important to remember that, on average, Chinese middle-class people have less spending power than middle-class people in developed countries.

How Big Is the "Middle Class"?

There are as many estimates of the size of China's middle class as there are consulting firms with consumer-goods clients. As we have just shown, "middle class" is an amorphous concept, so it can be plausibly defined in many ways, producing estimates of widely differing size. Bearing this caution in mind, we offer two calculations that define the upper and lower bounds.

The first is that of the World Bank, which defines the middle class in all countries as the people who spend US$10 to $100 each day on consumer goods and services. On this definition, the World Bank calculated China had 157 million middle-class consumers in 2010, or about 11 percent of the population. This was a large increase from just 2 percent in 2000, but considerably lower than the middle-class share of the populations in Brazil and South Korea when those countries were at China's present level of development.[8] Simple extrapolation suggests that by 2015, about 15 percent of China's population (roughly 200 million people) qualified as middle class according to the World Bank's standard.

A broader calculation relies on well-established income thresholds at which people in most countries start to buy important categories of goods and services. Households with incomes of at least $8,000 a year start to buy brand-name goods rather than cheap knockoffs. At $13,000 a year they start to buy automobiles—and since purchases of cars and houses are tightly correlated, this is also roughly the threshold level for widespread home ownership. At $20,000, they become significant purchasers of modern services: healthcare, education, tourism and leisure, and financial services.[9] If we define home ownership as an important criterion for a middle-class lifestyle, the middle class consists of households with an income of at least $13,000. We can define a larger "consuming class"—that is, people who are already active purchasers of some consumer goods, and may soon graduate to a middle-class lifestyle—by including all households whose income is at least $8,000 a year.

By this measure, China had a middle class of about 330 million people in 2012—one-quarter of the national population. (The narrower group of people we call "affluent" in the table below, with a household income of at least $20,000, roughly corresponds to the World Bank's definition of the middle class.) In addition, there were

Table 10.2 How Big Is China's Middle Class? Estimate for 2012

Income bracket	Millions of people	% of national population
Affluent	173	13
Established consumers	155	11
"Middle class"	328	24
Emerging consumers	228	17
Total consumer class	556	41
Lower incomes	805	59

Definitions:
Affluent: in households with income above $20,550
Established: household income between $13,500 and $20,550
Emerging: household income between $8,100 and $13,500
Lower incomes: household income below $8,100

Source: Adapted from Gatley 2013.

about 230 million "emerging consumers" with the potential to break into the middle class within the next decade. (See Table 10.2 for a full breakdown of the estimates of China's middle class.)

In short, depending on one's definition, one can say that the Chinese middle class is somewhere between 200 million and 300 million people, or 15 to 25 percent of the national population. At the high end, China's middle class is almost as big as the population of the United States—but has a median income far below the US median household income of $53,000 a year.

What Do China's Consumers Buy?

Over the past few decades, China's urban consumers have gone through successive waves of buying trends. In the 1980s, when incomes were very low, people focused on things like bicycles, electric fans, and basic furniture sets. In the 1990s they started to buy pricier household goods such as washing machines and air conditioners, and by the end of the decade China became the world's fastest-growing cell phone market. The early 2000s brought a huge upsurge in purchases of automobiles, and the private housing boom created large new markets for home furnishings and appliances. The average shopping basket for "affluent" Chinese consumers (the 13 percent or so of the population whose household income is above $20,000) is now fairly similar to that of ordinary households in South Korea and Taiwan.

One important shift is the rapid adoption of online commerce. E-commerce still accounts for just 5 percent of all retail sales—up from near zero as recently as 2009—but in some categories the online share is much higher. More than 20 percent of appliances and consumer electronics, and around 15 percent of clothes and cosmetics, are now bought over the Internet.[10] The retail landscape of Chinese cities will remain a hodgepodge of traditional markets, where most people still prefer to buy their fresh produce; modern supermarkets, department stores, and shopping malls, which offer a valued social experience; and online shopping. But e-commerce will certainly see the fastest growth. The potential growth of the market was reflected in the September 2014 initial public offering of China's biggest e-commerce firm, Alibaba, which valued the company at over $230 billion—significantly more than Amazon, even though Amazon's annual sales are about ten times Alibaba's.

There are several reasons for this swing. One is that the government has invested heavily to ensure that Internet access is cheap and virtually universal in urban areas: an estimated 650 million Chinese had Internet access in 2014, a sevenfold increase from a decade earlier. China is also home to a plethora of hardware manufacturers offering low-cost computers and smartphones. A Chinese firm, Lenovo, has the largest share of global personal-computer sales, largely because of its command of the China market. Lenovo and two other Chinese firms, Huawei and Xiaomi, are the world's third- through fifth-biggest suppliers of cellphones (behind Apple and Samsung), again because of their popularity in China.[11] Another factor is that an abundance of low-cost labor made it possible for e-commerce companies to hire armies of delivery people, who roam the cities on electric bicycles and motorcycles, delivering most goods within one or two days after an online order is placed.

Aside from the rise of e-commerce, the biggest trend in Chinese consumer behavior—and one with greater macroeconomic significance than online shopping—is a sharp rise in consumption of services. As we noted above, service consumption begins to pick up sharply among households making more than $20,000 a year. Such households have already satisfied their main material needs, and devote an increasing share of their income to extras like leisure and tourism; additional spending on education for their children (or perhaps even for themselves); more expensive healthcare; health and retirement services for their parents; and financial services to generate a higher return on their savings than that afforded by bank deposits.

This is important because, since 2010, the fastest-growing income bracket among China's consumer classes has been the "affluent" ($20,000-plus) category. And it is likely that most of the increase in Chinese consumer spending over the next decade will come from this group.[12] As one might expect, the last few years have seen a dramatic rise in service consumption. Overall, the services share of GDP rose from 43 percent in 2010 to 48 percent in 2014, and the service sector is now larger and growing faster than the traditional growth engines of industry and construction.

This growth is broad-based. We noted above the big increase in Chinese international tourism, which followed an even larger rise in domestic leisure travel. The boom in "wealth management products" around 2010, which we described in chapter 7, clearly reflects the emergence of a critical mass of high-end households that already owned property and were hungry for ways to diversify their financial portfolios. Between 2005 and 2013, the number of hospital beds nationwide rose by 75 percent, after nearly two decades of stagnation, and total healthcare spending rose from 4.5 percent to 5.2 percent of GDP.

How Good Is China's "Social Safety Net," and Would Making It Stronger Help Consumption?

Much discussion of consumption in China has focused on the relative lack of a social "safety net": public programs for health insurance, unemployment insurance, pensions, and so on. A common story is that consumer spending in China is relatively weak because families feel compelled to engage in "precautionary saving," devoting an ever-larger share of their income to finance expected future healthcare, education, and retirement costs. The evidence for this story is that the household savings rate has risen from less than 20 cents for every dollar of disposable income in the late 1990s to around 30 cents today. An improved social insurance system is therefore an important precondition for a more robust consumer economy.

This story sounds plausible. The traditional social safety net for urban workers until the late 1990s came through state-owned enterprises, which provided guaranteed employment, housing, medical care, pensions, and schooling for employees and their children. This welfare system was dismantled by the SOE reforms of 1995–2005, and at first there was no replacement for it. Urban families had to buy their own housing, and increasingly paid medical expenses and school fees out-of-pocket. Rural families suffered in different ways. Their main traditional safety net was simply the family farm, which could provide a subsistence living if all else failed; and this was unaffected. But the availability of state-provided medical care in rural areas deteriorated sharply in the 1990s.

These failures of government social welfare spending coincided with a rise in the household saving rate, and a decline in the consumption share of GDP. So it was natural to conclude that lower welfare spending contributed to weaker consumption, and that strengthening the social safety net would boost consumer spending. On closer inspection, the argument does not really hold up.

For one thing, growth in household consumption began to accelerate just as the old social safety net fell apart. In 2001, the trend growth rate in per capita consumer spending was just 5.6 percent a year; by 2008, when new social programs had been launched but not yet fully funded, this figure had risen to 7.6 percent. By 2013 trend consumption growth had climbed to 8.4 percent, even though the household saving rate continued to rise.[13] This acceleration is not consistent with the "precautionary savings" story. But it does square well with the story we told earlier in the chapter, about how rapid industrialization can create large income gains that enable the average consumer to spend a lot more dollars each year, even as she saves a higher percentage of each dollar she earns.

Another interesting point is that, at least in their early stages, expensive social welfare programs are more likely to be negative than positive for household incomes. This is because they have to be funded, and the main source of funding is levies on employers and employees that fall disproportionately on workers. Once a welfare system is up and running, present workers can benefit from the contributions that earlier workers made into social security funds. But the first generation of workers enjoys no such benefit. Moreover, the largest share of healthcare and pension benefits goes to older retirees. Today China has about five people of working age for every one of retirement age, meaning that more people are paying into social welfare funds than are extracting benefits. This is obviously good in the long run, but it is hard to see how it could be beneficial for total consumer spending in the short run.[14]

The conclusion is that creating a social safety net is likely to have a modest impact at best on consumer behavior, especially during the period when households are putting more into the welfare system through tax payments than they are receiving in benefits. Much more important is the rate of income growth. If household income grows fast, so will consumer spending, even if the safety net is riddled with holes. A social safety net is an important component of a just and equitable society, but it is not a consumption policy.

What Sort of Safety Net Is the Government Weaving?

One of the significant achievements of the Hu Jintao administration was the establishment of a comprehensive set of nationwide social programs, replacing the old SOE-based welfare system. In addition to expanding the minimum-income program that ensures a basic livelihood for the poor who are unable to find work, Hu's government established separate nationwide health insurance programs for urban and rural residents; abolished tuition and other fees for the nine years of education that are compulsory under Chinese law; greatly expanded coverage of basic pension schemes; and began a large-scale program to subsidize housing for low-income urban residents.

The minimum income program began in 1997 as a measure to prevent laid-off SOE workers from falling into destitution. In 2007 it was extended to include poor rural families, and about 3 percent of the urban population and 8 percent of the rural population are beneficiaries. Comprehensive national health insurance began to be rolled out in 2009 and consists of two urban insurance schemes (a mandatory one for formal-sector workers, funded mainly by employer and employee contributions, and a voluntary one for informal-sector workers, which relies more on government subsidies) and one for rural residents. At least 95 percent of households, both urban and rural, are now covered by government health insurance. However benefit levels, though rising, remain very meager. The number of people covered by government pensions has risen to about 700 million, from 200 million in 2002, although again the benefit levels in most cases are very basic. Another important initiative was the establishment of "social housing" programs in 2010 in order to increase the availability of affordable housing for low-income urban households. Between 2005 and 2013, total government spending on health, education, and social security rose from 5 percent to 8 percent of GDP, and from 28 percent to nearly 33 percent of the government budget. These figures would be even higher if subsidies for social housing were included.[15]

These achievements are substantial, but it is obvious that much more needs to be done. Many urban and rural workers still need to be brought into the pension system, and benefit levels for both pensions and health insurance must be raised significantly. More important, most social programs do a poor job of covering the migrant workers who constitute as much as a third of the urban population. Extending coverage to these disadvantaged workers, and financing increased benefits, will be very hard. A particular difficulty is that benefit levels must be raised to make them meaningful—but not raised so much that they impose an unbearable fiscal burden in thirty to forty years when China becomes a much older society, with far fewer workers supporting far more retirees. Yet solving the social welfare puzzle is essential if China is to bridge the vast gulf of income and social inequality that has arisen as a result of the fast economic growth of the past three decades.

What Policies Should the Government Take to Promote Consumption?

Earlier we made the point that the government need not bend over backward to boost consumer spending, which has been growing quite robustly for many years. We also argued that expansion of the social safety net, while important for other reasons, is unlikely to have much impact on consumer spending, at least in the short run. Does this mean the government should do nothing to make the economy more consumer-friendly? Not at all. There are two broad policy areas where the government can reasonably act to increase the scope for a vibrant consumer economy to emerge.

The first relates to income distribution. The main reason that household consumption is such a small share of the economy is not that consumers are reluctant to spend, but that the household share of national income is relatively small. The best way to get households to spend more is to increase their incomes.

As one would expect during an era of capital-intensive industrialization, an increasing share of national income over the past fifteen years has gone to companies that have reaped large profits from their investments, and mostly reinvested those profits in more industrial capacity. A goal of economic policy should now be to ensure that this trend is reversed, and that the household share of national income starts to rise. There are several ways to do this. Increased environmental and resource taxes can reduce corporate profits that arise simply from ignoring the true costs of "externalities" such as environmental damage or resource depletion. Allowing the cost of capital to be determined by the market, rather than by government policy, will effectively raise costs for heavy-industrial firms (especially SOEs). This means that firms will have to make their investments more efficient; it will also encourage them to simply forgo new investments when the prospective returns are not high enough. Then, instead of constantly recycling profits into new investment, they may choose to return some of their profits to shareholders through higher dividends; and that money becomes available for consumption spending. Ensuring stronger competition will also tend to reduce corporate profits; consumers benefit through lower prices, and will have more money left over to spend elsewhere.

The second major area where government policy can be useful is in promoting the development of services and deemphasizing industry. A shift from industry to services tends to redirect income away from the corporate sector and into households, because services generally use much more labor and much less capital than does industry. So a higher share of a service company's revenue goes into workers' pockets, in the form of wages.

Most of these initiatives have been built into government policy, at least in theory. The twelfth Five-Year Plan (2011–2015) explicitly targeted raising the household share of national income, and it also embraced the aim of making services replace industry as the main driver of economic production. Under its Third Plenum policy agenda of 2013, the Xi Jinping government has moved to raise resource taxes, make the pricing of capital more market-driven, and increase competition. Another bit of good news comes from demographics. As we documented in chapter 9, the supply of young workers is shrinking rapidly, forcing employers to raise wages more sharply than in the past. A number of market and policy factors are thus conspiring to give households a bigger share of national income, and this should be beneficial for consumer markets in the future.

Unfortunately, there are also a lot of obstacles. Much of the bias toward industry and investment arises from incentives built into the fiscal system, so a great deal depends on the ability of the central government to push through its very complex fiscal reform plan. Corporations (both state-owned and private) and officials at all levels of government profit handsomely from the present system, and will fiercely resist the necessary reforms. The next two chapters will examine in more detail the costs of the present growth model, and what the government needs to do to change it.

11

THE SOCIAL COMPACT

INEQUALITY AND CORRUPTION

So far we have painted a relatively positive picture: China's growth has been sustained at a high rate for over three decades, most of the population has benefited, and its political and economic systems have adapted fairly well to constantly changing conditions. But any process of rapid change such as China has experienced inevitably creates huge social stresses. In this chapter we will focus on two interlinked problems that, if left unaddressed, could undermine the political and economic order: inequality and corruption.

How Bad Is Income Inequality in China?

As is frequently pointed out by both Chinese officials and international agencies such as the World Bank, China's economic growth since the 1980s has lifted hundreds of millions of people out of poverty. This is a great achievement. But the fruits of growth have been distributed very unevenly. By virtually any measure of income or wealth, China is now one of the more unequal societies on earth. Perhaps more important, it is the country where inequality has grown most rapidly in the past few decades.

One standard measure of income inequality is the Gini index, developed by the Italian economist Corrado Gini a century ago, in which 0 represents perfect equality and 1 the state where all income is controlled by a single person. In practice, most countries have a Gini index of somewhere between 0.3 and 0.6. Rich countries with well-developed social welfare systems (e.g., in Scandinavia) fall at the bottom of the range; commodity-based economies where wealth is very concentrated (e.g., in Africa and Latin America) tend to be near the top.

Estimates of China's Gini index vary widely, but virtually all agree on two basic conclusions: China's income inequality is very high, and it rose substantially at least until 2008. The Chinese government's official Gini index peaked at 0.49 in 2008–2009 and since then has declined only marginally, to 0.47 in 2014. Some private estimates put the number as high as 0.55. If we accept the government's figure, China's income inequality is substantially greater than that of all developed countries. More important, it is much greater than in the successful East Asian economies it emulates (Japan, South Korea, and Taiwan), or even India—a country long infamous for its extremes of wealth and poverty.[1]

Perhaps more important is the trend: there is almost no doubt that during its economic reform era, China has seen its income inequality grow far more rapidly than that of any other region. Figure 11.1, drawn from the work of Branko Milanovic, a leading scholar of global inequality issues, shows that China's Gini index rose dramatically from 1988 to 2008, while inequality in other major regions stayed roughly constant or rose modestly. This general pattern is recognized by most serious scholars in China as well as by the government. No serious person disputes that income inequality

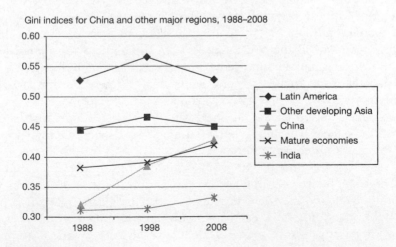

Figure 11.1 Global Inequality

Source: Laker and Milanovic, 2013.

in China has grown dramatically during the reform era and that correcting this trend is an urgent task.[2]

Why Hasn't Widening Inequality Caused More Social Unrest?

On the face of it, one might expect that rapidly widening income inequality would lead to a lot of social unrest, as the people with lower incomes grow angry at the rich people at the top who are skimming off most of the benefits of the growing economy. This should be especially true in China, where a Communist ideology of equality was strictly enforced for over three decades before the reform era.

Yet the available evidence does not indicate China is a simmering cauldron of discontent, at least not more than any other large and complex society. Journalists often point to Chinese government data showing that "mass incidents" or "public order disturbances" are on the rise, but these terms are hazy and the data is spotty. It is likely that most incidents that find their way into these statistics are small-scale events arising from local grievances.[3] Survey work suggests that Chinese citizens are not unusually unhappy with their lot and have a generally positive outlook for their personal economic prospects. The annual Global Attitudes and Trends survey by the Pew Research Center shows that, since 2007, well over 80 percent of Chinese respondents say they are "satisfied" with general national conditions and the state of the economy. In 2014, 89 percent of Chinese rated their economy "good," the highest score among the forty-five nations surveyed, and far higher than in India (64 percent), the United States (40 percent), or Brazil (32 percent). Similarly, a set of surveys by Harvard sociologist Martin Whyte in 2004 and 2009 concluded that despite increasing concerns over unfairness, "China's social volcano of potential anger at distributive injustice was clearly still dormant in 2009."[4]

It is possible that people would like to protest much more, but China's authoritarian political system simply crushes all demonstrations before they have time to spread. There is definitely truth to this: the Communist Party maintains an elaborate internal security apparatus, whose budget rivals that of the military, and is quite vigilant about cracking down on all forms of social disturbance.[5] But by itself, this answer is incomplete. Regimes that rely purely on repression and fail to deal with underlying causes do not last long, and China's record of sustained economic success, relative political stability over three generations of leaders since 1989, and the broadly positive attitudes revealed by surveys are not consistent with a simplistic picture of a cowed populace suppressing its anger from fear.

One answer to the question of why rising inequality has not spawned greater obvious discontent is that inequality is a by-product of even faster gains in average incomes. For most of the past three decades, all boats have been rising, and most people pay more attention to their own boat than to the boats that have risen higher. The same researchers whose data produced the chart above found that in 1988–2008, average per capita income in China grew by an astonishing 229 percent, ten times the global average of 24 percent, and far ahead of the rates for India (34 percent) and other developing Asian economies (68 percent). It may be (we have no way to prove it) that for many Chinese, the huge improvement in their own opportunities is a more important fact than the general rise in inequality. They may, in short, have bought into Deng Xiaoping's motto early in the reform era that "some people and some regions should be allowed to prosper before others." This psychology may seem alien to people from highly egalitarian societies, such as Scandinavia or Japan. But it is not that different from the prevailing ethos in the less egalitarian United States, where most people apparently believe that unequal economic outcomes are an acceptable counterpart of wide-open opportunity for bettering one's own lot.

Another factor is that, for the past fifteen years, Chinese policy-makers have devoted a lot of energy to addressing some (though not all) inequality issues. Here it is important to note that inequality has several dimensions. The dimension measured by the Gini coefficient is inequality among the incomes of all individuals. Not captured by the Gini are aspects of inequality that may be at least as visible and important to many people: the gap between urban and rural incomes; and the disparity between the rich coastal provinces, which benefited from foreign direct investment and exports, and the hinterland provinces that had been left behind.

The government has done relatively little to address individual income inequality, but over the past fifteen years has launched a host of policies specifically designed to reduce urban-rural inequality and inequalities between poor and rich regions. Programs to boost rural incomes have included: a relaxation of rules requiring farmers to grow grain, enabling them to increase production of more profitable cash crops; the easing and finally abolition of taxes and fees on agricultural production; a major push to build farm-to-market roads, helping farmers gain access to richer urban consumers; and stepped-up investments in food processing industries. To address the coast/hinterland divide, Beijing unleashed a series of infrastructure development programs targeting first the far west, then the rustbelt northeast, and finally the central provinces.

All these programs are subject to criticism on efficiency grounds, but they contributed to arresting or reversing the two types of inequality they intended to address. By 2004, growth in rural consumption began to catch up to urban levels, and the urban-rural income gap began to shrink in 2009.[6] As late as 2005, only a half-dozen provinces had urban wages within 10 percent of the national average. The rest of the country was divided between a handful of provinces, mainly on the coast, with much higher than average wages, and a vast mass of interior provinces with much lower incomes. By 2011 this provincial wage gap had closed: half of provinces had urban wages within 10 percent of the national average, and only the coastal megacities of Beijing, Tianjin, and Shanghai had wages more than 10 percent above the national norm.[7]

What Are the Sources of the Current Income Inequality?

Despite this progress, inequality at the individual level remains very high and is an increasing concern of Chinese citizens. By the Chinese government's own measurement, the Gini index was an uncomfortable 0.47 in 2014. Inequality of wealth—though harder to measure—appears to be more extreme. One credible estimate suggests that the top 10 percent of Chinese households own about 85 percent of assets in the country, much higher than their 57 percent share of total income. Pew's 2012 survey found that inequality ranked third on the list of urban residents' biggest worries, behind inflation and official corruption, but ahead of food safety and air pollution. About 45 percent of respondents agreed that hard work would be rewarded by success, but a significant minority, 33 percent, disagreed.[8]

The sources of this inequality can be divided into two broad categories. To some extent, increased inequality is the natural outcome of a period of rapid economic development, when a country shifts from agriculture to industry. The reason, as outlined by the economist Simon Kuznets in 1955 and elaborated by later development economists, is that in the early stages of economic development, the relatively few people lucky enough to have access to the modern economy—either through ownership of capital or by having the skills to get a job in the modern sector—see their incomes rise very quickly, while those left behind in traditional agriculture face relatively stagnant incomes. As development continues, a greater proportion of the population gets drawn into the modern economy, and inequality tends to moderate.[9] There is little doubt that this process is part of what lies behind China's high inequality.

Second are factors specific to China that have made its inequality problem far worse than those experienced by other fast-growing East Asian countries—especially Japan, South Korea, and Taiwan, which appear to have managed the industrial transition without big rises in inequality. Chief among these is the different property rights regimes for rural and urban households, which led to unequal access to capital. Urban households enjoyed a gigantic wealth transfer in the 1998–2003 housing privatization (see chapter 4); by contrast, farmers often had their land confiscated at below-market rates by local governments. On top of that, China imposes no taxes on capital gains of any kind. So the urban owners of property and financial assets such as stocks were able to enjoy tax-free windfall gains.

Is There Any Hope That Income Inequality Will Start to Decrease?

There are some signs that income inequality may have peaked. In the early 2000s, incomes for the lowest 40 percent of the population grew much more slowly than those for the top 40 percent. By 2007 the two groups had converged, and beginning in 2010 incomes were growing faster for lower-income people than for high-income people (see Figure 11.2). This trend is consistent with the government finding that the nation's Gini index peaked at 0.49 in 2009 and edged down to 0.47 by 2014. Income inequality remains quite high, although it no longer seems to be rising.

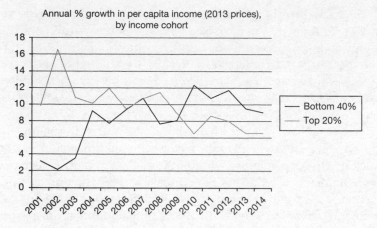

Figure 11.2 Income Growth

Source: NBS, Gavekal Dragonomics.

For the most part, this shift owes more to organic changes in the economy than to specific government policies. Chief among these is demographics: as the supply of young migrant workers has begun to shrink, firms must bid their wages higher. Meanwhile, the supply of young people competing for high-end jobs in management, finance, and technology has grown rapidly, thanks to a huge increase in the number of college graduates, from one million a year in 2000 to over six million a year today. As a result, since 2009 wages in predominantly blue-collar sectors (construction, manufacturing, retail, and agriculture) have grown much faster than those in white-collar sectors. This trend was reinforced by the government's massive infrastructure stimulus program in 2009–2010, which created millions of new construction jobs.[10] This progress is heartening, but modest. A tightening labor market may ameliorate inequity in wage income; it will do nothing to improve the distribution of assets and reduce inequality arising from ownership of capital.

The government is aware of these issues, but its policies so far are well short of what is needed. The twelfth Five Year Plan (2011–2015) was the first to highlight the need to make income distribution less unequal. The plan's approach was a set of policies designed to reduce incentives for capital-intensive investments and to encourage the growth of service sectors that are much more labor-intensive. All else being equal, this will tend to reduce the growth of income from capital and to accelerate wage growth for ordinary Chinese.

Such measures are helpful, as are efforts since 2005 to build a more comprehensive social safety net comprising unemployment protection, minimum income schemes, universal health insurance, and urban and rural pension plans. Progress in building these social insurance programs has been slow but steady; the government is anxious to avoid building a system promising overly generous benefits, because such a system could prove impossible to finance in a few decades' time when the population is much older. Nonetheless, pensions and health insurance are now available to the large majority of both urban and rural residents, albeit with relatively low benefit levels.

Yet to bring China's inequality in line with the much lower levels seen in the advanced East Asian economies, much more aggressive policies will be required. In particular, the government must put in place taxes on capital income as well as rolling back the vast accumulations of assets in the hands of a small number of officials and tycoons. In other words, it must tackle the problem of corruption.

How Bad Is China's Corruption Problem?

Corruption has clearly been endemic throughout the reform era, although its shape has shifted with time. In the 1980s, one of the biggest sources of corruption was the two-track price system, under which factories committed to sell a certain amount of their output at relatively low planned prices, but they could sell any excess production on the free market at higher prices. This created an incentive for officials to use their influence to purchase goods at low plan prices and then resell them at higher market prices. Outrage at this kind of corruption was an important contributor to the Tiananmen Square protests of 1989.

The subsequent price reforms, which eliminated the two-track system and led to the acceptance of market pricing for almost all goods except a handful of strategic commodities, eliminated this channel of corruption. In the booming 1990s, an important source of corruption was smuggling. This was profitable because high tariffs and nontariff barriers made many goods far more expensive in China than on the global market. In 1992, China's weighted average tariff was 32 percent, and duties on some popular goods (such as automobiles) were 100 percent or more. In addition, more than half of imports were subject to various kinds of nontariff restrictions that impeded their import.[11] By the mid-1990s, smuggling was a gigantic business turning over billions of dollars a year. The effect was visible in macroeconomic statistics. In 1998, foreign exchange reserves grew by only $5 billion, even though the official trade surplus and foreign direct investment inflows were each around $45 billion. The difference of more than $80 billion—nearly 8 percent of GDP—mostly represented money that flew out of China in payment for smuggled goods and other forms of capital flight. Smuggling disappeared as a major form of corruption thanks to draconian crackdowns on big smuggling rings in south China; but more importantly it was because tariffs and nontariff barriers were sharply reduced in the late 1990s and early 2000s, making the game not worth the candle.

In the first decade of the 2000s, the construction boom in urban China offered rich opportunities for rake-offs from land deals and infrastructure projects. Because local governments controlled the land supply, officials could extract bribes for directing prime plots to particular developers. And, as in any construction boom, officials routinely received kickbacks on infrastructure contracts. Since China was undergoing the biggest construction boom in history, the scale of corruption was similarly unprecedented, with top officials frequently squirreling away hundreds of millions of dollars in black income. Construction-related corruption almost certainly surged in 2009–2010, when the government launched its economic stimulus program, most of which went into infrastructure spending.[12]

There have of course been numerous other channels for corruption. Officials could get payoffs for delivering any of the many licenses and approvals required for setting up a new business or for executing any major investment project. In many jurisdictions, official appointments and promotions were for sale. And for the elite sitting at the top of the system, initial public offerings (IPOs) of major companies offered a comparatively clean way to get rich quick. Either to speed up the tortuous IPO approval process, or more likely to buy influence for other purposes, company officials often gave officials or their family members cheap or free shares ahead of the listing, enabling them to pocket huge profits when the shares started trading.[13]

Profiteering from corruption ran right to the top of the political system. The biggest case that the government has acknowledged was that of Zhou Yongkang, who served on the Politburo standing committee in 2007–2012 and ran the nation's security services. In 2014 Zhou was formally investigated for corruption and expelled from the party; police claimed to have confiscated assets of $14.5 billion from Zhou, his family members, and his business associates. That amount would rank Zhou as seventh in the list of China's richest people compiled annually by the Shanghai-based *Hurun Report*. Foreign media have also documented extensive wealth in the immediate family of former prime minister Wen Jiabao (US$3 billion, according to the *New York Times*) and current president Xi Jinping (US$55 million in Hong Kong property, and investments in companies worth US$2 billion, according to Bloomberg News). The widespread perception that, in the party and government, no one's hands are clean of corruption is probably accurate.[14]

Why Hasn't Corruption Stopped Economic Growth?

Given the magnitude and ubiquity of corruption—and its apparently rising scale over the last two decades—it is worth asking why the wheels haven't come off the Chinese system by now. A solid body of research finds a robust inverse correlation between corruption and economic growth: the more corrupt a country is, the lower its long-run growth rate. And of course, recent history is filled with examples of dictators who accumulated vast wealth by looting their countries but eventually saw their regimes crumble: the Duvaliers in Haiti, Mobutu Sese Seko in Zaire, presidents Marcos and Suharto in the Philippines and Indonesia, and so on. China has managed to be incredibly corrupt while at the same time sustaining an economic growth rate of around 10 percent for three decades and creating a political system that does not look in the least fragile. How could this be?

One answer, offered periodically by pessimistic analysts, is that it is just a matter of time: uncontrollable corruption will eventually force the system into either political collapse or economic sclerosis.[15] But despite the passage of time, these predictions have failed to pan out. Something else is going on, and three factors seem to be at play.

First, for much of the reform era, corruption was in essence a side effect of reforms that also brought powerful economic benefits. As long as the benefits from restructuring outweighed the stealing by corruption, the system as a whole was sustainable. And especially in the 1980s and 1990s, certain types of corruption (not all) could be seen as rational economic behavior, rather than just looting. The most obvious examples are the arbitrage of plan and market prices in the 1980s, and some of the smuggling activity in the 1990s. Under the dual-track price system, the authorities tried to maintain in-plan price controls for many goods, not because those prices were appropriate or economically efficient, but simply because it was politically inconvenient to dismantle the old planned-economy price system all at once. The result was artificial shortages of some goods and chronically high inflation. Officials who diverted goods from the plan to the market were, among other things, responding to the market signal that those goods were in high demand and short supply. Once prices were marketized, this type of graft disappeared.

The case of smuggling is in some ways even clearer. Some smuggling was just crime, as when Fujian entrepreneur Lai Changxing bribed dozens of officials to enable him to bring in billions of dollars' worth of crude oil and luxury cars without paying duties.[16] But much of it could be seen as a private-sector effort to reduce import tariffs. In Guangdong in the late 1990s, it was routine for businesses to import some of their materials and components, or finished goods they wanted to sell on the mainland, indirectly via Hong Kong. First the goods would be sold to an agent, or "converter," in Hong Kong. A week or two later those same goods would be purchased by the business in Guangdong from another agent, at a markup of 15 to 20 percent over what the converter paid. Everyone knew that customs officials had been paid off in between, but no one asked questions, and the practice was considered virtually legitimate. In these sorts of transactions, businesspeople were in effect reducing the import tariff from a noneconomic rate (typically 40 percent to 70 percent) to one that made commerce profitable. As with corruption related to dual-track pricing, this practice vanished once tariffs fell to more reasonable levels.

A second factor was that allowing some degree of official corruption was the deal that the leadership offered to officials in order to marshal their support for reforms. At the start of the reform era and for years after, many officials had reached their positions by toeing the line of Communist ideology, and they did not necessarily know how to conduct their new job of promoting business activity. Letting them keep part of the proceeds from the new market economy—giving them some "skin in the game"—provided a material incentive for officials to go along with market reforms.

Finally, this tacit license to steal was not unlimited. Beginning in the early 1980s, the Communist Party waged a continuous and occasionally intense fight against corruption. "Economic crime" cases recorded by the central prosecution agency surged from less than 10,000 in 1980 to nearly 80,000 in 1989 in the aftermath of the Tiananmen protests. Prosecutions continued at a rate of more than 50,000 a year until the late 1990s, when they dropped—most likely because opportunities for large-scale corruption abated with the elimination of controlled prices and high tariffs, and the legitimation of private-sector economic activity reduced officials' incentive to extract bribes simply to let private companies stay in business.

Prosecutions averaged 30,000 a year in the decade leading up to the 2008 global financial crisis. At the same time, though, the number of higher-level officials prosecuted continued to rise, as did the severity of penalties. Researchers have found that at most one in ten corrupt officials are ever charged with corruption; but those that are charged are almost invariably convicted, and they face harsh sanctions including prison terms of ten years or more or even death sentences, of which 700 were handed down in corruption cases in the decade to 2008. The point about this activity is not that it was comprehensive, but that it established some constraints, so that corruption was confined to the role of successful parasite: it lived off its host (a rapidly growing economy) without killing it.[17]

This description of why corruption and robust economic growth could coexist is plausible for the first quarter-century or so of the reform period, but becomes less convincing after about 2005, when the construction-led corruption boom was in full swing. The more recent corruption seems less a side effect of a generally beneficial economic reform process and more purely predatory. The two single biggest sources of corrupt wealth during the last decade were skim-offs from infrastructure projects (which may have been economically useful but could not be seen as part of "economic reform") and profits from land extracted from farmers at far below its true market value (which was simply exploitation of farmers' inadequate legal property rights). Moreover, the scale of the thieving—routinely running into the hundreds of millions if not billions of dollars—was extraordinary. By the end of the Hu Jintao era, many in the Chinese elite began to fear that economic reform had run aground, corruption had run out of control, and that the country was at serious risk of running off the rails.

Is Xi Jinping's Anticorruption Campaign a Real Solution to the Problem, or Just Window Dressing?

After Xi Jinping took over from Hu Jintao as secretary-general of the Communist Party (in November 2012) and as state president and head of the military (in March 2013), he immediately launched a massive anticorruption campaign, pledging that he would spare no efforts to snare "both tigers and flies"—in other words, both high- and low-level offenders. This campaign, led by Wang Qishan, a member of the Politburo standing committee and head of the party's internal disciplinary agency, has continued at full force for three years, through 2015. By the end of 2014 over 75,000 officials, SOE executives, military officers, and businesspeople had been disciplined, and virtually every province and every agency of the party-state was affected. It is by a wide margin the longest-lasting and most intense antigraft drive in the party's history.

The central question is whether this campaign is really a serious effort to root out corruption, or if it is—like many previous anticorruption surges—simply a witch-hunt to crush the current leader's political enemies. Since we cannot read Xi's mind, we can't know for sure, but most likely the campaign has at least three dimensions. There is little doubt that it is, in part, designed to destroy rival political networks. Key "tiger" targets have been Zhou Yongkang, the former security boss, who had turned the intelligence services into an almost autonomous power base; two senior generals closely linked to former president Jiang Zemin; and Ling Jihua, the powerful former private secretary for Hu Jintao.

But the extraordinary breadth and duration of the campaign, along with other parallel initiatives such as an intraparty ideological campaign, a fiscal reform program, and crackdowns on the media and academia, suggest the antigraft drive is part of a bigger governance strategy. And in fact the party document outlining the goals of the anticorruption campaign presents it as exactly that: an element of a broad-based effort to improve the party's governance capacity.[18] One specific governance objective may be to break down resistance to future major reforms in local government and in the organization of state-owned enterprises.

At the deepest level, the crackdown may aim to renegotiate the implicit political-economy bargain that has been in place since the early 1980s: a relatively high tolerance of corruption as part of the price to be paid for giving officials incentives to prioritize economic growth. That bargain worked tolerably well so long as the main economic task was installing basic industries, housing, and infrastructure: the idea was to get as much of these things built as possible, with efficiency a secondary concern. In the future (as will be discussed in the next chapter), China's growth will need to come much more from efficiency gains. Corruption is far more cancerous in an efficiency-oriented economy than in a stock-building one. In order to achieve the ambitious restructuring of China's economy that he claims to intend, Xi Jinping must first reform the governing structure, and this involves permanently reducing the level of corruption.

This is a speculative explanation, and many serious students of Chinese politics see the antigraft drive more simply, as a power grab by Xi. Yet even if one accepts the more generous hypothesis that Xi aims for a comprehensive overhaul of China's governance structures, it is very much an open question whether the effort to bring corruption under control will succeed. There is a good argument that the fundamental cause of corruption in modern China is a system in which weak rule of law is institutionalized by the insistence that the Communist Party hold a monopoly on political power and be exempt from the legal processes that apply to everyone else. So long as the party operates without checks and without external accountability, this argument goes, a high level of ongoing corruption is unavoidable.

12

CHANGING THE GROWTH MODEL

Why Do People Say China Must "Change Its Growth Model"?

Since reforms began in 1979, China has become one of the world's greatest economic success stories. At no point during those decades did success come easily: the economic miracle required persistent hard work and creativity by millions of Chinese workers and entrepreneurs, as well as skillful management by policymakers, under conditions that never seemed to stabilize for more than three or four years at a time. But today, China faces a challenge arguably greater than any it has had to overcome in the past. This challenge is to shift away from a growth model based mainly on the *mobilization of resources* to one based mainly on the *efficiency of resource use*. Another way of putting it is that China has spent the last three decades installing the assets needed for a modern economy. Now its job is to maximize the return on those assets.

As we have seen in the preceding chapters, since 1979 China has executed a move away from a state-dominated, planned economy to a dynamic mixed economy in which market forces and the private sector have played ever more important roles. Seen from one perspective, this task was complex, requiring an intricate series of reforms in financial, fiscal, enterprise, governance, and legal systems and an ability to respond flexibly to the often-unintended consequences of these changes. But from another point of view, the underlying task was quite straightforward: to put more resources to use.

This mandate—put more resources to use—mainly meant putting more capital into the system. China has always had an abundant labor supply, and even at the beginning of the reform era its workers were relatively healthy and well educated by the standards of low-income countries, so they had plenty of productive potential. But for that productive potential to be unleashed, these workers needed to be brought out of their low-productivity agricultural occupations and paired with capital in all its forms. This shift included industrial technology and modern management techniques, the network infrastructure needed to run these modern businesses (electricity and telecoms), the infrastructure linking these businesses with global markets (ports and airports), the infrastructure required to enable workers to move to where the jobs were, and infrastructure needed to knit together the domestic market (roads, railways, and housing).

In short, the biggest single task for China over the past thirty-five years was to increase its *capital stock*: the total value of equipment, buildings, and other forms of physical capital. An advanced economy like the United States typically has a capital stock with a value of a bit over three times its annual output or GDP. A poor country, such as China was in the early 1980s, might have a capital stock that is one-and-half times its annual GDP, or even less. The primary job for any country that wants to move from poor to rich is therefore to increase its capital stock to a degree approaching rich-country levels.

Three conclusions follow from this observation. First, by simple arithmetic, in order for the capital stock to rise relative to GDP, investment in capital must obviously grow quite a bit faster than GDP for a long time. Here's a simple example. Let's say a country starts out with a capital stock one-and-a-half times its GDP, and aims to reach the rich country's capital/GDP ratio of three-to-one over thirty years, with the economy growing at an average rate of 6 percent a year. For this country to achieve its aim, the capital stock must grow each year by 8.5 percent—more than a third faster than GDP. If we further assume that capital in this country depreciates at a rate of 5 percent a year, then the country's *investment rate*—that is, the share of annual GDP that is devoted to new capital investments—will nearly double over the three-decade period, from 19 percent to 37 percent.

This is obviously a simplified example, but it captures fairly well the experience of the successful post–World War II East Asian economies (see Figure 12.1). All of them invested intensively in industry, infrastructure, and housing over several decades, building up their

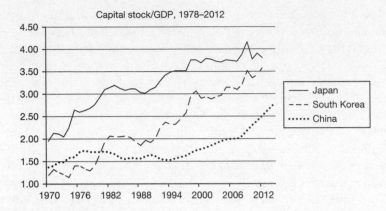

Figure 12.1 Capital Stock

Source: Gavekal Dragonomics, Asian Productivity Organization.

capital stock; all of them saw their investment rates rise from somewhere in the twenties to somewhere in the high thirties; and at the end of the process Japan, South Korea, and Taiwan all achieved at least upper-middle-income status, with household living standards half or more of the US average. In China's case, between 1980 and 2010 the investment rate rose from 28 percent to an unusually high 46 percent, and the capital stock rose from about 1.8 to 2.4 times the GDP.[1] Conversely, the crucial characteristic of countries that have failed to sustain a drive into the club of upper-income nations (for instance Brazil, India, and Thailand) is that they have been unable to keep capital investment growing at a sufficiently high rate.

The second point is that, at least during the early stages of this capital accumulation phase, the marginal efficiency with which capital is used, while not irrelevant, is of secondary importance. Obviously, new capital projects must meet some basic productivity standard: building a bridge that is not connected to a road on either end is a pure waste of money, as is building an export-oriented sneaker factory a thousand miles from the nearest port. Capital investments must be broadly appropriate to the country's level of economic development, and linked to well-functioning markets, so that industries do not keep producing goods for which there is no demand and infrastructure helps enable the creation of new productive businesses. These conditions differentiate an effective period of capital accumulation, such as China has enjoyed over the past three decades, from misguided capital accumulation—which is what China endured in the preceding Maoist era. During Mao's time, there was plenty of investment in capital stock, but because much of this investment was inappropriate to China's level of development (too many steel plants, not enough farm-to-market roads or consumer goods factories), and because markets were not allowed to signal where new investments might be most appropriate, this capital spending generated very poor economic returns.

On the whole, though, it is more vital for poor countries to focus on putting in as much appropriate capital as possible than to try to maximize the marginal productivity of each individual project—so long as they have functioning market institutions, a decent labor force, a reasonable standard of governance, and economic policies that create a predictable investment environment for businesses. Under these conditions, most new capital investments are likely to generate very large returns quite quickly, thanks to the ability of infrastructure and new technology to dramatically boost productivity from its very low starting point. This is the "advantage of backwardness" that we talked about in chapter 3. The aggregate benefit of adding lots of new capital to the system far outweighs the marginal loss incurred by having each dollar of capital generate a return a couple of percentage points lower than in a more perfect system.

The third point, though, is that even if this capital-intensive stage of growth is perfectly executed, it has an expiration date. At some stage, a country's capital stock approaches the rich-country level. There is then little benefit to be achieved by simply throwing more capital into the system. Businesses already have the equipment they need to compete effectively. Workers are already so productive that their output cannot be increased by a factor of two or three simply by pairing them up with a new machine. Most of the roads, railways, ports, and power plants that the country needs have been built. When this happens, robust economic growth can no longer be achieved simply by adding capital. Instead, growth must come from increasing the amount of output that a given unit of capital can produce—that is, by increasing the efficiency of resource use. One consequence of this shift is that the economy will grow much more slowly than in the past, because instead of two major sources of growth (addition of new capital and improved productivity), there is really only one (productivity).

The relevance of this discussion to China is clear. The high economic growth rates of the reform era can be boiled down to two factors: (1) the mobilization of resources that greatly increased the country's capital stock; and (2) the gradual shift of control of those resources from the state sector to the private sector, which ensured that over time and on average, the efficiency of resource use gradually improved, even if some investment got wasted along the way. Now, however, China has installed so much capital that the era of resource mobilization is drawing to an end. In the future, growth must rely less on additions of capital and more on efficiency gains.

Why Do People Say China's Growth Was "Imbalanced"?

Many analysts describe China's economic problems today in terms of "imbalances." In the past, the story goes, China relied far too much on investment and exports to power its growth and too little on household consumption. Household spending typically represents 60 to 70 percent of final demand in rich countries, but in recent years has accounted for less than 40 percent of Chinese demand. China's main task, according to this school of thought, is to achieve a better "balance" among the different sources of growth: investment, consumption, and exports. In practice the prescription is usually to cut back the investment rate and increase consumer spending.

The concept of "imbalances" is in some respects a good way to describe China's position, but it also presents problems. The most basic is that, as we have just shown, every country that has grown rich through industrialization has done so thanks to a long period of "unbalanced" growth, when investment grows much faster than GDP so that a modern capital stock can be built up. Since investment is the converse of consumption (every dollar that is not invested must be consumed), the inescapable corollary is that during this period of intensive capital spending, the consumption share of GDP must fall. During this phase, a declining consumption rate is perfectly normal and does not necessarily signal a faulty growth model or "insufficient" reliance on household spending. In fact, as we showed in chapter 10, China's consumer spending has grown at a very fast rate for over a decade, and the fall in the consumption share of GDP is not out of line with the earlier experience of Japan and South Korea.

That said, one can have too much of a good thing, and there are solid reasons to think that China's reliance on exports before the global financial crisis, and on investment spending since then, were excessive. The idea that China's growth was dangerously "imbalanced" began to take hold in the early 2000s, when both the trade surplus and the investment share of GDP began to expand rapidly. From 1990 to 2004, China consistently ran a positive balance of trade, with annual surpluses of around 2 percent of GDP. Exports grew fast, but so did imports—both of raw materials and capital goods—so the trade balance stayed fairly stable relative to the whole economy. Starting in 2005 the surplus began to balloon, reaching a peak of nearly 9 percent of GDP in 2007. In the same year, the broader current account balance (which includes trade in services and income on international investments in addition to goods trade) hit 10 percent of GDP. These are extremely high numbers for a large economy. The United States, whose trade deficits are legendary, usually runs a current account deficit of 1 to 2 percent of GDP, which rose to a peak of just under 6 percent on the eve of the financial crisis.

Similarly, the investment share of GDP, which fluctuated at 32 to 36 percent in the decade up to 2002, began to surge as China poured billions of dollars into manufacturing, housing, and infrastructure. By 2008, investment was about 41 percent of GDP, exceeding the top levels reached by Japan, South Korea, and Taiwan during their most capital-intensive phases of growth.

These trends partly reflected the natural peak of the capital-intensive growth phase, but were exacerbated by peculiarities of the Chinese economic situation and policy environment. Investment surged to an unusual degree in the early 2000s because of housing privatization, which suddenly unleashed a wave of pent-up demand for urban housing. Exports boomed because investments by foreign companies in outsourced production facilities in the late 1990s and early 2000s began to pay off, especially after China joined the WTO in late 2001 and became a full participant in the global trading system. And for much of the period 2002–2007, policymakers kept interest rates and energy prices lower than they would have been in a market economy (making it cheaper to invest), and they also tolerated an exchange rate that was increasingly undervalued in real terms (boosting exports).

Chinese leaders had begun to recognize these problems and to take limited action: the renminbi was allowed to appreciate beginning in 2005, and energy efficiency targets adopted in 2006 had in part the goal of raising the cost of investment. These steps were very cautious and did little to rein in the growth of exports and investment—a fact acknowledged by Premier Wen Jiabao, who in his annual work report in 2007 described China's economy as "unbalanced, unstable, uncoordinated and unsustainable." But whatever plans the government may have had to address these problems were thrown off course by the events of 2008.

What Was the Impact of the 2008 Global Financial Crisis?

The global financial crisis that began in September 2008 had a profound impact on China, despite the fact that its own, closed financial system was not directly affected. The main effect came through exports. As trade finance dried up and the global economy weakened, demand for Chinese exports plummeted by 20 percent over the next year—by far the biggest annual fall in export value in Chinese history. The impact on employment was swift: an estimated 23 million workers in export-oriented factories were laid off by the Lunar New Year holiday in February 2009, and told not to come back to work after the vacation. In response, China unleashed an infrastructure-focused economic stimulus program with a headline value of Rmb 4 trillion (about US$590 billion at the then-current exchange rate), or 12 percent of GDP. Over the next two years, the actual stimulus was probably closer to Rmb 11 trillion.[2] At a time when every government in the world was launching stimulus programs, China's was the biggest both relative to the size of its economy and in absolute terms.

The announced, immediate objective of the stimulus program was to maintain an economic growth rate of at least 8 percent—the rate Chinese leaders believed was necessary to ensure satisfactory employment growth. In this they were successful: GDP growth averaged over 9.5 percent a year in 2009–2011.

At a deeper level, the stimulus program and a variety of subsequent policy measures reflected a shift of course in economic strategy. The leadership realized that China's unusually large export sector—with exports equal to 35 percent of GDP (triple the figure for Japan) and a current account surplus of 10 percent of GDP (by far the largest of any major economy)—was more of a vulnerability than a strength. The problem with relying so much on exports is that if your trading partners run into trouble, so do you. Chinese policymakers decided that future economic growth would have to come mainly from domestic demand, not exports. In this they were also successful: the current account surplus fell from 10 percent in 2007 to under 2 percent by 2013 (see Figure 12.2).

Domestic demand, of course, has two main components: investment spending and household consumption. In the short run, it was unrealistic to expect Chinese consumers to suddenly start spending a lot more money—especially since many of them had lost their jobs in the export slowdown. And in general, changes in consumption patterns tend to occur very slowly. So to stimulate domestic demand, the leaders did the only thing they could: push up investment through government spending on infrastructure and private spending on housing. As a result, investment surged from 41 percent of GDP in 2008 to an astonishing 46 percent of GDP in 2010, a level it roughly maintained for the next four years (see Figure 12.3). In other words, China reduced its external "imbalance" (the trade surplus) by increasing its domestic "imbalance" (the high investment rate).

Another consequence of the global crisis was that it prompted a decision to make the renminbi an international currency, rather

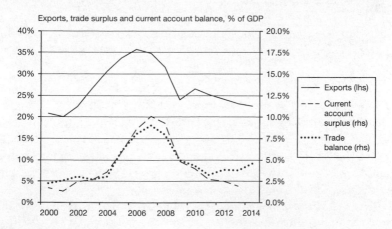

Figure 12.2 Export Reliance

Source: NBS/CEIC

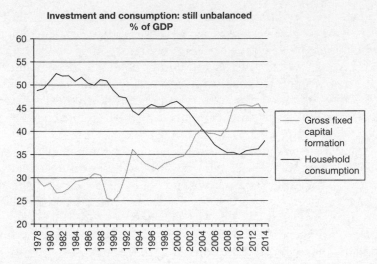

Figure 12.3 Investment Consumption
Source: NBS, CEIC.

than a purely domestic one. The basic reasons that policymakers decided to push on this front were (a) they believed the global crisis was caused in part by the US government's abuse of the dollar's position as the main global currency; and (b) they worried that over-reliance on the dollar for trade invoicing made China vulnerable at times—as in late 2008—when dollar-denominated trade finance dried up (see chapter 7 for more detail).

Why Is the Return on Capital Falling?

The stimulus program got China past the global crisis in better shape than any other major economy. But the artificial boost it gave to the economy papered over the fundamental structural challenge: the "mobilization" phase of growth was at the end of its natural lifespan, and important reforms were needed to ensure that the "efficiency" phase of growth could begin.

The last three years of the Hu Jintao administration (2010–2012) saw very few concrete structural reform achievements. This failure seems to have stemmed less from an inability to diagnose the problems than from an incapacity to enforce solutions. The twelfth Five

Year Plan, for 2011–2015, contains a number of targets showing an understanding that many of the traditional growth sources were exhausted and that new ones needed to be cultivated. In particular, the plan expressed the intent to increase consumption's share in the economy, and to promote that aim by ensuring that a higher proportion of national income flowed to households (who are likely to spend their income), rather than corporations or the government (which mainly invest).

But the authorities did not come up with specific policies to realize these goals. Unable to attack the economy's structural problems, but fearful of letting GDP growth slip, the government instead tolerated a huge buildup of debt by local governments and corporations, mainly to fund investment projects that propped up reported growth while the money was being spent, but whose returns—and hence contribution to future growth—were quite low. Virtually every indicator of investment efficiency shows a severe deterioration in the five years after the global financial crisis. According to a recent report by the OECD, the average return on capital, which rose from 10 percent to a spectacular 17 percent between 2000 and 2006, had fallen to 9 percent by 2014. The "incremental capital output ratio," which measures how many dollars of new investment are required to create a dollar of GDP growth, was fairly steady at between 3 and 4 for virtually all of the reform period up through 2007. It began to climb after the global crisis and by 2013 exceeded 5 for the first time.

Perhaps most tellingly, the contribution to growth from productivity began to shrivel. The OECD found that, between 2000 and 2007, economic growth came about equally from capital accumulation and productivity. This accords with the story we just told that China's growth in the first three decades of the reform era came in roughly equal parts from the state's ability to marshal capital resources and from productivity gains achieved by gradually moving more and more of the economy into private hands. But in the years 2008–2012, the OECD found that about three-quarters of growth on average came from capital accumulation, and a quarter or less from productivity growth. By 2012 productivity contributed only about one-sixth of GDP growth.[3] This deterioration can be explained in part by the corporate-sector dynamics we described back in chapter 5. Returns in state-owned companies fell sharply after 2008, but despite their poor performance, SOEs maintained an unreasonably large share of the economy, thanks to their political connections.

Measures of the productivity of capital are necessarily rather technical. A clearer picture of China's productivity problem emerges from a single indicator: debt, or more precisely the level of debt compared to the size of the economy. This debt-to-GDP ratio is commonly termed "leverage." As Figure 12.4 shows, the total borrowings of households, nonfinancial companies, and the government stayed roughly stable at a bit less than 140 percent of GDP for several years, until the financial crisis. After the crisis the debt ratio surged by about 90 percentage points in five years, reaching 230 percent of GDP in 2015.

What this means is quite straightforward. Most debt is taken on to finance productive investments. So long as the return on those investments is reasonably high, debt and GDP grow at about the same rate, and the ratio between the two remains stable. A rising debt-to-GDP ratio can mean one of two things. It could be that the financial system is becoming more sophisticated, enabling households and companies sustainably to take on more debt. This is what happened in the United States between 1960 and 2000 with the rise

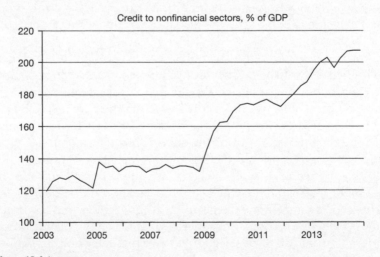

Figure 12.4 Leverage

Source: NBS, Gavekal Dragonomics.

of credit cards, home equity loans, and other forms of consumer finance. Or it could be that people are taking on more and more debt to finance projects with a lower and lower return. While it is true that China's financial system has become more sophisticated in recent years, the evidence is strong that most of the extra debt incurred since 2008 was taken on by local governments and SOEs to finance low-productivity projects.

Obviously, this process cannot continue forever: at some point the return on investment becomes so low that the debts cannot be repaid. At that point one of two things can happen: there can be a financial crisis (because many loans go into default, hurting the banks); or the economy can go into recession (because even if special arrangements enable borrowers to avoid default, too much capital is tied up in projects delivering no economic benefit).

Whatever indicator you choose, the conclusion is clear: China's economy has become much less productive, and much more reliant on debt, since 2008. This state of affairs derives in part from ineffective macroeconomic policy during the latter years of the Hu Jintao administration. But more importantly, it reflects the central fact we stressed at the beginning of this chapter. The days when China could grow at a fast pace in large part by accumulating capital, secure in the knowledge that this capital would almost automatically deliver high returns, are over. Policymakers must focus on fostering an economy where efficient use of resources, rather than addition of new resources, becomes the main source of growth. And the time to make that transition without first hitting a recession or financial crisis is fast running out.

What Is Xi Jinping's Plan to Reform the Economy?

The new leadership that took power between November 2012 and March 2013 under president Xi Jinping quickly showed both a keener awareness of this challenge than the preceding government and a greater political ability to get things done. In his first year in office, Xi unveiled a reform program that included three main elements:

- a draconian anticorruption drive;
- a broad ideological campaign, to tighten the party's control over the media, academia, and civil society; and

- a comprehensive economic reform roadmap encompassing major changes in fiscal, financial, and enterprise systems.

It is important to understand all three parts of this agenda, and not imagine economic reform as a set of technical measures disconnected from the nation's political fabric. It is evident that Xi and his aides have diagnosed China's ills as political-economic in nature and believe that success in economic reforms can only be achieved by first making significant changes in the way the country is governed. In this they are almost certainly correct: virtually all of the inefficiencies and distortions in the Chinese economy can be traced to problems in the political or governance systems that create incentives for officials and businesspeople to act in economically unproductive ways. With that in mind, let us review the three elements of Xi's agenda in turn.

What Is the Anticorruption Campaign All About?

We discussed the antigraft drive in detail in the previous chapter, noting that it serves several purposes. For the present discussion the key points are that the campaign seeks to renegotiate the long-standing implicit bargain with government and party officials, and to remove entrenched figures (such as local government bosses and senior SOE executives) who might be expected to oppose economic reforms.

The basic political-economy bargain, established in the early years of the reform era and not seriously challenged until now, was that one of the primary responsibilities of officials at all levels—but especially in local governments—was to promote economic growth, and that the central authorities would tacitly permit officials to skim off a percentage of that growth for themselves. This arrangement worked reasonably well so long as the main source of growth was installing new physical capital. But it becomes pernicious when the economy needs to shift to efficiency-led growth: corruption is a pure tax on efficiency.

Evidently, one purpose of Xi's unusually long-lasting and unusually far-reaching anticorruption campaign is to set a new, and much lower, tolerance level for corruption. If successful, and if combined with other measures, the long-run effect could be to shift the incentives of officials away from the mindless pursuit of the next big investment project (steel mill, property development, airport, etc.) and toward the promotion of more sustainable economic growth, and to encourage them to view government less as a glorified chamber of commerce and more as an institution for setting rules and providing social services. The risk is that it spreads a climate of fear that discourages officials from making the policy experiments that have been such a key part of China's success.

Why Is the Ideological Campaign Important?

An overarching theme of Xi's first three years at the helm is that power is being concentrated within the party, at the expense of other social institutions; and within the party, power is being concentrated at the very top. For those who hoped that, as China grew richer, it would also grow more open and pluralistic, this is a great disappointment. Xi has curbed the power of the Internet by detaining or intimidating individuals with large followings on microblogs or other forms of social media; instituting new rules that will make it easier to punish people who use instant-messaging programs to spread ideas the government finds inconvenient; and interrupting the virtual private networks (VPNs) that people use to access international websites that are blocked in China.[4] He has also promoted rules to discourage the dissemination of "foreign ideas" in university classrooms and textbooks.

The message is clear: the party is to be the gatekeeper of all information flows in Chinese society. These rules cannot be completely enforced, obviously, in an age where tens of millions of people are tweeting and blogging. But perfect enforcement is not the goal: the objective is to make the potential cost of running afoul of the censors sufficiently high that most people choose to censor themselves.[5] Finally, Xi has tightened the reins on nongovernmental organizations (NGOs) and other civil society organizations, making it clear that the main function of civil society organizations should be to act as subcontractors who deliver social services that for one reason or another the government cannot.

From a human rights standpoint, these developments are depressing. From a political perspective, the intent is obvious: to ensure that the party is the sole source of authority. And within the party, it is clear that Xi would himself be the sole source of authority—more so than was the case with his predecessors in the reform era. Deng Xiaoping shared power uneasily with his rival Chen Yun and delegated many key tasks to his lieutenants: Hu Yaobang, Zhao Ziyang, and finally Jiang Zemin. Jiang, when he became president, lived for a time in Deng's shadow, and then delegated economic management to his strong-willed and powerful premier Zhu Rongji. Hu Jintao was forced to wait two years into his term before Jiang handed over control of the military to him; again let his premier Wen Jiabao handle most economic affairs; and presided over a fractious Politburo standing committee, several of whose members, notably security boss Zhou Yongkang, created virtually independent fiefdoms.

Xi by contrast quickly amassed a large degree of personal power. The quickest index of the range of his power is visible in the "leading small groups" (LSGs) that the party uses to coordinate policy on complex topics. In his second term, Hu Jintao headed four of the ten LSGs. Xi Jinping now heads six of eleven LSGs, including the ones covering the economy, foreign affairs, state security, the Internet, and a new one of his creation on "comprehensive deepening reform."[6] Evidently, Xi's vision of reform is of an uncompromising top-down nature. While centralizing power in this way may ease the process of pushing through technocratic reforms in the short run, it is very questionable whether the kind of tightly controlled authoritarian state that Xi is building is compatible in the long run with the dynamic and innovative economy that he and other Chinese leaders say they want.

What Is Xi's Economic Reform Agenda?

The outlines of Xi's economic reform agenda were laid out in considerable detail in the "Decision" released in November 2013 by the Third Plenum of the Eighteenth Party Congress.[7] By the standards of these rather turgid documents, this Decision was fairly impressive. The key terminological move it made was to announce that, in future, market forces would play a "decisive" role in resource allocation. Prior party documents had assigned market forces a merely "important" role. Specific agenda items included the removal of remaining price controls, a bigger role for private investment, and deregulation of protected markets.

But the Decision also reaffirmed a long-standing principle that the state sector should have a "dominant role" in the economy. This stands in direct contradiction to the idea of a "decisive" role for market forces. If market forces are really decisive, then the dominant role of the state cannot be guaranteed (state firms might lose out to private ones in the market). Conversely, if the dominant role of the state is guaranteed, then market outcomes must sometimes be suppressed and therefore cannot be "decisive."

The vision that emerges from the Decision—and from the progress of reforms since its publication—is of an economy where the state remains firmly in command, not least through its control of "commanding heights" state enterprises, but where market tools are used to improve efficiency. In practice, this means the government will pursue reforms that increase the role of the market in setting prices, but will avoid reforms that permit the market to transfer control of assets from the state to the private sector. Given that one of the biggest problems in the Chinese economy is the very low productivity of state-owned assets, it is questionable whether this reform program will deliver the boost needed to sustain high-speed growth in the long run.

What Specific Reforms Have Occurred since the Third Plenum? And Which Ones Are We Still Waiting For?

The most important reform measure introduced so far is a comprehensive restructuring of the fiscal system, which began in July 2014 and was scheduled to be complete within two years. We looked at the details of this package earlier in chapter 6. The three main elements are a restructuring of local government debts; revisions of the central-local tax-sharing arrangements so that local governments' revenues more closely align with their expenditure responsibilities; and various measures to improve accountability throughout the budgetary system. Although it has received relatively little media coverage (because it is so technical and complex), the fiscal reform is important. If successful, it can play a role in shifting the incentives of government officials into alignment with a more efficiency-oriented economy. It is best seen as the policy complement to the anticorruption campaign: together they constitute the most sustained effort in decades to make Chinese governance more effective.

Another set of technical but significant reforms relates to energy pricing. Opaque, rigid, and/or inappropriate pricing structures for oil products, natural gas, coal, and electricity have long been key distortions in the economy. In particular, the ability to manipulate power prices for favored users has been an element of local governments' ability to skew the structure of production in favor of electricity-hungry heavy industry, and to keep inefficient factories in operation. In addition to improvements in the oil and gas pricing systems, taxes on coal were reformed to discourage excess production, and work was begun on a long-overdue revamp of electricity pricing to make it more responsive to market conditions.

In the financial sector, there has been a series of incremental steps. The key moves have been the abolition of controls on deposit interest rates; the introduction of a full-fledged deposit insurance scheme; the linkage of the Shanghai and Hong Kong stock markets, providing a significantly wider window for outward flows of private capital; and a significant adjustment in exchange rate policy to make the renminbi a more free-floating currency.

In the crucial area of enterprise reform, however, progress has been slow. The one significant positive step was the abolition in early 2014 of registered-capital and other onerous administrative requirements for new businesses. Before that move, according to the World Bank, China had one of the world's most restrictive regimes for business start-ups. In the year after these regulations were removed, new company formation shot up by 23 percent, even though the economy was slowing.[8]

But in reality China has always done a fairly good job of allowing new, small businesses to spring up. The bigger problem is that it has not done so well in forcing the big, inefficient state enterprises to give up their positions. As we outlined in chapter 5, the strategy seems to be to force provincial governments to open up local-level SOEs for new shareholders. So far, virtually every provincial government has published a plan for these so-called mixed ownership schemes. In the few transactions that have occurred, a trend has emerged for provincial governments to transfer shares not to private-sector shareholders but to state-owned firms. The logic seems to be that the efficiency of SOEs can be improved by wresting them away from local governments (which may view these firms mainly as patronage networks) and giving control to commercially oriented state firms that are more interested in profit. This may be true, but it is almost certainly the case that the productivity gains from this kind of ownership reshuffle will be far less than those possible under outright privatization.

Finally, in the areas of land tenure, hukou, and the urbanization system in general, little of substance has occurred. Despite a relaxation in 2014, hukou rules still unreasonably restrict migration into the largest, most vibrant cities, and no solution has yet been found to the problem of incorporating migrant worker families into the social safety net. A plan for "new style urbanization" (focusing less on construction and more on social services) was released, but omitted crucial details on how these services would be paid for and how rules for acquisition of agricultural land would be changed to make them fairer to farmers.

The overall assessment is that there has been spotty progress in several areas, but much more needs to be done. More structural economic reform was achieved in the two years after the Third Plenum than in the entire five years of Hu Jintao's second term. Many of the individual reform steps had been under discussion for years, but it was only after the publication of the Third Plenum Decision that they began to be realized. And although the reforms so far consist of many small steps, rather than a highly visible "big bang," it should be borne in mind that most of the changes laid out in the Third Plenum decision carried a target completion date of 2020, so it is unreasonable to expect that they would all bear fruit instantly. But the overall design of the reform program, and the state-enterprise reforms in particular, suggest that Xi Jinping—unlike his predecessors Deng Xiaoping and Jiang Zemin—is unwilling to contemplate the bold retreats from state control that have been essential to China's impressive economic growth throughout the reform era.

Is China's Growth Model Changing?

At the end of the day, what matters is results. There is already evidence that China's growth model is beginning to shift. The question is whether these changes are broad enough, or happening fast enough, to avert a financial crisis or severe economic slowdown.

On the positive side, the economy has begun the transition away from its traditional industry/investment focus and toward a new services/consumption focus. As noted above, reliance on exports has declined steadily since 2008 and is now back at 1990s levels. In 2013, the value of services surpassed the combined value of industry and construction for the first time, and this shift accelerated in 2014, when services accounted for 48 percent of the economy and industry and construction for just 42 percent. Household consumption's share of the economy bottomed at 35 percent in 2010 and has crept up to just over 36 percent since then. Housing construction seems to have peaked in 2012, and steel demand (which follows housing construction very closely) began to decline in 2014. Coal use has also begun to fall, bringing down carbon dioxide emissions along with it.

These are all significant changes, some of which have been driven by policy and some by the market. And so far, they have occurred in the context of continued strong economic growth: 6.9 percent in 2015, with a very solid rate of job creation. So can we conclude that China has figured out how to have it all—a steady transition to a new and more sustainable growth model, without a wrenching recession or financial crisis?

Not yet. For one thing, the high growth rates disguise the fact that parts of China's economy are already in recession. By the middle of 2015, several provinces in northeast and central China, which have traditionally relied mainly on resource extraction and heavy industry, were reporting negative GDP growth rates. Even if it is successfully carried off, the economic transition is likely to be extremely painful for many individuals and industries, in much the same way that the SOE reforms of the late 1990s were. In 2016–2017, China will be very lucky to sustain GDP growth above the 6 percent mark.

Even more worrying is that there is as yet no evidence of an improvement in the productivity of capital. Leverage continues to rise, and indeed it is plausible to argue that the only reason why the Chinese economy has continued to grow so smartly in the past few years is that the government has let companies, households, and local governments pile on more and more debt. As the United

States discovered in 2008, growth fueled mainly by debt accumulation cannot be sustained for very long. And there has been no obvious progress in addressing the root cause of low capital productivity: the excessive size and decreasing efficiency of the SOE sector. Until we see clear signs that SOEs are being restructured and privatized, and that the sectors they dominate are being opened up to much more vigorous competition from private firms, it is likely that capital productivity will continue to languish, growth will continue to slow, leverage will continue to rise, and questions will persist about whether China can make a smooth transition to its new growth model.

Can Economic Reforms Succeed without Political Reforms?

For as long as China has tried to combine a dynamic and ever more market-driven economy with an authoritarian political system, observers from the West, and numerous domestic critics, have argued that this combination was unsustainable. Eventually, the argument goes, China would have to change its political system to become more open and representative, or the economy would stop growing.[9]

This prediction is based on plausible precedents. In nineteenth-century Europe, industrialization and the rise of an urban middle class led to the destruction of old aristocratic orders and the gradual emergence of representative government. In Asia after World War II, both South Korea and Taiwan experienced rapid growth under authoritarian regimes, and then made the transition to democracy in the late 1980s and early 1990s as their growing middle classes demanded more voice in government. And the most successful post-Communist countries in Eastern Europe, such as Poland, Hungary, and the Czech Republic, embraced capitalism and liberal democracy together. Of the fifty-six economies whose per capita GDP exceeded the global average in 2013, all but four are at least nominally democracies, in the sense that they hold regular contested elections for the country's top leader in which all adult citizens can vote. The exceptions—Qatar, Equatorial Guinea, Saudi Arabia, and Kazakhstan—are all countries with small populations whose economies depend mainly on exports of oil and gas, a natural formula for authoritarian oligarchy. Among major economies, the only one

other than China that is not really democratic in any meaningful
sense is Russia. It seems likely that the Communist Party's twin
desires to turn China into a great economic power and to retain its
own political monopoly are incompatible, and sooner or later one of
those goals must give way.

So far, though, this prediction has proved wrong. Xi Jinping's
top-down reform program aims at a sort of "Leninist capitalism" in
which the economy will be driven more by market efficiency, while
the party's power will be strengthened, not weakened. There are
several reasons to think this strategy could be effective, at least for
the next few years.

First, the acquiescence of the governed appears to remain relatively high. China is a large country and many people have many
grievances, about inequality, corruption, pollution, expropriation of
land, and so on. But such discontent is natural in any fast-changing
society. As we saw in chapter 11, surveys suggest that the large
majority of Chinese remain satisfied with the country's direction,
and their discontent is largely directed at the abuses of local officials, not at the system as a whole.

Second, the party does not simply crush dissent; it also makes
a real effort to address the underlying material causes of discontent. Many elements of Xi's reform program, if successfully implemented, may address some of the most serious causes of social
unrest. The anticorruption campaign could constrain the rapacity
of local officials. The drive for industrial efficiency, and changes in
the tax system, may drive many polluting factories out of business,
and make it more cost-effective for the remaining plants to install
pollution-abatement equipment. Deregulation of state-dominated
sectors could open up more opportunities for private entrepreneurs. If it succeeds, Xi's economic reform program will enhance
the party's legitimacy, by showing that it is capable of delivering
difficult changes that are beneficial not just to a narrow elite but to a
broad majority of people. (Admittedly, there are a lot of "ifs" in this
prognosis.)

Third, the natural class advocate of a more open political system
is not obviously interested in change. The urban middle class is
generally seen as the group that pushes hardest for political openness. This group has been growing fast in China, but it is still a
minority: at the very outside it might comprise 300 million people,

or less than a quarter of the population. On the whole, members of this group have benefited disproportionately from economic reforms—notably through the privatization of state-owned housing, which gave them a valuable tax-free asset; and through the quotas for university admission, which are heavily skewed in favor of urbanites. In a more representative system, the interests of this group would almost certainly lose out to the interests of poor rural people, who are twice as numerous as the urban middle class. So long as the party continues to deliver the goods, in the form of a rising standard of living (not just financial but environmental), expanding opportunities, and reasonably secure property rights, the urban middle class is unlikely to agitate for political change.

Finally, we ought to question the premise of this whole discussion, namely that China's economy has changed dramatically while its political system has been static. This is not really true. The governance system of 2014 bears little resemblance to that of 1979. Back then, China was literally a land without laws—Mao had dispensed with laws and courts, preferring to rule by decree—and the majority of officials had no qualifications other than obedience to the ruler. The only reliable means by which a new ruler could come to power was for the old one to die. In the intervening thirty-five years, China has established a comprehensive body of law and regulation that enables the country to be governed, for the most part, in a rational and predictable way (though not always fairly). Officials must demonstrate some kind of competence to be promoted, and the technocratic skills of the upper echelons of the bureaucracy are formidable. Starting in 1993, the party has pulled off three successive peaceful transfers of power from one living leader to another. These achievements represent a significant improvement in the systems of governance, even if they fall short of the Western ideal of representative democracy or the Chinese ideal of benevolent government.

So there is a fair chance that Xi's "Leninist capitalism" strategy will succeed in sustaining China's unique combination of market economy and authoritarian political system, at least until the end of Xi's term of office in 2022. But this strategy is far from cost-free. The obvious victims of this approach are innovation and creativity. Although its leaders often mouth the idea that China must become a more innovative society, it is impossible to imagine creativity blossoming so long as the state places draconian restrictions on the right of people to express their views, share information, organize independently to solve social problems, challenge authority, and freely collaborate with like-minded people from other countries. In the short run, this lack of innovation need not stifle the economy, since there is plenty of growth yet to be squeezed out from things like industrial efficiency and service-sector deregulation. Ultimately, though, a more open and less paranoid political system will be required for Chinese society to remain vibrant as it grows older and richer.

13

CONCLUSION

CHINA AND THE WORLD

What Is the Nature of the Present Global Political-Economic Order?

Before we consider China's position in the world, it is useful to define what we mean by "the world," namely its overall political and economic arrangements. These arrangements, since 1945, have been built around the position of the United States as the dominant military power, the global technological leader, and the biggest national economy. The unique status of the United States at the end of the devastation of World War II—when, by some estimates, it accounted for about half of the entire world economy—enabled it to take the leading role in establishing a set of global institutions including the United Nations, the World Bank, the International Monetary Fund, the Organization for Economic Cooperation and Development (OECD), and the General Agreement on Tariffs and Trade (GATT, later the World Trade Organization or WTO), which defined the "rules of the game" for international politics, trade, and investment. In addition, less formal institutions such as the G-7 group of large economies enable US leaders to share ideas and coordinate actions with the leaders of other important, friendly countries.

The United States undergirds this multilateral civil architecture with a military alliance structure encompassing Canada; most Western European nations; key Asian nations, including Japan, South Korea, and Australia; a global naval presence that polices the seas, much as the British navy did in the two centuries before World War II; and a network of over seven hundred military installations in thirty-eight countries.[1]

The final component of this system is financial: the international economic and trade system is built around the US dollar. The dollar was the anchor of the so-called Bretton Woods system of fixed exchange rates that lasted from the end of World War II until 1971, when President Richard Nixon took the dollar off the gold standard and the present system of freely floating exchange rates came into existence. Since then, the dollar has continued as the main global currency. On average, around 60 percent of central bank currency reserves are held in dollars, around two-thirds of global trade is conducted in dollars, and the prices of virtually all globally traded commodities (such as oil, iron ore, copper, wheat, and soybeans) are quoted in dollars. The benefit to the United States is that, as the issuer of the global currency, it uniquely has an unconstrained ability to use its own money to buy all its imports and borrow from foreigners. (Other countries must at least occasionally use a foreign currency—usually dollars—to settle their import bills or borrow.) Therefore the United States never has to worry, as other nations do, that its debts will suddenly become unmanageable due to a currency depreciation. Because it can safely borrow more than other countries, the United States can finance expensive luxuries—such as a large military—to a degree that other large countries are hard-pressed to match.[2]

This system—sometimes described as the "established world order" by its supporters, and as "US hegemony" by its critics—has proved to be powerful and resilient. It outlasted its only significant rival so far, the international Communist bloc led by the Soviet Union, which collapsed in 1991. It also survived the breakup of the postwar fixed exchange rate system and efforts by the major oil-producing nations via the Organization of Petroleum Exporting Countries (OPEC) to push up the price of oil in the 1970s. And this system has endured despite a steady diminution in the relative economic position of the United States, as the rise of powerful economies including Japan and Germany in the 1970s, and China, India, and Brazil more recently, reduced its share of global economic output to 22 percent.

What Will Happen When (and If) China Becomes the World's Biggest Economy?

The one challenge that the present global system has not yet had to face is the United States' loss of its position as the world's biggest single economy, a status it has held since the 1870s, when it surpassed the United Kingdom. At some point in the next two decades it is likely—though by no means certain—that China will overtake the United States and become the world's biggest economy.[3] It is not easy to say when this will occur, and the shifts of the past few years counsel caution in making forecasts of this kind. In the aftermath of the 2008 global crisis, when China was still growing at double-digit rates and the United States was mired in low growth and pessimism, straight-line extrapolations suggested China could become number one before the end of this decade. Today, with the United States in a solid recovery and China facing a slowdown, extrapolations tell a different story. In 2014 the US economy produced a bit over $17 trillion in goods and services, while China produced $10 trillion. If both countries maintain their present trend of nominal GDP growth rates (4 percent for the United States and 8 percent for China), China will finally become the world's biggest economy in 2029.[4]

Obviously, a lot could happen in the next decade and a half to speed up or slow down China's march to the top. But let's just suppose for a moment that a decade from now China overtakes the United States to become the world's biggest economy. What will that mean?

The short answer is: not very much. China's population is more than four times that of the United States, so it is hardly odd that China should eventually have a bigger output. Economic historians estimate that for about a thousand years, ending in the early 1800s, China was the world's biggest economy. This reflected the fact that, before the Industrial Revolution, all countries were agrarian, and the average standard of living was not that different from one country to another. So the country with the biggest population (China) naturally had the biggest economy. The Industrial Revolution changed that, because it created new and much more powerful forms of capital that enabled incomes to grow far faster than they did in agrarian economies. This made it possible for an industrialized country with a small population (like the United Kingdom) to have a bigger economy than a nonindustrialized economy with a large population (like China or India). That state of affairs could well be temporary.

If we assume that eventually industrial technology will spread across the world in the same way that agricultural technology did around ten thousand years ago, we can imagine that over the next century or two all countries may industrialize, and living standards around the globe will be much more equal than they are today. If that happens, the biggest economy will be the one with the most people, as in the days when the whole world was agrarian. But the fact that a country has the biggest economy will tell us nothing about that country, other than that it has a large population.

Moreover, the evidence so far is that this hypothetical convergence of incomes is unlikely to be anywhere near complete on any timescale (say thirty to forty years) for which it is possible to have a meaningful discussion. The most successful non-European economies since World War II—Japan, South Korea, and Taiwan—grew much more rapidly than the advanced economies until their per capita incomes reached 60 to 90 percent of the US level in the 1990s. Then their rapid "convergence growth" stopped, and they are no closer to matching US incomes than they were fifteen years ago. Other countries, which got stuck in the "middle income trap," have seen their average incomes stagnate at 20 to 40 percent of the US level. When China surpasses the United States as the world's biggest economy, it will by definition have a per capita income only one-fourth as high (because its population is four times greater). So it will be a larger economy than that of the United States, but also a poorer one. Whether it can subsequently sustain rapid convergence growth until per capita income crosses around 50 percent of US GDP is questionable. For one thing, current demographic projections suggest that China's population will start shrinking in the early 2030s. And as we showed in chapter 9, by 2050 its society will be as old as Japan's today. The United States is projected to have a younger population that is still growing.[5]

The bottom line of all these considerations is clear. It is probable that at some point China will become the world's biggest economy, thanks to the successful deployment of established industrial technology over a very large population. The more interesting and difficult question is how this economic bulk will translate into global influence. History suggests that the key variables here are not sheer economic size but technological capacity and political positioning. In 1800 China was still the world's biggest economy. But its global influence was far less than that of the European nations led by Great Britain, because it had fallen far behind Europe in the pace of technological change. It was the superiority of European technology, rather than the size of European economies in GDP terms, that proved the decisive factor in the nineteenth century.

Conversely, the United States became the world's biggest economy in the mid-1870s and was already a leader in the invention of new technologies. But it was not until seven decades later, after World War II, that it emerged decisively as the most important power. In the interim, Britain's vast colonial empire and control of trade networks, the dominant status of the pound sterling, London's position as the hub of global finance, and a strongly isolationist tilt to American policy meant that the United Kingdom still exerted greater influence.

So to address the question of China's future global impact, we need to think less about the size of its economy and more about its technological capacities and its leaders' desire and ability to modify or even supplant the present geopolitical order.

How Close Is China to Becoming a Global Technological Leader?

China has undeniably made rapid technological *progress* over the last three decades. But there is little concrete evidence to suggest it is becoming a technological *leader*.

One can justify this conclusion in several ways. One is simply to look at the structure of exports. A country with a strong position in industrial technology will tend to have a lot of manufactured exports, because its technological edge means it can make things that other countries can't. This is obviously true of the countries that have long been recognized as technological leaders—the United States, Germany, and Japan. All of them export large volumes and a broad range of manufactured goods. So does China—in fact, China now exports more manufactures, by value, than any other country in the world. Close to 30 percent of its exports are categorized by the Chinese government as "high technology" goods. This fact has led some commentators to talk about China's looming technological dominance.[6]

A closer look at the data exposes this as a myth. As we showed in chapter 3, nearly half of China's exports, and around 70 percent of its "high-tech" exports, are produced by foreign firms. This is not the case—not even close—in the United States, Germany, and Japan, where the vast majority of exports are produced by domestic firms. China's role in global production chains remains principally as the final assembly point for products put together out of components made elsewhere or made by other foreign firms in China. China gets to book the full export value of the finished product, but this tells us nothing about China's technological contribution. In many cases, this is small.

Take, for instance, the world's most popular consumer-technology item, the iPhone. Virtually all the world's iPhones are assembled in China, and their wholesale value shows up as part of China's trade surplus. None of the technology embedded in an iPhone comes from China. The operating software and the overall design emerged from Apple's labs in California. The integrated circuit chip that is the crucial part of the hardware was designed and fabricated by Samsung in South Korea. The touch screens depend on materials science research conducted in the United States, Europe, and Japan and are produced by Toshiba. Many of the other electronic components, such as the wireless transceiver and camera, are produced by Infineon, a Germany company. Even the assembly process (which counts as a form of "soft" technology) is managed by Foxconn, a Taiwanese company.[7]

One may further observe that few Chinese companies are recognized global leaders in their fields; those that are typically have large sales volumes by virtue of the enormous China market, but little claim to leadership in quality, process, or technology. The United States has many globally important firms of course; one can easily tick off several names for most major countries (Germany, France, Britain, Japan), and even quite small countries have a few recognizable names. South Korea, for instance, has Samsung, Hyundai, and LG. Canada and Brazil each has a globally successful maker of passenger aircraft; but China, despite its enormous aviation market, has none. If China is a global technological leader, where are the firms that embody this leadership?

It might be that China excels in industrial products whose makers may not be household names. Yet here too, the list of Chinese firms that have achieved sustained, large-scale international success based on technological leadership is tiny. The most frequently cited success story is Huawei, the world's second-biggest maker of telephone network switches, two-thirds of whose sales occur outside

China. Huawei is frequently cited because other examples are hard to come by. Chinese civil engineering firms are emerging as important builders of infrastructure throughout the world, and it is likely that they will dominate this market, in terms of total construction volumes, in the coming decades. Yet for the most part, they conform to the "80 percent of the quality for 60 percent of the price" business model we described in chapter 3.

One could also argue that it is still early days yet for China. Most of its private companies are less than twenty years old, and it is only a matter of time before they emulate the international success of their Japanese and Korean peers. A comparison with Japan gives cause for doubt. In the early 1970s Japan's per capita GDP, adjusted for purchasing power, was about the same as China's is today. By then Japan already had a large number of firms with important positions in international markets for technology-intensive goods: Canon and Nikon in cameras, Seiko in watches, Toyota and Honda in cars, Sony and Panasonic in consumer electronics, and NEC in semiconductors. Not only does China lack a single such company, it has few plausible candidates for firms that might achieve this sort of global prominence.

It is sometimes suggested that China is quickly moving to a leadership position in basic research fields, where the results do not necessarily show up in economic statistics. China is spending a great deal more money on basic scientific research than most countries. But a willingness to spend money does not equal results. A crude but handy test of a country's prowess in basic scientific research is a count of Nobel Prizes in physics, chemistry, and medicine. Between 1990 and 2015, two-thirds of these prizes went to researchers in North American institutions, another quarter to Europe, and 5 percent to Japan. China got its first prize in 2015, for work done in the 1960s and 1970s on malaria cures.

None of this is to deny that China has made substantial technological progress in many industries over the past two decades, nor that the pace of innovation is picking up. Numerous studies show that China's manufactured goods and its export mix have steadily become more technologically advanced.[8] Chinese companies have proven expert at developing products and services, often based on models invented elsewhere, that do better in the Chinese market than foreign brands; this is a legitimate and important type of innovation. Exemplars of this kind of success are China's "big three" Internet companies: Alibaba (e-commerce), Tencent (gaming and social networks), and Baidu (search). All three are considered by industry insiders to be technologically proficient and very innovative. Compared to other large developing countries, such as India or Brazil, China's technical progress and record of commercial innovation are indeed impressive.

The question we posed, though, is not how far China has progressed, but how close it is to becoming a technological *leader*—that is, a country whose innovations are widely adopted or emulated elsewhere. There is little evidence of such leadership so far. In the commercial realm, the big three Internet firms may have the strongest prospects for leadership. They are dominant at home but have no meaningful presence anywhere else, making it hard to judge how much of their success derives from superior technology and how much from state controls on the Internet and other forms of protection, which have made it difficult or impossible for their global competitors to operate in China.

As we argued at the end of chapter 3, China's innovative capacity, and hence its potential for global technology leadership, is compromised by the state's obsession with technological autonomy and with information control. The quest for autonomy means that the state will always support a second-best solution, so long as it is homegrown, over a superior foreign one. This creates an environment in which firms find it more profitable to be just good enough for the domestic market than to make the extra effort to be globally competitive. Information control stifles the knowledge sharing and collaboration across disciplinary and national boundaries that is essential for large-scale innovation. Continued technological progress is perfectly possible under such conditions; technological leadership is not.

How Does China's Economic Strength Translate into Political Influence?

Even without technological leadership, it is quite conceivable that China could leverage its burgeoning economic muscle into greater influence of various kinds, or greater ability to act unilaterally in ways that might harm other countries. It is worth breaking this down into three distinct questions, which we will treat separately below:

- Does China succeed economically in world markets by "cheating," or breaking the rules of global competition?
- What kind of political leverage does China gain from its economic strength?
- To what extent is China trying to replace existing global institutions with new ones of its own creation?

Is China's Economic Success the Result of "Cheating" on Global Trade and Investment Rules?

We have already dealt with the "cheating" question in chapter 3. For the most part, China's trade and investment activities conform to the established pattern of sharp business practice by developing countries struggling to muscle their way up to rich-country status. The claim that China's success results from an unusual degree of "cheating" or undermining global economic rules does not stand up to serious scrutiny.

China has opened up its domestic market to foreign investment and international competition far more than any of its East Asian models (Japan, South Korea, and Taiwan) or any of its large developing-country peers (Brazil, India, and Russia). It has joined virtually every major international economic agreement or convention, and plays by the rules of those agreements at least as consistently as do other major economic powers, including the United States. (It has in fact joined some agreements that the United States has refused to, notably the United Nations Convention on the Law of the Sea, or UNCLOS.) It is actively negotiating bilateral investment treaties (BITs) with the United States and the European Union, indicating a willingness to submit further to internationally determined rules in order to gain more secure access to developed-country markets.

The charge that China gains unfair advantage in international markets by subsidies, cheap financing, and other benefits showered on state-owned enterprises is undermined by the evidence we presented in chapter 5, showing that the financial performance of SOEs is far worse than that of Chinese private companies and deteriorating. To the extent that these subsidies and benefits exist, they ultimately weaken rather than strengthen the global competitiveness of China's firms.[9]

What Kind of Political Leverage Does China Gain from Its Economic Strength?

On the second question, China's economic strength is undoubtedly translating into increased political strength. The only reason this obvious development causes concern in the United States and Europe is that, unlike the two previous economic powers to arise since World War II (Germany and Japan), China is not part of the US alliance structure and is an independent geopolitical actor with its own military capability. So far, however, China's gain in political influence has been less than one might reasonably expect given its economic record.

One reason for this is that, until recently, China pursued a deliberately restrained foreign policy, under a cautious slogan coined by Deng Xiaoping in the early 1990s: *taoguang yanghui*, meaning roughly "lie low and bide your time."[10] In practice this meant focusing diplomatic efforts on fostering stable and reasonably cordial ties with as many countries as possible, and avoiding both provocations and leadership roles in the international arena. A key objective in the early days of the reform era was to ensure that most countries broke diplomatic relations with Taiwan and recognized the People's Republic. This strategy was successful. From a position of almost complete diplomatic isolation in the late 1970s, China succeeded in establishing productive relations with virtually every country in the world by 2000, and in reducing the number of nations recognizing Taiwan to an insignificant handful.

In the early 2000s, China's foreign policy became a bit more proactive. The government started encouraging its companies to "go out" (*zou chuqu*) and invest globally, in part to secure access to natural resources like oil, iron ore, and copper that it needed for its capital-intensive growth at home. After a slow start, Chinese outward direct investment started to pick up sharply from 2007, and now averages about US$80 billion a year. This puts China second behind the United States in terms of annual flows; but of course since the United States has been investing abroad for much longer, its total stock of outward investments is much larger: about $3.5 trillion compared to China's approximately $600 billion.[11]

Generally speaking, China takes the position that its involvement in other countries is purely economic, and it maintains a principle of noninterference in the internal political affairs of other nations. The more money China has tied up in other countries, the more concerned it will become that the political regime of those countries does not change in a way that threatens China's investments. One must assume that China's foreign relations will become more activist with time. But "more activist" does not necessarily mean "as activist as the United States." There is as yet no hard evidence that China has either the desire or the ability to dictate or preach to other countries how they should organize their political or economic systems—a prerogative that the United States frequently asserts.

Chinese foreign policy took a decidedly activist turn in 2013 under new president Xi Jinping. The new approach included a more aggressive assertion of China's territorial claims in the South China Sea (which are disputed by Vietnam, the Philippines, and other neighbors), the establishment of an air defense identification zone in the East China Sea, and a policy of what one might call "infrastructure diplomacy" in Southeast and Central Asia (discussed in more detail below). There can be little doubt that China has abandoned the "lie low" approach and will progressively take a stronger role in both regional and global affairs.

This shift has occasioned much anxiety and criticism, but should be kept in perspective. First, American and European officials have been asking for years that China take a more active role in global affairs.[12] Many of Xi's initiatives can be interpreted as a response to this call. At a meeting in Beijing with President Obama in November 2014, Xi pledged to work together with the United States to achieve a global accord to combat climate change—a significant shift from five years earlier, when a crucial climate policy meeting in Copenhagen failed to reach agreement, largely because of antagonism between the United States and China. And China's bid to spearhead infrastructure investment in neighboring countries of Asia, while incorporating a healthy dose of self-interest, is also in part a legitimate effort to finance international "public goods" that will provide widespread material benefit.

Second, China's efforts to expand its influence have in the main been limited to its immediate neighborhood in Asia, and have met with modest success and considerable resistance. Japan and South Korea are firm members of the US military alliance system, as is Taiwan de facto if not de jure. China's influence in the weakest countries of Southeast Asia (Cambodia and Laos) is growing, but its sway elsewhere is contested. Vietnam harbors centuries-old resentment against its large northern neighbor and has actively courted closer ties with and greater investment flows from Japan. Myanmar had very tight relations with Beijing under its former military regime, but fear of becoming a Chinese vassal state was one factor contributing to a dramatic political and economic liberalization that led to dissolution of the military junta in 2011 and strengthened ties with the West. Central Asian nations such as Kazakhstan and Turkmenistan welcome Chinese investment to unlock their mineral wealth and improve transport infrastructure, but they also strive to maintain their independence by playing off China against their traditional patron, Russia.

Third, the factual record shows that during the reform era China has been no more inclined to use force outside its own borders than has India, and significantly less so than China itself during the Maoist era.[13] Its record of intervention pales in comparison to that of the United States over the past 125 years. Even if one excludes the many rearrangements of other countries' governments that the United States orchestrated during the Cold War in the name of containing Soviet influence, American military interventions have long been a routine feature of global affairs. Countries affected include the Philippines, Cuba, Panama, and Nicaragua before World War II, and Afghanistan, Iraq, the former Yugoslavia, and Libya since the end of the Cold War.

In sum, there can be little doubt that China's leaders now seek to translate their country's economic strength into greater influence in Asia and the world. This is natural and, to the extent that China channels its energies into economic development programs, broadly beneficial. China will certainly gain influence relative to established regional powers (Russia in Central Asia, Japan in Southeast Asia), but it is very far from becoming a regional hegemon. Beyond its immediate periphery, China's political influence is modest.[14]

Is China Trying to Replace Existing Global Institutions with New Ones of Its Own Creation?

China has been a willing participant in existing global institutions, but it has become increasingly frustrated by its limited role in the governance of those institutions. Two recent instances have been especially irksome. One is its failure to obtain greater voting rights in the International Monetary Fund (IMF). China's IMF voting rights are much smaller than its share of global GDP. Changes in IMF voting shares require ratification by member states, and the US Congress persistently declined to pass legislation that would enable an increase in the Chinese vote. (It finally approved this increase, after a five-year delay, in December 2015.) A second is the US effort to build a high-level trade and investment agreement—the Trans-Pacific Partnership (TPP)—among most of the major nations in Asia, but not including China. China's view on the TPP is conflicted. On the one hand, it is reluctant to join because this would require major concessions in liberalizing the service sector and government procurement rules. On the other, it is worried about being left out of a major trade agreement that could benefit all of its neighbors.

These issues are symptoms of a deeper anxiety in China about being a supporting player in a global order whose rules are essentially set in Washington, DC. The overarching project during the reform era has been to restore China to its historical position as a major political and economic power, and this ultimate aim is incompatible with simply accepting as an unchangeable fact a world system that is usually described in Beijing as "American hegemony."

China has therefore dabbled in creating multilateral institutions of its own, where American influence is limited or absent. These include the Shanghai Cooperation Organization (SCO), a political and security grouping founded in 2001 comprising China, Russia, and several Central Asian republics; a free-trade agreement with the Association of Southeast Asian Nations (ASEAN) members; and a New Development Bank (originally called the BRICS Bank), with Brazil, Russia, India, and South Africa as the other founding members. The impact of these early efforts was limited.

In 2014, however, Xi Jinping's government formalized a number of regional infrastructure initiatives that had been brewing for some time, under the rubric of "One Belt, One Road." The "Belt" refers to a "New Silk Road" set of transport projects that aim to link western China with Central Asia and, ultimately, Europe. The "Road" refers to a "Maritime Silk Road" program consisting of rail, road, and port projects connecting southwest China with the Indian Ocean. To help finance these projects Xi authorized the creation of a Silk Road Fund from China's own budget and, more ambitiously, a multilateral Asian Infrastructure Investment Bank (AIIB). Combined with the New Development Bank, these new Chinese-led financial institutions have authorized capital of US$240 billion. But this headline number is misleadingly high. Most of this notional capital will never be paid in; the true capital base of these three funds may be US$40–50 billion by the early 2020s, about the same as the World Bank.[15] China invited dozens of nations, including most significant economies in Asia and Europe, to join the AIIB as founding members. The US government urged many of its allies, notably Australia and South Korea, not to participate, but in the end around sixty countries, including many US allies in Europe and Asia, joined.

Several motivations lie behind this "infrastructure diplomacy." At one level, China is responding to the need for improved transport infrastructure in developing Asia. The ADB, a multilateral institution essentially controlled by Japan and the United States, has estimated that Southeast Asia alone requires $8 trillion in infrastructure investment over the next decade. Until China stepped up, existing national and multilateral resources were nowhere near enough to meet this need.[16] National self-interest also clearly plays a role, in several respects. Much of the proposed infrastructure will help China secure supplies of energy and other natural resources, via routes that cannot easily be interdicted by the US military. It will also create new corridors of economic activity, and linkages to the rich markets of Europe, that could enhance economic development in China's landlocked central and western regions. The construction projects themselves will provide much-needed business for Chinese engineering firms and materials suppliers, which now face a stagnant market at home. Finally, there can be little doubt that China would like to have a multilateral financing institution where it, and not the United States or its allies, calls the shots.

But before we get too excited about China setting up a parallel architecture to existing global institutions, let us step back for a moment. The AIIB is an interesting experiment, but until it actually starts lending on a large scale its impact is unknown. It could well wind up being simply a second ADB, which has long played a useful role in financing Asian infrastructure but is essentially irrelevant to regional or global economic governance. The importance of organizations such as the World Bank, IMF, and OECD stems less from the money they disburse than from the immense depth of their technical and intellectual resources, accumulated over many years of practice and research. Thus far, there is little evidence that China possesses the intellectual resources to compel a substantial readjustment of the basic "rules of the game" of international trade and investment that have developed over the last two centuries as the consequence of European expansionism, and that have been cemented under the American-led system in the seven decades since the end of World War II.[17]

A final observation is that China's embrace of multilateralism in its infrastructure diplomacy is a clear advance over its previous approach, which relied heavily on lending by a single, rather opaque domestic institution, the China Development Bank (CDB). The CDB rapidly expanded its international lending portfolio in 2007–2012, but under the Xi Jinping government these activities have been curtailed and the CDB has been ordered to refocus its energies on its traditional role of domestic policy lending.[18] Another policy lender, the China Export-Import Bank, is an important and growing source of finance for China's international development objectives. But the increased reliance on multilateral finance should be welcomed.

Can China's Growth Model be Replicated in Other Countries?

One dimension in which it is reasonable to ask whether China can exercise intellectual leadership is in development strategy. China has an enviable record of economic success over the past three decades. Is it possible that its growth model can be replicated in the dozens of poor countries that are still waiting their turn to join the industrial age and the club of upper-income nations?

One of China's leading economists believes that it can. Justin Yifu Lin, who established China's top economic think tank in the 1990s and served from 2008 to 2011 as chief economist of the World Bank, argues that African countries are in a good position to emulate China's experience of economic development, using state-led infrastructure investment to attract FDI from companies (including Chinese ones) that no longer find China attractive as a site for low-cost manufacturing.[19] Two African countries, Rwanda and Ethiopia, have adopted a more or less explicit policy of imitating the Chinese growth model. Over the past decade Ethiopia has been the fastest-growing economy in Africa, with an average GDP growth rate of 11 percent since 2004. Rwanda is not far behind, at 8 percent.

There are, however, grounds for skepticism about the transferability of the Chinese growth experience. Throughout this book we have shown that China's record is in part the product of special conditions: the proximity of Hong Kong as a link to the global market and modern financial and legal institutions; China's location right next to the established industrial and trade hubs of Japan, South Korea, and Taiwan, which made it easy to relocate production to China to save costs; the unusual institutional glue of the Chinese Communist Party; and the coincidence of China's reform era with a boom in global trade that appears to have ended in 2008.

Furthermore, Lin's "Leading Dragons" model is an updated version of the "Flying Geese" model popularized in the 1960s by Japanese economists, who argued that Southeast Asian countries were well placed to follow Japan (the leading goose in this metaphor), occupying industrial niches being driven out of Japan by rising costs, and taking advantage of direct investment by Japanese firms. In retrospect, the "Flying Geese" model did not fare so well. Southeast Asian countries did indeed grow quite rapidly from the end of the Vietnam War into the mid-1990s, but they never fully industrialized. One reason was that local political structures, combined with a reliance on foreign investment and borrowing, created incentives for local entrepreneurs to invest in monopolistic commodity and services businesses, leaving the hard work of competitive manufacturing to foreigners. Following the 1997 Asian financial crisis, inflows from abroad dried up, and Southeast Asia lost its growth momentum. This indicates that copying other countries' growth models is a lot harder than it might seem at first. It also suggests a hazard to the FDI-driven approach, which we have already discussed in chapter 3: putting too much of one's industrial structure in the hands of foreign firms may retard the emergence of domestic companies needed to drive the long-run innovation processes that will push a country into upper-income status.[20]

Lin agrees that there is no simple recipe for the "Chinese model" that other countries can simply copy. He argues the most important lesson other developing countries can glean from China's experience is the value of pragmatism. Instead of hewing to a particular development theory, or putting too much weight on the opinions of experts from the outside, countries should experiment and stick with policies that work, regardless of whether they conform to theory or the desires of rich countries.[21] This is a sensible prescription.

Lin is also correct to observe that to the extent poor countries seek models, they are better off looking at other recent development success stories than at rich countries. This simple point was often forgotten by neoclassical economists and development agencies like the World Bank in the 1990s, when poor countries were often told that stronger property rights, freer markets, and more open financial systems—essentially, the luxuries that rich countries obtained after centuries of development—were their key to progress. China's success has reminded us of the crucial importance of infrastructure, pragmatic industrial policies, and an appropriate role for the state in maintaining a stable investment environment. It is a useful corrective to the free-market fundamentalism propagated by rich-country experts.

What Is the Impact of Chinese Trade, Investment, and Aid in the Rest of the World?

Leaving behind the speculative questions about what sort of "leadership" China wishes to exert in the world, it is worth briefly considering the concrete impact that its economic activities have on the world right now.

The most straightforward effect is through trade. China is the world's biggest trading nation, and is the leading trade partner for over 35 countries; it is second only to the United States, which is the top partner for 44 nations.[22] For rich countries, China is an important supplier of low-cost consumer goods, especially electronics. It is also a big buyer of capital goods such as industrial equipment, airplanes, and components such as semiconductors. For commodity-producing countries China has become the most important customer for products like crude oil, iron ore, copper, other metals, soybeans, palm oil, and sugar.

In the broadest terms, China's emergence as a major buyer of raw materials and capital goods, and a major supplier of low-cost consumer products, has been beneficial for the world economy as a whole and for most individual countries. But the impact has not been uniform, and China's rapid emergence on the global trading scene generated some important problems and frictions. Three in particular are worth attention.

First, the rise of China as a low-cost outsourcing destination for multinational companies in the early 2000s created a view that China was "stealing" manufacturing jobs from developed countries, in particular the United States. For several years the media was filled with stories about the "China price" (supposedly lower than anyone else's), China as "the workshop of the world," and Chinese "currency manipulation" as the source of its unusual competitive advantage. Much of the air has gone out of these criticisms thanks to a 40 percent appreciation of the renminbi between 2005 and 2013, along with the rapid rise in Chinese labor costs that we documented in chapter 9. There can be little doubt, however, that the introduction of several hundred million Chinese workers into the global economy has permanently weakened the bargaining position of workers in high-wage economies.

A second impact subject to wide discussion was China's large current account surplus, which grew to around 10 percent of GDP at its peak in 2007 and, along with the widening US trade deficit at the same time, was considered to be one of the major "global imbalances" that may have contributed to the 2008 global financial crisis. Again, the urgency of this concern has abated as China has managed to reduce its current account surplus to around 2 percent of GDP. But its merchandise trade surplus is about 5 percent of GDP and at around $600 billion is now larger than ever in absolute terms.[23] China continues to pick up global market share in manufactured exports, and it is increasing the sophistication of the products it sells abroad. Trade theory suggests that on balance the world economy will benefit from the increased supply of low-cost, high-quality goods from China. But the phrase "on balance" conceals the fact that individual producers in many countries will find it increasingly difficult to keep pace with Chinese competition.

A third point is that commodity-producing economies benefited disproportionately from China's investment boom, as the prices of things like crude oil, iron ore, and copper rose by a factor of five or so between 2000 and 2010. But then they suffered disproportionately when the investment surge leveled off, and commodity prices fell by half or more in 2014. The main lesson is an age-old one that has little to do with China: if you are a commodity exporter, make sure you wisely invest your gains from commodity booms, because such booms never last for very long.

The conclusion from all this is that China's domestic economic policies now matter a great deal to virtually every country in the world because virtually every country counts China as one of its biggest suppliers or customers, and for an increasing number China is one of the most important outside investors. The only other nation whose internal policies have such wide-ranging impact and are followed so closely is the United States. Many smaller countries have long wished that the United States kept their interests in mind while setting its domestic economic policies; for the most part it does not. China is unlikely to be much different. That said, China does increasingly pay attention to its external impact, and responds constructively in some cases when that impact causes problems. Its reduction of its current account surplus since 2007 is one example; its shift from a bilateral to a multilateral approach in regional infrastructure investment is another; and its determined efforts to reduce energy intensity and play a more positive role in global climate negotiations is a third.

As China's economy matures, its outward investments will eventually exert at least as great an influence on the rest of the world as its trade flows. We have already examined its "infrastructure diplomacy," but its outward direct investment is already a much more complex story than the traditional tale of building oil fields, copper mines, roads, and railways. By value, about three-quarters of China's outward investment is conducted by SOEs and is in these sectors. By number of deals, however, three-quarters is conducted by private firms who are much more interested in acquiring technology, distribution channels, and market access in rich countries. Over the next decade, it is probable that the private-sector share of Chinese outward investment will rise and that manufacturing and service-related deals will become as important as negotiating deals in infrastructure and resources.

China's outward investments have prompted two sorts of anxieties. Rich countries—more the United States than Europe—worry that Chinese investment could somehow compromise national security. In the United States, this concern is much more evident among bureaucrats and politicians in Washington, DC, than in state capitals, which eagerly court Chinese investment.[24] It can sometimes reach absurd heights, as when some members of Congress argued against the proposed acquisition of pork producer Smithfield Foods by a Chinese firm on national-security grounds. In reality, the vast majority of cross-border investments, regardless of the buyer, have no national-security implications whatever. For the tiny fraction that do, the United States and most other countries have adequate formal review processes.[25] For its part, China has shown a strong interest in trying to create consistent, workable rules of the road for cross-border investment through bilateral investment treaties with the United States and the European Union.

In poor countries, notably in Africa, a different concern has been raised: that China's natural resource investments are extractive, neocolonialist, and of little benefit to local communities. Some activists worried that because of its nondemocratic political system, China would offer blank checks to dictators, and that its investments would undermine efforts to improve standards of governance. These worries have not been borne out by serious research. There is little evidence China's resource investments are conducted with dramatically lower standards than those by firms from other countries, nor is there substance to the related claim that Chinese aid money propped up despotic regimes. China's involvement in Africa is subject to the same complexities, and a similar mix of benefits and costs, as the involvement by other countries. The efforts by some African countries to see if the Chinese development model can be replicated there are at least as valid as the many, largely failed attempts to transplant Western ideas.[26]

What Challenges Does China's Economic Rise Pose for the Rest of the World?

It is time now to conclude with a discussion about the appropriate response in the rest of the world to China's economic and political rise. The starting point is a realistic assessment of China's actual position today, and the probable changes to that position over the next decade or so.

Economically, China is a great success story. In the past three decades it has risen from a marginal position to become the world's second-biggest economy, the largest trading nation, and one of the most important manufacturing bases. The average income has risen from not much above subsistence to a global middle-income level, and the number of people living in absolute poverty has fallen from over 800 million to around 80 million. China has achieved this result through the successful adaptation of a robust economic growth model borrowed from its East Asian neighbors, pragmatic and flexible economic policies, and the good fortune of occupying a geographically favorable position that enabled it to take advantage of the previous success of other Asian nations and the extraordinary growth in global trade. It is likely to continue growing relatively rapidly and to expand its already large position in global trade and investment flows.

China's economic and social development challenges nevertheless remain daunting. The investment- and export-intensive growth model that has served it well since 1980 is nearing the end of its useful life. Its trend economic growth rate has already fallen from the 10 percent rate of 1980–2010 to around 7 percent, and it is likely to decline further to around 5 percent in the 2020s if not earlier. Its per capita income is at the lower end of the range defined as "middle income" by the World Bank, and inequalities of wealth, income, and opportunity are large. Within a generation China will have a population age structure similar to that of Japan's today—that is, very old—and will struggle to maintain vibrant economic growth while at the same time bearing the healthcare and pension costs of this older population.

Politically, China is a resilient authoritarian system whose legitimacy is based on effective governance rather than on democratic elections. This system has strengthened substantially since the political crisis of 1989, managed three peaceful leadership transitions, responded competently to changing circumstances, and appears to enjoy a high degree of citizen support or at least acquiescence. The hypothesis that market-driven economic change would force the political system to become more open and pluralistic has proved wrong so far.

On the international front, China enjoys productive relations with most countries, but has no allies. Diplomatically, it is thus fully engaged, but also in an important sense isolated. China has sought to mitigate this isolation both through active and mainly constructive participation in global institutions and through creation of new multilateral institutions, such as the Asian Infrastructure Investment Bank. Most of its neighbors in Asia welcome the economic benefits arising from their trade and investment relationships with China, but remain wary of China's strategic intentions. They therefore seek to balance their China relationship with relationships with other big powers, notably Japan, Russia, and in particular the United States.

Finally, although China is now a large and powerful nation in most dimensions, it is not much of a leader. Technologically it remains well behind the advanced economies of North America, Europe, and Japan. Politically its bureaucratic-authoritarian system, though apparently well adapted for conditions in China, lies outside the mainstream for middle- and upper-income countries, which continue generally to prefer more open systems. China has made little effort to export its economic development model, although two small African countries have emulated it, apparently with some success. Intellectually and culturally, China exerts very little influence in the world, and its own cultural trends tend to be driven by influences from the world's dominant culture (the United States) and the most vibrant Asian pop-culture exporter (South Korea).[27]

With this assessment in mind, we can consider the appropriate range of responses to China's rise. Generally speaking, China's increased prosperity is beneficial not only for itself but for the rest of the world and most people in it. Its demand for natural resources has been broadly positive for many low-income countries that depend on commodity exports. Whether those countries can take best advantage of such temporary windfall gains is a separate question, and if they cannot do so then the blame does not really rest with China. China's expertise in infrastructure has lowered its cost and made it cheaper for other developing nations to install the transport and communications systems required to build a modern economy. Its efficiency as a platform for manufacturing has lowered the costs of household goods throughout the world. And the rising purchasing power of China's large and increasingly mobile middle class is creating an important new source of demand for goods and services both in China and abroad.

This average beneficial effect, however, comes with some real and concentrated costs. One of the largest is the impact on rich-country wages by the introduction of several hundred million Chinese workers into the global workforce. It is hard to measure this effect precisely, or to determine its importance relative to other forces that may exert similar effects, notably the rapid spread of sophisticated low-cost automation, which has enabled many manufacturing and service jobs to be replaced by robots and software programs. But there is certainly a plausible case to be made that the integration of China and other low-wage economies into the global economy has contributed to the loss of high-paying manufacturing jobs and stagnation of real wages in rich economies, and to the rise in income inequality that many countries have seen since 1980. One recent study found that competition from cheap imports—mainly from China—accounted for one-quarter of the decline in US manufacturing jobs between 1990 and 2007. Another estimate is that low-cost imports account for 85 percent of the fall in the labor share of national income in the United States between 1985 and 2010.[28]

The other set of concentrated costs is borne by producers in many countries both rich and poor, which often find it hard to compete with the low prices of Chinese goods. Some researchers have found that competition from cheap Chinese exports has had a significant negative impact on exports from a wide range of European countries.[29] Another significant question, which has not been well studied, is whether China's great competitiveness across a broad range of industries makes it more difficult for poorer developing countries to develop their own manufacturing sectors.

These impacts on individual lives and national economies must be recognized. Yet in almost all cases the appropriate response to these pressures is to reform one's own domestic economic system in ways that encourage innovation and investment; improve education so that workers can take advantage of opportunities in the rapidly changing global economy rather than be left behind; ensure that tax and social welfare systems create a minimum acceptable standard of living and limit inequalities of wealth and income; and increase openness to trade, foreign investment, and the flow of ideas, with selective protection measures to safeguard critical industries and smooth out the losses of employment and income in sectors that are no longer competitive.

Countries that consistently follow these prescriptions have managed to prosper in a wide range of circumstances. Those that spend their time blaming their ills on external forces (China, Japan, commodity prices, American imperialism, European colonialism), or building protectionist walls to limit flows of goods, investment, and ideas, have consistently lagged. In any country the true enemies in the struggle for broad-based prosperity are not external competitors, but domestic elites that constantly strive to preserve their own privileges at everyone else's expense. Innovation, education, openness, and a redistributive state are reliable weapons in this struggle.

How Should Other Countries in Asia Respond to the Political Rise of China?

The tougher set of challenges posed by a rising China is political, in part because political power, unlike economic growth, is essentially a zero-sum game: economic growth in one country may very well enhance growth in other countries, but an increase in one country's political power inevitably requires a reduction in power somewhere else. The specific challenges differ depending on where one is situated.

For the smaller countries on China's periphery—essentially, Southeast and Central Asia—the problem is how to extract maximum economic benefit from Chinese trade and investment, while ceding as little political sovereignty as possible. This is the problem that small countries on the outskirts of big ones have always faced. Most of these nations are fairly well placed to manage this issue, for several reasons. First, the international system in place since World War II, and embodied in the United Nations, enshrines national sovereignty and the sanctity of international borders. Second, China has consistently and loudly espoused a principle of noninterference in other countries' internal political affairs—in part for defensive reasons, since it does not want other countries questioning its own political arrangements. These factors mean that for China to intrude in an obvious way on another nation's sovereignty, through an invasion or the establishment of a puppet government, would be quite costly.

Costly, but not utterly impossible. The ultimate guarantor of sovereignty is military power, if not one's own then that of the international order's policeman, the United States. The United States went to war to defend national sovereignty and the sanctity of borders (and of course, its own oil interests) when Iraq invaded Kuwait in 1990; it did not do so when Russia snatched Crimea away from Ukraine in 2014. The lesson for those on China's periphery is that they need to ensure that enough powerful countries have a large enough stake in their independence so that the potential cost of an incursion by China would be deemed unacceptably high in Beijing. This calculation lies behind Myanmar's political opening, Vietnam's courting of Japan, and the Central Asian balancing act between Russia and China. (It is important to emphasize that we are describing long-term hedging strategies, not responses to imminent threats. So far, China has been consistently respectful of the economic and political integrity of its neighbors, in a way that Vladimir Putin's Russia, for instance, has not.)

For the other regional powers in Asia—Japan, Russia, and India—China's rise means a diminution of influence, and the question is not how to reverse that trend but how to deal with it. Russia is in the weakest position, in part because its commodity-dependent economy is relatively fragile, and it has done little to counteract China's rising sway in Central Asia. On the other hand its significance as a supplier of energy and military equipment, and its considerable military capability, mean it can remain confident that China will treat it respectfully.

Japan's response to China's surging influence was to elect a government in 2012, under the nationalist premier Shinzo Abe, that promised to restore the nation's economic vitality and roll back some of the restrictions on its military imposed by the pacifist postwar constitution. Although the economic reforms have mostly stalled, the strengthening of military capacity has occurred, as has a swelling of industrial and infrastructure investment in Southeast Asia, especially in Vietnam. Japan may no longer have an economy capable of much growth, but it remains wealthy, technologically advanced, and highly desirable in Southeast Asia as a counterweight to Chinese influence.

India presents an interesting case because it is by far the poorest and least influential of the regional Asian powers, but the only one with a chance to grow much faster than China in the coming years. Unlike China, which faces a slowing economy and an aging population, India is still right in the heart of its "demographic dividend" period, and has the potential to sustain a couple of decades of East Asian–style fast growth. Historically, however, India has done a worse job than China and other East Asian countries of capitalizing on its natural advantages, mainly because it never achieved elite consensus that economic growth should be prioritized above everything else.

One consequence has been an erosion of influence in its own South Asian neighborhood: Chinese firms are building pipelines and dams in Myanmar, ports in Sri Lanka, and textile factories in Bangladesh. The central issue for India therefore is whether it can gin up enough sustained growth to become a credible competitor to China for economic and political influence in South and Southeast Asia. In 2014 India elected a new government under a nationalist economic reformer, Narendra Modi, whose ambition is to achieve precisely this kind of growth. Modi is a dynamic and impressive leader; it will be very interesting to see how successful he is in transforming India's notoriously slow-moving and intractable system.

How Should the United States Respond to the Rise of China?

The challenge that generates the most comment by far is the challenge that China supposedly poses to the global order and to its central power, the United States. "Realist" diplomatic historians argue that the transition from one great power to another has never gone smoothly and that the United States and China are doomed to face off in a great political or military confrontation sooner or later. Media pundits trumpet every new action by China as yet another sign of the "inexorable march of power from West to East."[30] Apparatchiks of the gigantic American military-industrial complex are quick to claim that every quiver of the Chinese state betrays an existential threat justifying a large increase in their budgets. A recent global public opinion survey shows that majorities in most countries believe that China will replace or has already replaced the United States as the world's leading power.[31]

As our discussion so far has shown, this perception is at odds with reality. China's rise is a large fact, and raises a host of strategic questions that must be taken seriously. Yet much of the anxiety about China's capacity to challenge the United States for global leadership, or to disrupt the US-led global system, is misplaced or overdone. We can separate our discussion of these issues into two parts, one on facts and one on values.

On the facts, remember the description we gave of the global system at the beginning of this chapter. This system is complex, multilayered, and robust, and has already survived severe tests. It depends not just on the economic size and technological capacities of the United States, but on a sophisticated array of multilateral institutions, knowledge and financial networks, and military alliances. It has been built up over seven decades since the end of World War II, upon deep foundations laid over the previous century through the emergence of modern industrial capitalism in Europe and the United States; the creation of flexible and responsive liberal political systems; and the statecraft of running a global commercial empire, which Great Britain pioneered and the United States has inherited and improved.[32]

The breadth, depth, and strength of this global system renders one-on-one comparisons between China and the United States irrelevant. China's economy may at some point be bigger than that of the United States, but so what? Its economic growth will still depend to a substantial degree on its ability to integrate with the global system. As its weight grows, China will gain a greater voice in how that system is run, as it should. But its ability to transform the deeply rooted principles on which that system rests will be modest.

China's capacity to conjure up some alternative, competing system should not be overrated. What would be the basis for such a system? It cannot be technological leadership, since China is a technological laggard. It cannot be a military alliance structure, since China has no alliances and no credible prospects of creating any. It cannot be a regional power bloc, since all of its neighbors view China with a degree of mistrust and are busy with hedging and balancing strategies to constrain China's influence. It could perhaps be a claim that China has discovered more effective methods of governance and economic management, and hence a stronger claim to global legitimacy and moral leadership. Here we must turn to the values side of the equation.

Perhaps the deepest anxiety caused by China's rise stems from the supposed paradox of its dynamic economy and its authoritarian political system. For years, critics have claimed this combination was unsustainable and that eventually China would be forced to accept the true faith of liberal democracy. For years this critique has proved wrong. The worry—especially in the United States, whose elites subscribe to a monotheistic view of the unique rightness of the American system and the essential imperfection of all other systems—is that China has shown how to combine economic growth with repressive politics. The risk therefore is that more countries will be seduced into this path and away from the combination of free-market capitalism and electoral democracy favored by the United States and its allies.

It is true that China's governance system is founded on principles quite different to those of Western democracies. In particular, the party rejects elections as the criterion of political legitimacy, in favor of effective governance. This stance achieves broad acquiescence in Chinese society because it is little more than a restatement of the principle of *tian ming* or the Mandate of Heaven, which was the basis of legitimacy in China's imperial system. For 1,500 years China's bureaucracy and ruling house justified their rule by claiming to run a well-ordered land where roads, canals, irrigation systems, and dikes were maintained; commercial activities were vibrant and well regulated; and social stability was maintained. Breakdowns in this order signaled the loss of the right to rule. The Communist Party makes essentially the same claim, but in the context of a high-growth industrial economy rather than a low-growth agrarian one.

The pragmatic response from the United States and other liberal democracies should begin with the recognition that China's system of values differs substantially from that of the West, that this system of values is not some fragile recent invention but is deeply rooted in Chinese traditions of governance, and that it is validated for most Chinese people by the nation's developmental successes since 1980. China's governance system has many flaws but has generally proved effective, and has in fact changed substantially in response to shifting conditions, even if the Communist Party's monopoly remains intact. Most important, outsiders can do nothing to change it—just outsiders can do nothing to change the aspects of the American system they deplore, such as the capture of the political system by big campaign donors, institutionalized racism, excessive consumption of energy and other resources, capital punishment, and so on. When the majority of Chinese people feel this system no longer meets their needs, they may seek to change it, as people across the world have changed their governance systems over the past two centuries.

Second, greater participation by Chinese companies and the Chinese government in the world outside China is a good thing, and there is no reason why all this participation must occur within the preexisting frameworks of the US-led system. The world is a large place, with diverse needs, and different sources of funding and ideas should be encouraged, not rebuffed. Only after much more of this sort of international engagement will we be able to see which elements of the Chinese model are exportable and which are applicable only in the special conditions of China. (My personal suspicion is that few will prove exportable.) Moreover, the more Chinese companies and agencies work abroad, the more they will absorb international norms and practices, and the gulf between "Chinese" and "Western" values that now seems so scary will lessen. It is also possible that Westerners, once they discard their ideological blinkers, will find aspects of the Chinese way of doing things that are genuinely worth emulating or adapting.

Last, it should be recognized that China will never be content to be a US vassal, and that this is entirely reasonable. Equally, however, the deep uncertainty over its long-run demographic and economic outlook, and the untapped expansive potential of the US economy, not to mention the richness and robustness of the US-led world order, make it unlikely that China will ever unseat the United States as the world's technological, cultural, and political leader. Given China's demonstrated pragmatism and caution under successive leaders over the past thirty-five years, there is reason to believe that an accommodation can be reached under which China enjoys increased prestige and influence—to the extent it can earn it—but the US-led system remains the core of the world's political and economic arrangements. Twenty-first-century China is not the reincarnation of Kaiser Wilhelm's Germany or the Soviet Union. Recognizing the fact and durability of its distinct value system does not constitute appeasement. And "containment"—the strategy that ultimately proved successful against the brittle and stagnant Soviet system—is a foolish idea when applied to China, which has proved itself dynamic and adaptable. There is plenty of room in the world for both the US and the Chinese systems, so long as people on both sides can agree that this peaceful coexistence is a goal worth striving for.

APPENDIX

Are China's Economic Statistics Reliable?

This book, like all works of practical economics, relies heavily on statistics. Most of the official Chinese government data are sourced from the CEIC database, which is the authorized online reseller for China's National Bureau of Statistics (NBS). Some data not available from the CEIC is sourced from Chinese government publications, notably the yearbooks published by various agencies, the Ministry of Finance's annual budget reports to the National People's Congress, and occasional ad hoc reports that appear on government websites.

Academic researchers have made good use of Chinese data for decades, but from time to time claims surface that Chinese economic statistics are intrinsically untrustworthy. These claims come in two varieties, the serious and the unserious. The unserious ones are those advanced by nonspecialists, typically analysts for hedge funds or other financial firms, alleging that Chinese data on GDP, or energy consumption, or inflation, or whatnot are falsified by the government in order to cover up some major problem. These claims, often hyped by the media, are best ignored. Economic data in all places are subject to various problems and distortions, which are addressed by the constant revision of published data and the underlying methods used by national statistical agencies, as well as by enormous volumes of academic econometric research that seek to refine our understanding of how numbers relate to reality.

Chinese data suffer from two additional problems. First, the country is enormous, decentralized, and undergoing rapid structural change. This makes the collection of consistent data much harder than in a slower-growing economy with a more stable structure. Second, the Chinese government is unusually secretive about the sources and methods used to generate its statistics, making it hard for researchers to do the independent cross-checks that they would like to do, and arousing understandable suspicions about what the government might be trying to hide.

Many serious analysts do believe that the government tends to smooth out the quarterly GDP growth numbers, underreporting growth when it is very hot and nudging the figures upward when it is cool. Most other data problems and inconsistencies can be explained by ordinary analytic econometric work, without resort to conspiracy theories about deliberate falsification. Those interested in making sensible use of Chinese data should consult Tom Orlik's excellent *Understanding China's Economic Indicators* (FT Press, 2012).

The falsification theory also fails a simple logical test. If the government publishes false data, it must either rely on this false data to make economic policy, or it must keep a secret set of true data. If it uses false data, economic policy will quickly run aground, as it did during the Great Leap Forward of the 1950s, when reliance on bogus agricultural production numbers led within a couple of years to a catastrophic famine that killed tens of millions of people. China's sustained economic success since 1978 simply could not have occurred if the government had relied on faulty data.

This leaves the possibility that the government uses a secret set of true data to form policy, while feeding lies to the public. No evidence has ever been presented that such a secret data set exists. There are certainly a few data series that are not published but are reserved for the internal use of government officials. What is interesting is how boring these prove to be when occasionally they come to light through a leak—as, for instance, when a classified unemployment figure was accidentally disclosed at a press conference. The figure was 5 percent, compared to the published "registered unemployment" figure of 4 percent. In any case, if the government really kept a full set of secret accounts, the falsity of the published data could be exposed by the same statistical tests used by forensic accountants to prove chicanery in corporate balance sheets. These tests have been applied, and have failed to show any evidence of systemic falsification.[1]

The more serious claim, made by several economists, is that China's long-run growth rate has been systematically overstated, not because China sought to bamboozle the world but because its statisticians employed faulty techniques. The most recent version of this argument is by Harry X. Wu of The Conference Board, who heroically reconstructed China's national accounts for the sixty-year period 1952–2012 in order to arrive at a better understanding of long-term trends in productivity growth. Wu concluded that, thanks mainly to weaker than reported productivity gains, China's average annual real GDP growth during the reform era (1978–2012) was 7.2 percent, well below the official figure of 9.8 percent.[2]

This is an interesting exercise, but it raises some conceptual problems. If we assume that the size of the Chinese economy was accurately measured in 1978, then the lower growth rate compounded over thirty-four years implies that China's economy in 2012 was less than half as big as the official data say it was. This is impossible, because the economy's present size is roughly confirmed by a wealth of information, including the government's own economic censuses, and indicators including exports, foreign exchange reserves and consumption of physical items such as automobiles, oil, steel, and cement that are independently verifiable and not subject to falsification. If, on the other hand, we assume that the economy's reported size today is correct, then the lower growth rate compounded back thirty-four years implies that China's economy was more than twice as big in 1978 as the government believed it to be. This is slightly more plausible than the first case, but not much. Alternatively, we can try to pick values for China's 1978 and 2012 GDP that are not so obviously incredible, for instance that the economy was two-thirds bigger than reported in 1978 and one-quarter smaller in 2012 (in which case we need merely explain away $2 trillion—an India's worth—of phantom output). Any way you slice it, it is quite hard to reconcile the arithmetic of these alternative growth calculations with observed reality.

To anyone who has spent much time in China since the 1980s, it is clear that (a) China has grown very rapidly for a long time; and (b) the speed and nature of that growth was roughly comparable to that of Japan, South Korea, and Taiwan, each of which uncontroversially grew at 8 to 10 percent a year for about a quarter-century in the post–World War II era. The reluctance of some observers to accept that China achieved similar results to those of its neighbors, using essentially the same economic playbook, is odd. It probably reflects the belief that because China's government is secretive, authoritarian, and untrustworthy in many political matters, its economic data must also be untrustworthy. The feeling is understandable, but the conclusion is supported by neither logic nor the preponderance of evidence. A government so dependent on sustained economic growth for its legitimacy, and so keenly aware (thanks to its own recent history) of the disastrous consequences of relying on bad data, has a strong self-interest in maintaining statistics that are approximately right, at least with regard to trends, even if they do not meet the highest standards of modern statistical science. Like all economic data, China's must be used with care; but they are useable.

FOR FURTHER READING

These suggestions present the most important easily accessible sources for each chapter in the book, to guide readers who wish to delve further into particular topics. Additional sources are in the detailed endnotes. As this book is aimed at a non-specialist readership in English, the sources cited in this bibliographic note and in the endnotes are for the most part in English. Readers with Chinese-language reading ability will find abundant references to Chinese academic work and primary sources in the books and articles listed here. All cited articles from the *China Economic Quarterly* or the Gavekal Dragonomics research service are available to the public at the website: http://www.china-economy-book.com.

General Overviews

Those who want a more detailed understanding of China's economic development during the reform era, and the challenges it now faces, are referred to four weighty tomes. The authoritative textbook treatment is Barry Naughton, *The Chinese Economy: Transitions and Growth* (MIT Press, 2007). Loren Brandt and Thomas G. Rawski, eds., *China's Great Economic Transformation* (Cambridge University Press, 2008) is an excellent, though often dense, collection of essays by the world's top China scholars. Both volumes are comprehensive, but unfortunately somewhat dated.

A more contemporary and forward-looking set of views can be found in two big reports prepared jointly by the World Bank and the Development Research Center of the State Council, China's leading think tank. These are *China 2030: Building a Modern, Harmonious and Creative Society* (2013, http://documents.worldbank.org/curated/en/2013/03/17494829/); and *Urban China: Toward Efficient, Inclusive and Sustainable Urbanization* (2014, http://www.worldbank.org/en/country/china/publication/urban-china-toward-efficient-inclusive-sustainable-urbanization). Both reports are invaluable compendia of the best current economic research on China, and are cited extensively throughout this book. In the rest of this section and in the notes, *China 2030* is cited as World Bank/DRC 2013, and *Urban China* as World Bank/DRC 2014.

Chapter 1: Overview: China's Political Economy

For an accessible and up-to-date introduction to China's governance system, see Tony Saich, *Governance and Politics of China*, 3rd ed. (Palgrave Macmillan, 2011). An older but still useful discussion is Kenneth Lieberthal, *Governing China: From Revolution to Reform*, 2nd ed. (W. W. Norton, 2003). The indispensable introduction to China's Communist Party is Richard McGregor, *The Party: The Secret World of China's Communist Rulers* (Penguin Books, 2011), by a former *Financial Times* bureau chief in Beijing. David Shambaugh, *China's Communist Party: Atrophy and Adaptation* (University of California Press, 2009) is more academic, but quite readable, and especially good on the lessons learned from the fall of the Soviet Union. Ezra Vogel, *Deng Xiaoping and the Transformation of China* (Belknap Press, 2013), offers a wealth of valuable party's-eye detail of the critical 1980s, when the parameters of China's reform era were laid down. Finally, a dense but provocative analysis of the tensions between central and local governments is in Pierre Landry, *Decentralized Authoritarianism in China: The Communist Party's Control of Local Elites in the Post-Mao Era* (Cambridge University Press, 2008).

A readable distillation of the literature on East Asian developmental states, and how China's development strategy compares to that of its neighbors, is Joe Studwell, *How Asia Works: Success and Failure in the World's Most Dynamic Region* (Grove Press, 2013). The classic academic accounts include Robert Wade, *Governing the Market: Economic Theory and the Role of Government in East Asian Industrialization* (Princeton University Press, 2003); Alice Amsden, *Asia's Next Giant: South Korea and Late Industrialization* (Oxford University Press, 1992); and Chalmers Johnson, *MITI and the Japanese Miracle: The Growth of Industrial Policy, 1925–75* (MIT Press, 1982).

Last but not least, an academic exposition of a basic thesis very similar to my own—that China must be considered as a unique combination of East Asian developmental state and post-Communist transitional economy—is Barry Naughton and Kellee S. Tsai, eds., *State Capitalism, Institutional Adaptation, and the Chinese Miracle* (Cambridge University Press, 2015), especially the introductory chapter by Tsai and Naughton, "State Capitalism and the Chinese Economic Miracle" (1–24).

Chapter 2: Agriculture, Land, and the Rural Economy

A good summary of China's agricultural development is Jikun Huang, Keijiro Otsuka, and Scott Rozelle, "Agriculture in China's Development: Past Disappointments, Recent Successes, and Future Challenges," in Brandt and Rawski, eds., *China's Great Economic Transformation*, 467–505. A standard description of the rise of rural industry under the aegis of local governments is Jean C. Oi, *Rural China Takes Off: Institutional Foundations of Economic Reform* (Stanford University Press, 1999). Land issues are comprehensively covered in World Bank/DRC 2014.

Chapter 3: Industry and the Rise of the Export Economy

The classic account of China's industrial reforms in the early reform era is Barry Naughton, *Growing Out of the Plan: Chinese Economic Reform, 1978–1993* (Cambridge University Press, 1996). More detail, for a longer period of time, is available in Naughton 2007 (referred to above under General Overviews). A concise summary of the reforms that led to the shift from the import-substitution to the export-led model is Nicholas Lardy, *Foreign Trade and Economic Reform in China, 1978–1991* (Cambridge University Press, 1993). A later treatment of China's foreign trade, on the eve of WTO accession, is Lardy, *Integrating China into the Global Economy* (Brookings Institution, 2001).

Reaching further back into history, Angus Maddison in *The World Economy* (OECD, 2007), presents the standard estimates of China's GDP over the past 2,000 years. A still-controversial view of China's economic position around 1800 is Kenneth Pomeranz, *The Great Divergence: China, Europe and the Making of the Modern World* (Princeton University Press, 2001). A vivid fictional, but deeply researched, description of the opium trade that also contains interesting insights into the foundations of China's manufacturing process is Amitav Ghosh, *River of Smoke* (Farrar, Straus, & Giroux, 2011).

Chapter 4: Urbanization and Infrastructure

World Bank/DRC 2014 is an exhaustive treatment of urbanization issues, with extensive references to scholarly literature in English and Chinese. Another detailed overview is *OECD Urban Policy Reviews: China 2015* (OECD Publishing, 2015). A lively popular treatment of China's urbanization push is by my colleague Tom Miller, *China's Urban Billion: The Story behind the Biggest Migration in Human History* (Asian Arguments, 2012).

Chapter 5: The Enterprise System

Four sources were especially important for this chapter. Nicholas Lardy, *Markets over Mao: The Rise of Private Business in China* (Peterson Institute of International Economics, 2014), forcefully advances the thesis that the private sector has steadily advanced throughout the reform era, and that China's impressive economic growth has depended heavily on this advance. Yasheng Huang, *Capitalism with Chinese Characteristics: Entrepreneurship and the State* (Cambridge University Press, 2008) argues in contrast that a brief experiment with a relatively free private sector in the 1980s gave way to a state-driven economic model in the 1990s and 2000s. Tsai and Naughton 2014 (cited above under chapter 1) also make a compelling case against underestimating the state role. My account of the structure of state-owned enterprise groups is drawn mainly from Li-Wen Lin and Curtis J. Milhaupt, "We Are the (National) Champions: Understanding the Mechanisms of State Capitalism in China," *Stanford Law Review* 65 (April 2013), http://works.bepress.com/curtis_milhaupt/20.

Chapter 6: The Fiscal System and Central-Local Government Relations

An accessible overview of China's fiscal system, is Lou Jiwei, ed., *Public Finance in China: Reform and Growth for a Harmonious Society* (World Bank, 2008). (Lou Jiwei was one of the architects of the 1994 tax reform and since 2013 has been minister of finance.) World Bank/DRC 2014 contains a good discussion of fiscal issues (54–62 and 371–446). *OECD Urban Policy Reviews: China 2015* has a comprehensive treatment of the fiscal system and related governance issues (159–228). A technical discussion of the central-local transfer system is Xiao Wang and Richard Herd, "The System of Revenue Sharing and Fiscal Transfers in China," *OECD Economics Department Working Papers*, No. 1030 (OECD Publishing, 2013). An easy-to-read comparison of central-local governance problems in both China and India—which reminds us that the problems of effectively managing a huge country are not unique to China—is William Antholis, *Inside Out India and China: Local Politics Go Global* (Brookings Institution, 2013).

Chapter 7: The Financial System

The dean of China financial experts is Nicholas Lardy, who has devoted much of his time since the late 1990s untangling the mysteries of this opaque system. Those interested in a deeper understanding of Chinese finance should consult three of his books. *China's Unfinished Economic Revolution* (Brookings Institution, 1998) describes the evolution of the banking system in the first two decades of reform and how it led to the effective bankruptcy of Chinese banks in the late 1990s. *Sustaining China's Economic Growth after the Global Financial Crisis* (Peterson Institute of International Economics, 2012) analyzes the mechanisms of financial repression and makes the case for interest rate liberalization as the key to unlocking future growth. *Markets over Mao* (cited above under chapter 5) provocatively argues that a majority of bank credit now goes to the private sector. A curmudgeonly but intensely well-informed look at China's capital markets by two former bankers is Carl Walter and Fraser Howie, *Red Capitalism: The Fragile Financial Foundation of China's Extraordinary Rise* (John Wiley, 2012).

Chapter 8: Energy and the Environment

The most lucid and accessible overview of China's energy system is Daniel Rosen and Trevor Houser, *China Energy: A Guide for the Perplexed* (Peterson Institute for International Economics, 2007). It is now unfortunately somewhat out of date. A more recent, and also more academic, overview is Philip Andrews-Speed, *The Governance of Energy in China: Transition to a Low-Carbon Economy* (Palgrave Macmillan, 2012). The China Energy Group at the Lawrence Berkeley National Laboratory, under Mark Levine, has done excellent work monitoring the structure of China's energy use and modeling the future trajectory of energy consumption and greenhouse gas emissions. Two of its important publications are *Key China Energy Statistics 2014*, which is based on its invaluable China Energy Databook, (http://china.lbl.gov/research-projects/china-energy-databook); and Nan Zhou et al., "China's Energy and Emissions Outlook to 2050: Perspectives from Bottom-up Energy End-Use Model," *Energy Policy* 53 (February 2013), also available at: https://china.lbl.gov/sites/all/files/lbl-4472e-energy-2050april-2011.pdf.

For a general summary of China's environmental problems, see Elizabeth Economy, *The River Runs Black: The Environmental Challenge to China's Future*, 2nd ed. (Cornell University Press, 2010); Ma Jun, *China's Water Crisis* (Pacific Century Press, 2004); and Jonathan Watts, *When a Billion Chinese Jump: How China Will Save Mankind—Or Destroy It* (Scribner, 2010). The Yale Environmental Performance Index (http://epi.yale.edu/epi) provides excellent internationally comparable data on all types of environmental degradation. Comprehensive data on greenhouse gas emissions is in the World Resources Institute's Climate Analysis Indicators Tool (CAIT) database (http://cait.wri.org/historical).

Chapter 9: Demographics and the Labor Market

The standard work on China's demography is Judith Banister, *China's Changing Population* (Stanford University Press, 1987). Although it obviously does not cover recent developments, it is the authoritative account of deaths from China's great famine of 1958–1961, the subsequent population boom, and the efforts to control population growth in the 1970s and 1980s that culminated in the one-child policy.

For a detailed account of the great famine by a dogged and heroic Chinese journalist, see Yang Jisheng, *Tombstone: The Untold Story of Mao's Great Famine* (Farrar, Straus & Giroux, 2012). An excellent overview of labor market issues is Fang Cai, Albert Park, and Yaohui Zhao, "The Chinese Labor Market in the Reform Era," in Brandt and Rawski, *China's Great Economic Transformation*, 167–214. The idea of the "Lewis turning point" derives from W. Arthur Lewis, "Economic Development with Unlimited Supplies of Labour," *Manchester School of Economic and Social Studies* 22 (1954): 139–91, (http://www.globelicsacademy.net/2008/2008_lectures/lewis%20unlimited%20labor%20supply%201954.pdf). A brief summary and explanation of its relevance to China is in World Bank/DRC 2014, 89. This essay is essential reading for anyone who wants to understand the dynamics of growth in a developing economy and how they differ from those of rich countries.

Chapter 10: The Emerging Consumer Economy

Detailed scholarly study of the Chinese consumer economy is a thing of the future. I have instead relied heavily on commercial research, including work done by my colleagues at Gavekal Dragonomics, which is available at the firm's public website, http://www.china-economy-book.com. The best discussions of the size of China's middle class, the "middle-income trap," and the construction of the social safety net are in World Bank/DRC 2014, 104–5 and 198–214.

Chapter 11: The Social Compact: Inequality and Corruption

The classic statement of the view that inequality arises naturally during a period of rapid industrialization, and then declines as an economy matures, is Simon Kuznets, "Economic Growth and Income Inequality," *American Economic Review* 45, no. 1 (1955): 1–28; available at https://www.aeaweb.org/aer/top20/45.1.1-28.pdf. World Bank/DRC 2014 contains much good discussion of China's inequality problems, and the World Bank's Poverty and Inequality program is a good place for further exploration (http://web.worldbank.org/WBSITE/EXTERNAL/EXTDEC/EXTRESEARCH/EXTPROGRAMS/0,,contentMDK:20227695~menuPK:475424~pagePK:478091~piPK:475420~theSitePK:475417,00.html). For the discussion of corruption, I have relied extensively on Andrew Wedeman's excellent *Double Paradox: Rapid Growth and Rising Corruption in China* (Cornell University Press, 2012). The best statement of the view that rampant corruption risks stifling economic growth and undermining the political system is Minxin Pei, *China's Trapped Transition: The Limits of Developmental Autocracy* (Harvard University Press, 2006).

Chapter 12: Changing the Growth Model

Amid the flood of discussions since the 2008 global financial crisis about China's need to "rebalance" or "change its growth model," two works stand out. One is World Bank/DRC 2013, which was consciously designed as a comprehensive reform agenda for the next two decades. The other is the *Economic Survey of China 2015* by the Organization for Economic Cooperation and Development (OECD; available at http://www.oecd.org/eco/surveys/economic-survey-china.htm), a detailed and rigorous assessment of China's current challenges and the reforms needed to address them.

Chapter 13: Conclusion: China and the World

Because China's emergence as a global economic power is so recent, measured discussions of its impact and how other countries might respond are rare. Instead we face a huge volume of breathless media coverage and politically motivated advocacy documents. Three books are worth consulting to get a more balanced view. Deborah Brautigam's *The Dragon's Gift: The Real Story of China in Africa* (Oxford University Press, 2011) is a clear-eyed account of the pluses and minuses of China's engagement in Africa, and a good corrective to early hyperbolic accounts suggesting that China was simply a neocolonialist invader intent on extracting natural resources and propping up dictators. A careful study of China's growing military capability is George J. Gilboy and Eric Heginbotham, *Chinese and Indian Strategic Behavior: Growing Power and Alarm* (Cambridge University Press, 2012). Finally, there is Edward Steinfeld's *Playing Our Game: Why China's Rise Doesn't Threaten the West* (Oxford University Press, 2010), which underscores the enormous power and resilience of existing global institutions and the great difficulty China will face in modifying them.

NOTES

CHAPTER 1

1. All these generalizations are subject to the caveat that the party's internal workings are kept secret, so there are many details we don't know about how power is exercised. I try to present an account that represents the consensus view of Chinese political scholars. But scholars differ on some basic points, for instance the degree of power held by the current president, Xi Jinping. Some believe that he wields a breadth of personal authority unmatched since Mao Zedong, and this is certainly the impression one gets from the Chinese media. Others, notably the eminent Stanford scholar Alice L. Miller, argue from a close reading of published party documents that Xi operates within, and is constrained by, the consensus mechanisms of the inner party circle. (See, e.g., Alice Lyman Miller, "The Trouble with Factions," *China Leadership Monitor* No. 46 (March 2015) (http://www.hoover.org/sites/default/files/research/docs/clm46am.pdf.)

2. Strictly speaking, the power transitions are spread out over several months, with control of the party transferred at the Party Congress in the autumn, and of the government and military at the National People's Congress session the following March. For the 1992 succession specifically, see Ezra Vogel, *Deng Xiaoping and the Transformation of China* (Harvard University Press, 2012), 684–88.

3. Technically, several other parties exist, but in practice they have no influence on government nor the right to contest elections.

4. Richard McGregor, *The Party: The Secret Life of China's Communist Rulers* (Allen Lane, 2010), 72.

5. See Philip C. C. Huang et al., "Development 'Planning' in Present-Day China—Systems, Process and Mechanism," in *Modern China* 20, no. 10 (2013): 1–78, for a detailed discussion from both Chinese and Western perspectives of the policy planning process.

6. Actually, a misnomer, since numerous exceptions enabled many families to have more than one child. See chapter 8 for details.

7. Pierre Landry, *Decentralized Authoritarianism in China* (Cambridge University Press, 2008), 6–8; and China Ministry of Finance, *Report on the Implementation of the Central and Local Budgets in 2013 and on the Draft Central and Local Budgets for 2014*, March 15, 2014 (http://www.npc.gov.cn/english-npc/Speeches/2014-03/18/content_1856702.htm).

8. Data in this paragraph is from Barry Naughton, *Growing Out of the Plan: Chinese Economic Reform 1978–1993* (Cambridge University Press, 1995), 40–50.

9. Varieties of this argument can be found in Susan Shirk, *China: Fragile Superpower* (Oxford University Press, 2008); Minxin Pei, *China's Trapped Transition* (Harvard University Press, 2006); and Will Hutton, *The Writing on the Wall* (Free Press, 2006).

10. Vogel 2012, 677.

11. Ibid., 677–81.

12. In Chinese, *fazhan cai shi ying daoli*. This is often translated as "Development is the only hard truth." I am grateful to Robert Kapp for the suggestion that "iron law" better captures the implication that development is a positive mandate imposed by the party, rather than an unavoidable and perhaps unpleasant necessity.

13. Vogel 2012, 423.

14. David Shambaugh, *China's Communist Party: Atrophy and Adaptation* (Woodrow Wilson Center, 2008), 60–81.

15. Andrew Batson, "Is China Heading for the Middle-Income Trap?" Gavekal Dragonomics research note, September 6, 2011.

16. The presentation of the East Asian development model from which this section is mainly drawn, is Joe Studwell, *How Asia Works* (Profile Books, 2013). For more detail, see the sources listed in "For Further Reading"; and also Arthur Kroeber, "Developmental Dreams: Policy and Reality in China's Economic Reforms," in Scott Kennedy, ed., *Beyond the Middle Kingdom: Comparative Perspectives on China's Capitalist Transformation* (Stanford University Press, 2011).

17. In addition to Studwell, this observation was also made by James Fallows in his useful 1980s survey of the rising Asian economies, *Looking at the Sun* (Vintage, 1995).

18. See Yasheng Huang, *Capitalism with Chinese Characteristics* (Cambridge University Press, 2008).

19. For a good discussion of Taiwan's calculations in this regard, see Jay Taylor's biography of Chiang Ching-kuo, *The Generalissimo's Son* (Harvard University Press, 2000).

20. The phrase "crossing the river by feeling for the stones" (*mozhe shitou guohe*) was frequently used by both Deng and his rival Chen Yun, a more conservative official who essentially ran China's economic planning bureaucracy throughout the 1980s. The Third Plenum Decision of 2013, an important economic strategy document outlining Xi Jinping's vision for economic development (to be discussed in more detail in chapter 11), uses the odd phrase "strengthen the combination of top-level design with crossing the river by feeling for the stones" (*jiaqiang dingceng sheji he mozhe shitou guohe xiang jiehe*), which nicely catches the tension between Chinese leaders'

desire for all-encompassing plans and the messy, intractable reality that they must confront.

21. This includes 22 provinces, 5 "autonomous regions" that are ostensibly organized to permit some self-government for large ethnic minorities, and 4 independent municipalities of which the largest (Chongqing) occupies an area the size of Austria. All these administrative units are at the same level in China's administrative hierarchy and will be referred to collectively as "provinces" in this book.

CHAPTER 2

1. Wing Thye Woo, "The Art of Reforming Centrally-Planned Economies: Comparing China, Poland and Russia," *Journal of Comparative Economics* (June 1994): 276–308.

2. Concise descriptions of socialist-era agriculture and the early agricultural reforms are in Naughton 2008, 252–66, and in Lardy 2014, 60–62. For a more detailed overview of China's agricultural development, see Jikun Huang, Keijiro Otsuka, and Scott Rozelle, "Agriculture in "China's Development: Past Disappointments, Recent Successes and Future Challenges," in Loren Brandt and Thomas G. Rawski, eds., *China's Great Economic Transformation* (Cambridge University Press 2008), 467–505. A detailed discussion of Chinese agriculture up through 1982 is in Nicholas Lardy, *Agriculture in China's Modern Economic Development* (Cambridge University Press, 1983).

3. This data from Naughton 2008, 260–65. Data on rural cash savings from Jean Oi, *Rural China Takes Off: Institutional Foundations of Economic Reform* (Stanford University Press, 1999), 26.

4. Naughton 1995, 153.

5. Naughton 2008, 285–88. In 1995 total employment in China was 680 million people, of which 120 million worked in rural enterprises (NBS/CEIC).

6. Chinese government data, sourced from the CEIC database. This is the ratio between urban per capita disposable income and rural per capita net income.

7. Gap between rural and urban incomes: *China 2030: Building a Modern, Harmonious and Creative Society* (2013, http://documents.worldbank.org/curated/en/2013/03/17494829/) hereafter World Bank/DRC 2013, 9; also see *Urban China: Toward Efficient, Inclusive and Sustainable Urbanization* (2014, http://www.worldbank.org/en/country/china/publication/urban-china-toward-efficient-inclusive-sustainable-urbanization) hereafter World Bank/DRC 2014, 105. Rural pension coverage: Thomas Gatley and Andrew Batson, "China's Welfare State: Mission Accomplished?" Gavekal Dragonomics research note, March 19, 2013.

8. The World Bank's definition of absolute poverty is daily expenditure of less than $1.25, in 2005 dollars adjusted for purchasing power parity (PPP). See http://povertydata.worldbank.org/poverty/country/CHN, which also enables one to display the reductions since 1990 in the number of people under other poverty thresholds: $2, $4, and $5 a day. By any measure, China's poverty-reduction efforts have been more successful than any other developing country's.

9. The Landesa survey, its fifth in China, is "China's Farmers Benefiting from Land Tenure Reform," February 2011, http://www.landesa.org/where-we-work/china/research-report-2010-findings-17-province-china-survey/. Specifically, Landesa found that 63 percent of farmers had land-right certificates, 53 percent had land-rights contracts, but only 44 percent had both as required by law. Landesa also found the persistence of many abuses, including inadequate compensation for land converted to urban use, and forced leases to agribusinesses. See also Lardy 2014, 61; and John Bruce, "China's Land System Reform: What Comes after the Third Plenum?" unpublished paper for World Bank Conference on Land Tenure, March 2015.
10. World Bank/DRC 2014, 17.
11. This arrangement may sound strange to Americans, who are used to freehold property rights, but it exists in other countries. Most apartments in England are leasehold, as is all real property in Hong Kong, where the normal term of the lease is ninety-nine years.
12. "Rural construction land" refers to rural land used for structures (mainly village housing, but also commercial and small-scale industrial buildings) rather than for cultivation.
13. This discussion largely follows Bruce 2015. For a good discussion of the most recent developments in the land reform discussion, see Barry Naughton, "Is There A 'Xi Model' of Economic Reform? Acceleration of Economic Reform since Fall 2014," *China Leadership Monitor* No. 46 (Winter 2015) (http://www.hoover.org/publications/china-leadership-monitor/spring-2015-issue-46).
14. A similar issue exists in regard to urban property, which has been overwhelmingly registered in men's names. See Leta Hong Fincher, *Leftover Women: The Resurgence of Gender Inequality in China* (Zed Books, 2014).
15. See Lester Brown, *Who Will Feed China* (Worldwatch Institute, 1995) and *Full Planet, Empty Plates: The New Geopolitics of Food Scarcity* (W. W. Norton, 2012).
16. Will Freeman, "How To Feed a Dragon," Gavekal Dragonomics research note, February 26, 2013.
17. The focus of food security is also being broadened beyond the mere minimization of imports, to include food safety, a rising concern among China's urban middle class. See Robert Ash, "A New Line on Food Security," *China Economic Quarterly* (September 2014): 45–48.

CHAPTER 3

1. Trade data from World Trade Organization. Manufacturing data calculated from United Nations National Accounts Main Aggregates Database (http://unstats.un.org/unsd/snaama/selbasicFast.asp). In 2013 China's manufacturing value added was US$2.74 trillion, or 23 percent of the world total; that of the United States, $2.03 trillion (17 percent). A good cross-country comparison is Daniel J. Meckstroth, "China Has a Dominant Share of World Manufacturing," Manufacturers Alliance for Productivity and Innovation, January 6, 2014, https://www.mapi.net/china-has-dominant-share-world-manufacturing.
2. For China's share of global GDP over the past 2,000 years, see Maddison 2007. For a still-controversial view of China's position around 1800, see Pomeranz 2001.

3. Seeking a commodity other than silver to balance its trade with China, Great Britain resorted to exports of opium grown in its Indian colonies. China prohibited imports of this drug, and its effort to enforce its ban led to the war. Britain won, and under the subsequent treaty it and other European powers gained greatly expanded trading rights within China. For a vivid fictional, but deeply researched, description of the opium trade, see Amitav Ghosh, *River of Smoke* (Farrar, Straus, & Giroux, 2011). See also Julia Lovell, *The Opium War: Drugs Dreams and the Making of Modern China* (Macmillan, 2011).

4. Prasannan Parthasarathi, *Why Europe Grew Rich and Asia Did Not* (Cambridge University Press, 2011).

5. For a convincing discussion of the importance of Hong Kong's "soft" legal infrastructure to China's economic development in the 1980s and 1990s, see Yasheng Huang, *Capitalism with Chinese Characteristics* (Cambridge University Press, 2008), 1–10.

6. For price data, see Lardy 2014. For SOE market share data, see Loren Brandt, Thomas Rawski, and John Sutton, "China's Industrial Development," in Loren Brandt and Thomas G. Rawski, eds. *China's Great Economic Transformation* (Cambridge University Press, 2008): 572.

7. For an accessible explanation of this "golden age" of Chinese exports, see Alexandra Harney, *The China Price* (Penguin Books, 2008).

8. The environmental scientist Vaclav Smil calculated that China used more cement in the three years 2011–2013 than the United States did during the entire twentieth century. This is a frightening statistic, but skewed by the fact that in China virtually all housing and many rural roads are built with concrete, whereas in the United States wood-frame housing and asphalt paving is the norm. Measured on a per capita basis against other big Asian countries, China's consumption of steel and cement still looks high, but not so outlandish. See http://www.independent.co.uk/news/world/asia/how-did-china-use-more-cement-between-2011-and-2013-than-the-us-used-in-the-entire-20th-century-10134079.html. For a good overview of the cement industry, see http://www.globalcement.com/magazine/articles/796-china-first-in-cement.

9. For a clear discussion of Made in China 2025, see Scott Kennedy, "Made in China 2025," Center for Strategic and International Studies, June 1, 2015, http://csis.org/publication/made-china-2025. The original policy document (in Chinese) is at http://news.china.com/domestic/945/20150519/19710486_all.html.

10. For this comparison, see Kroeber 2011.

11. Round-tripping is impossible to measure, but analysts have long used the one-third figure as a rule of thumb.

12. See Brandt, Rawski, and Sutton 2008.

13. See G. E. Anderson, *Designated Drivers: How China Plans to Dominate the Global Auto Industry* (John Wiley, 2012). For a condensed version, see Anderson, "Fat Profits, Fat Failures," *China Economic Quarterly* (June 2012): 43–47.

14. For US subsidies, see Lardy 2014, 35–36.

15. See Lardy 2014.

16. For most of this period the average pump price for regular gasoline in China was about Rmb 7.5 per liter, and the Rmb/USD exchange rate averaged around 6.3. This translates into an average price of $4.52 per gallon, compared to a US average pump price of $3.57 (calculated from Energy

Information Administration data, http://www.eia.gov/dnav/pet/pet_pri_gnd_dcus_nus_w.htm).

17. This partly reflects the pricing formula adopted by the government in late 2009 and adjusted since then. Under this formula, the price regulator must move pump prices in line with crude oil prices, but has discretion to limit the size of those moves—to stave off volatility—if the crude oil price goes below US$80 a barrel or above US$130 a barrel. In addition, the government offset some of the gasoline price fall by increasing excise taxes.

18. Electricity pricing is complicated, and there is no doubt local governments often force local grids to provide low-cost power to favored users. But research has failed to show systematic underpricing of power across the country. The latest US power prices are from the Energy Information Administration, which reported an average industrial price of 6.65 cents per kilowatt hour in December 2014 (http://www.eia.gov/electricity/monthly/epm_table_grapher.cfm?t=epmt_5_6_a). For China the figure was Rmb 0.79 or about 12.7 cents at the current exchange rate; data from CEIC.

19. China has for many years been one of a handful of countries on the "priority watch list" for intellectual property violations in the United States Trade Representative's annual "Special 301" report on IPR issues. See https://ustr.gov/sites/default/files/2015-Special-301-Report-FINAL.pdf.

20. Francis Cabot Lowell was unable to buy plans or drawings for the power looms that were essential for efficient production of modern textiles. So he talked his way into factories in Lancashire and made careful notes of the machinery so that he could replicate it back home. The role of textiles in the world economy of the 1820s was comparable to that of electronics today; what Lowell did would now be considered industrial espionage.

21. For an excellent, readable, and nontechnical introduction to the question of what innovation is, see Amar Bhidé, *The Venturesome Economy* (Princeton University Press, 2008).

22. Standard Chinese dictionaries translate *zizhu* as "independence, autonomy" (*Far East Chinese-English Dictionary* [Far East Book Company, 1993]) or "to act on one's own, decide for oneself" (*Hanying Cidian* [Commercial Press, 1995]). It is clearly related to the term *zizhuquan*, which is one of the Chinese words for "sovereignty."

23. As I document in chapter 11, virtually none of the value or technology embedded in an iPhone originates in China.

24. I am grateful to Mary Kay Magistad, author of a forthcoming book on Chinese innovation, and to Vijay Vaitheeswaran for discussions that informed these remarks. In the last couple of years, official publications have talked less about "indigenous innovation" and more about "innovation-led growth," which is an improvement. But the Made in China 2025 program clearly aims to increase the market share of Chinese-made goods, so the basic confusion between innovation and autonomy still holds.

CHAPTER 4

1. For historical US urban population data, see http://www.census.gov/population/www/censusdata/files/table-4.pdf. For South Korea, see the UN Population Division database, http://esa.un.org/unpd/wup. Combined size of New York and Boston metro areas drawn from http://www.census.gov/

popest/data/metro/totals/2013/. For international comparisons of urbanization rates, see World Bank/DRC 2014, 100–101.

2. Chinese officials and scholars have generally embraced the view that urbanization in and of itself is a driver of economic growth, and this is one reason
for ambitious urbanization targets. For a more skeptical view, that urbanization itself is not a proven cause of economic growth, see World Bank/DRC
2014, Box 1.1, 85.

3. Brookings Institution, Global Metro Monitor, http://www.brookings.edu/
research/reports2/2015/01/22-global-metro-monitor. The World Bank
defines the three stages of urbanization's economic impact as agglomera-
tion, specialization, and mobility; see World Bank/DRC 2014, 91ff.

4. Fang Cai and Dewen Wang, "The Sustainability of Economic Growth and
the Labor Contribution," *Economic Research Journal* 10 (1999): 62–68.

5. World Bank/DRC 2014, 74n1. "Natural increase" here means the growth in
urban population through births in urban households.

6. http://www.worldbank.org/en/news/press-release/2015/01/26/world-
bank-report-provides-new-data-to-help-ensure-urban-growth-benefits-the-
poor.

7. A good discussion of the problems of China's urban population data is
OECD 2015, 31–37.

8. World Bank/DRC 2014, 5. An even more pessimistic view was that of the
670 million urban residents identified by the 2010 census, 314 million or
47 percent did not hold urban hukou. See World Bank/DRC 2014, 89.

9. See Tom Miller, *China's Urban Billion: The Story behind the Biggest Migration in
Human History* (Asian Arguments, 2012), 33ff.

10. For the relative efficiency of larger and denser cities, see World Bank/DRC
2014, 7–8. An alternative view, which stresses that productivity benefits arise
not because of sheer population density but by "the ease with which people
can interact with large numbers of other people," is in OECD 2015, 44–47.

11. Relative wages: World Bank/DRC, 180; on social mobility see World Bank/
DRC, 179.

12. Rosealea Yao, "Housing and Construction Review," Gavekal Dragonomics
research note, November 2014. The government's full urbanization strategy document, *Guojia xinxing chengzhenhua guihua* ("National New-Style
Urbanization Program"), is available in Chinese at http://www.51baogao.
cn/free/xinxingchengzhenhua_pdf.shtml.

13. For a comprehensive discussion of these issues, see World Bank/DRC 2014,
186–95.

14. For the estimate of the value of the housing wealth transfer, see Arthur
Kroeber, Rosealea Yao, and Pei Zhuan, "Housing: A Room of One's Own,"
China Economic Quarterly (December 2007): 53–58.

15. Work by my colleague Rosealea Yao suggests that 46 percent of all urban
housing built in China from 2000 to 2012 satisfied upgrading demand, while
only 36 percent reflected new demand from the increased urban population. The remaining 18 percent was replacement of demolished housing.
Yao 2014.

16. World Bank/DRC 2014, 21. Given that migrants make up about 40 percent of
the urban population, this implies an overall urban home-ownership ratio
of around 50 percent. The US homeownership rate is now 65 percent. The

US rate can be viewed on the handy website of the St. Louis Federal Reserve, http://research.stlouisfed.org/fred2/series/USHOWN/.

17. House price rises calculated from official data on the average cost of housing per square meter, NBS/CEIC. House prices in the most desirable neighborhoods, such as central Beijing and Shanghai, rose much more, sometimes by a factor of eight or ten.

18. In the two decades before the US housing bubble of the early 2000s, the median US house price was 2.6 times the median household income, although figures for individual cities fluctuated between 2 and 5. See http://www.forbes.com/sites/zillow/2013/04/16/high-home-price-to-income-ratios-hiding-behind-low-mortgage-rates/.

19. The high down-payment requirements for investment properties were relaxed in most cities in 2014.

20. Yao 2014.

21. For a discussion of social housing programs, see World Bank/DRC 2014, 22–23.

22. Some officials in the Ministry of Housing and Urban-Rural Development have begun to argue publicly in favor of setting up a Fannie Mae–like agency in China.

23. Ports data courtesy of Charles de Trenck, a Hong Kong–based shipping analyst.

24. Electricity capacity: China Statistical Yearbook 2014 and China Daily http://www.chinadaily.com.cn/business/chinadata/2015-02/13/content_19582590.htm. Data on highways, railways, and Internet and mobile phone use compiled from the CEIC database by my colleague Rosealea Yao.

25. A detailed justification of the high-speed rail program is in Will Freeman, "High-speed Rail: The Iron Rooster Spiffs Up," *China Economic Quarterly* (June 2010), 7–9. By 2013, the high-speed network was carrying twice as many passengers as the national airline system. See Keith Bradsher, "Speedy Trains Transform China," *New York Times*, September 23, 2013.

26. A vivid account of the railway corruption scandal, and of the safety problems it caused, is in Evan Osnos, "Boss Rail," *New Yorker*, October 22, 2012, http://www.newyorker.com/magazine/2012/10/22/boss-rail. Hasty installation of signals on one high-speed rail route helped cause an infamous derailment in 2011 that killed 40 passengers and led to national outrage when photos circulated on the Internet of local officials trying to bury the derailed train.

CHAPTER 5

1. The most forceful expression of the private-sector advance story is Lardy 2014. An important articulation of the state-sector dominance view is Yasheng Huang 2008; a similar view is advanced by Tsai and Naughton, "State Capitalism and the Chinese Economic Miracle" in Barry Naughton and Kellee S. Tsai, eds., *State Capitalism, Institutional Adaptation, and the Chinese Miracle* (Cambridge University Press, 2015).

2. The best description of China's state-owned enterprise system is Li-Wen Lin and Curtis J. Milhaupt, "We are the (National) Champions: Understanding the Mechanisms of State Capitalism in China," *Stanford Law Review*, Vol 65: 697, April 2013 (http://works/bepress.com/curtis_milhaupt/20).

My account draws heavily on theirs. For a detailed understanding of SASAC and its role, the best source is a series of articles by Barry Naughton for the Hoover Institution's *China Leadership Monitor* (http://www.hoover.org/publications/china-leadership-monitor), specifically: "The State Asset Commission: A Powerful New Government Body" (Issue 8, October 2003); "SASAC Rising" (Issue 14, April 2005); "Claiming Profit for the State: SASAC and the Capital Management Budget" (Issue 18, July 2006); "SASAC and Rising Corporate Power in China" (Issue 24, March 2008); "Loans, Firms and Steel: Is the State Advancing at the Expense of the Private Sector?" (Issue 30, November 2009).

3. The idea of these "soft budget constraints" as an essential feature of Communist economies was pioneered by Janos Kornai, "The Soft Budget Constraint," *Kyklos*, 39 (1986): 3–30 (http://www.kornai-janos.hu/Kornai1986%20The%20Soft%20budget%20Constraint%20-%20Kyklos.pdf).

4. SASAC is the supervisory agency only for nonfinancial SOE groups. Financial SOEs such as the big banks and insurance companies are controlled by the Ministry of Finance, in many cases via an intermediate holding company called Central Huijin.

5. Lardy 2014, 51.

6. SASAC reported that as of the end of 2011, over 90 percent of SOEs nationally, and 72 percent of centrally controlled SOEs, had corporatized. In other words, over a quarter of central SOEs still had *not* corporatized. See "Report of the State Council on the Reform and Development of State-Owned Enterprises," October 26, 2012. Available at http://www.npc.gov.cn/npc/xinwen/2012-10/26/content_1740994.htm (in Chinese).

7. For the role of agencies other than SASAC, see Lin and Milhaupt 2013, 726; and Naughton March 2008. For bureaucratic rank, see Lin and Milhaupt 2013, 736. For control over senior appointments, see Lin and Milhaupt 2013, 738.

8. Again, these figures refer to individual SOE companies (layers 2 and 3 in the organizational structure we outlined above), not to the unlisted parent group companies.

9. Also see Barry Naughton, "SOE Policy: Profiting the SASAC Way," *China Economic Quarterly* (June 2008); and Andrew Batson, "Fixing China's State Sector," Paulson Institute Policy Memorandum, January 2014. Some analysts, notably the China Unirule Institute of Economics, argue that SOE profits in the 2000s were due entirely to preferential access to cheap land and capital. See Unirule Institute of Economics, "The Nature, Performance and Reform of the State-Owned Enterprises," April 12, 2011. This is implausible, since SOEs had just as much if not more access to cheap land and capital before 1998, and managed to rack up huge losses nonetheless. Hidden subsidies no doubt played a significant role in SOE profits, but they cannot explain the improvement in SOE financial performance between the 1990s and the 2000s.

10. Ministry of Finance, Finance Yearbook 2014.

11. See Przemyslaw Kowalski, Max Büge, Monika Sztajerowska, and Matias Egeland, "State-Owned Enterprises: Trade Effects and Policy Implications," OECD Trade Policy Papers No. 147 (2013), http://dx.doi.org/10.1787/5k4869ckqk7l-en. Technically, these data are expressed as a percentage of

Gross National Income (GNI), which is GDP plus net income from abroad. In practice the difference between GDP and GNI is small, so for simplicity I have used GDP rather than GNI.

12. This estimate comes from Zhang Bin of the Institute of World Politics and Economics at the Chinese Academy of Social Sciences, in a draft paper, *Zhongguo jingji zengsu weihe fangman? Jingji jiansu, jinrong gao honggan yu zhengfu gaige de san nan xuanze* (China's Trilemma: Economic Slowdown, Financial Leverage and Government Reform).
13. Lardy 2014, 24–33.
14. For the lack of market exit, see Kennedy, "Wanted: More Creative Destruction," Gavekal Dragonomics research note, February 10, 2014. On the antimonopoly law, see US Chamber of Commerce, "Competing Interests in China's Competition Law Enforcement: China's Anti-Monopoly Law Application and the Role of Industrial Policy," September 2014, https://www.uschamber.com/report/competing-interests-chinas-competition-law-enforcement-chinas-anti-monopoly-law-application.
15. See Scott Kennedy, *The Business of Lobbying in China* (Harvard University Press, 2008); and Erica Downs, "Business Interest Groups in Chinese Politics: The Case of the Oil Companies," in Cheng Li, ed., *China's Changing Political Landscape* (Brookings Institution, 2008).
16. Lin and Milhaupt (2013) insightfully describe the relationship between SOEs and the state as one of "networked hierarchy."
17. Lardy 2014 argues strongly that the private sector has continued to expand at the state sector's expense. For the number of Chinese millionaires and billionaires, see the Hurun Report, http://www.hurun.net/EN/HuList.aspx.
18. Specifically, company registrations include many categories, such as collectives and joint-stock firms, which include both private and state-owned firms.
19. Sean Dougherty, Richard Herd, and Ping He, "Has a Private Sector Emerged in China's Industry? Evidence from a Quarter of a Million Chinese Firms," *China Economic Review* 18, no. 3 (2007): 309–34.
20. Lardy 2014, 74.
21. Ibid., 81.
22. For a careful discussion of the *guojin mintui* phenomenon, see two articles by Scott Kennedy, "Private Firms: Pink Capitalists In Bloom," *China Economic Quarterly* (June 2012): 37–42; and "Wanted: More Creative Destruction," Gavekal Dragonomics research note, February 10, 2014.

CHAPTER 6

1. Until recently, when Xi Jinping began a systematic and long lasting antigraft drive (discussed in chapter 10), high-profile corruption investigations were often politically motivated. Prominent examples were the prosecutions of Beijing mayor Chen Xitong in 1995 and of Shanghai Party Secretary Chen Liangyu a decade later. Each case brought down an official with a strong local power base who was seen as a threat by the national leader. Other prominent anticorruption drives that targeted powerful local networks, though not competitors for the nation's top job, included the crackdown on smuggling in south China in the late 1990s, which basically gutted the city

governments in several cities, including Xiamen and Shantou; and a sweep of gangster-run local governments in the northeast's Heilongjiang in the early 2000s.

2. A good comparison of governance in China and India is William Antholis, *Inside Out India and China: Local Politics Go Global* (Brookings Institution, 2013).

3. The lack of accountability of local governments should not be exaggerated. An argument can be made that unelected local governments in China have historically been more accountable to the needs of their constituents than are democratically elected local governments in India, whose mandate is not to maximize economic growth but to garner spoils for particular caste, language, or religious groups. See Antholis 2013, 33, for a comparison; and Lily L. Tsai, *Accountability Without Democracy* (Cambridge University Press, 2007) for a study of accountability mechanisms in Chinese local government.

4. Local governments are far less able to restrict trade and competition than in the 1980s and 1990s. See Barry Naughton, "How Much Can Regional Integration Do to Unify China's Markets," in *How Far Across the River: Chinese Policy Reform at the Millennium,* ed. Nicholas C. Hope et al. (Stanford University Press, 2003). But it is also clear that weak companies exit the market far more slowly in China than elsewhere—especially if they are state-owned—and this has largely to do with local support. See Scott Kennedy, "Wanted: More Creative Destruction," Gavekal Dragonomics research note, February 10, 2014. For a true market economy, both the entry of new players *and* the speedy exit of weak players are essential.

5. This is necessarily a simplified explanation; reality was not quite so centralized. In practice, localities controlled "extrabudgetary funds," which accounted for nearly a third of the finance for investment in the late 1970s (Naughton 1995, 43).

6. It is not clear how much of the post-1996 increase in overall revenue was a real increase, or just a better accounting of revenue that was there all along but hidden in various extrabudgetary funds. (Similarly, the apparent decline in revenue in the 1980s may have been due in part to revenues being squirreled away off-budget.) To this day, China's budgetary accounting is loose: a long-running effort to force each government agency to run all its revenues and expenses through a single account, visible to the Ministry of Finance, is far from complete.

7. For details see He Yuxin, "China Development Bank: The Best Bank in China?" Gavekal Dragonomics research note, July 1, 2010.

8. Only about 40 percent of local liabilities were local government financing vehicle loans; the remainder were a patchwork of other types of borrowing, as well as guarantees and contingent liabilities that local governments were not directly responsible for, but could be forced to honor if economic conditions got worse. See National Audit Office, "Audit Results of Nationwide Governmental Debts," December 30, 2013, http://www.cnao.gov.cn/main/articleshow_ArtID_1335.htm.

9. For the IMF estimate, see IMF, Article IV Consultation, Staff Report (2014), http://www.imf.org/external/pubs/ft/scr/2014/cr14235.pdf, 9 and 26–27. Some private estimates put the total government debt burden higher, at around 70 percent of GDP, but these calculations include various items,

such as bills issued by the central bank and bonds issued by state-owned policy banks, that are not normally counted as sovereign debt. See Janet Zhang, "The Magic Mountain: China's Public Debt," Gavekal Dragonomics research note, April 20, 2011. The IMF notes that while the current *level* of government debt is not a concern, the rate of increase is a worry: the IMF estimates that the true combined budget deficit is around 7 percent of GDP, compared to the 2 percent reported by the government.

10. Problems of the transfer system are detailed in Lou Jiwei, ed., *Public Finance in China: Reform and Growth for a Harmonious Society* (World Bank, 2008), especially David Dollar and Bert Hofman, "Intergovernmental Fiscal Reforms, Expenditure Assignment, and Governance" (39–52); and Anwar Shah and Chunli Shen, "Fine-Tuning the Intergovernmental Transfer System to Create a Harmonious Society and Level Playing Field for Regional Development (129–54.) See also Xiao Wang and Richard Herd, "The System of Revenue Sharing and Fiscal Transfers in China," OECD Economics Department Working Papers, No. 1030 (OECD Publishing, 2013).

11. The reasons why the tax structure leads localities to overemphasize industry and infrastructure are complex and technical. For a good explanation, see World Bank/DRC 2014, 57; and Xinye Zheng and Li Zhang, "Fiscal Reform: A Better Way to Tax and Spend," *China Economic Quarterly*, March 2013, 26–30. A key factor is China's VAT system. In most countries VAT is effectively a consumption tax, since most of the net amount is paid by final goods consumers. China however has a "production VAT," in which much of the net receipts come from businesses, especially those investing heavily in capital equipment. And unlike in most other countries, services are excluded from VAT, and service firms instead pay a "business tax" on their revenues (see Ehtisham Ahmad, "Taxation Reforms and the Sequencing of Intergovernmental Reforms in China: Preconditions for a *Xiaokang* Society," in Lou 2008). This means that service enterprises are heavily taxed, and users of these services cannot deduct their payments from their VAT obligations as they can for purchases of materials. Another problem is that taxes shared by local and central governments, such as VAT and corporate income tax, are shared based on the location of collection. So cities are extremely reluctant to permit enterprises to move to new locations or to be absorbed by another enterprise that pays tax in a different jurisdiction. In order to keep VAT payments flowing from a struggling enterprise, local governments will often give the firm some kind of benefit that does not impose an immediate budgetary impact, such as access to loans from a friendly local bank branch, cheaper electricity, or a discount on land.

12. For a good discussion of the property tax and its problems, see World Bank/DRC 2014, 56 and 292–97.

13. For an outline of the priorities that eventually found their way into the fiscal reform package, see Lou Jiwei's first budget report as finance minister, "Report on the Implementation of the Central and Local Budgets in 2013 and on the Draft Central and Local Budgets for 2014" (Ministry of Finance 2014). For a discussion of the impact of the revised budget law (in Chinese), see Lou's interview with the *People's Daily*, "Xin yusuanfa: dajian xiandai caizheng zhidu kuangjia" ("The New Budget Law: Framework for Building

a Modern Fiscal System"), *People's Daily,* September 11, 2014, http://politics. people.com.cn/n/2014/0911/c1001-25637407.html.

14. In June 2015 a vice commissioner of the National Development and Reform Commission, Lian Weiliang, indicated in a speech that NDRC would not tolerate bond-market defaults. See http://www.sdpc.gov.cn/gzdt/201507/t20150701_710447.html.

15. In a strict economic sense, of course, all taxes in all countries are ultimately levied on individuals, and the only question is whether they are collected directly or indirectly via corporations. But practically and politically, it often makes a big difference whether taxes are seen to be collected from individuals or from corporations.

CHAPTER 7

1. Much of the following discussion is drawn from Nicholas Lardy *China's Unfinished Economic Revolution* (Brookings Institution, 1998) and Nicholas Lardy, *Markets Over Mao* (Peterson Institute of International Economics, 2014).

2. Naughton 2007, 462.

3. Lardy 1998, 119.

4. Agricultural Bank of China was the last of the Big Four to list, in 2010.

5. These are the China Development Bank (CDB), the Agricultural Development Bank of China, and the China Export-Import Bank. Of these three the CDB (which from 1997 to 2013 was run skillfully by Chen Yuan, the son of Deng's old rival Chen Yun) became by far the most important. It financed a wide range of infrastructure projects, pioneered the land-based financing mechanism for local governments, and beginning in the mid-2000s became a major financier of China's global resource investments. See Erica S. Downs, "Inside China, Inc: China Development Bank's Cross-Border Energy Deals," Brookings Institution China Center Monograph, March 21, 2011; and Michael Forsythe and Henry Sanderson, *China's Superbank* (Bloomberg Press, 2013).

6. Lardy 2014, 130.

7. In 1998 the banks got Rmb 270 billion in new capital by issuing special bonds that were purchased by MOF. But MOF did not actually have the money to pay for these bonds, so it gave the banks IOUs instead. Over the next several years, the banks earned high profits and paid a large chunk of those profits as dividends to MOF; and MOF then recycled these proceeds back into the banks, paying down their IOUs. In other words, the "capital" used to recapitalize the banks did not actually exist in 1998, but was created later out of bank profits. This sleight-of-hand worked because (a) the banks were part of a unified, closed system entirely owned by the government, without external shareholders or auditors who could force the banks into bankruptcy; and (b) structural reforms created vast new profitable lending opportunities.

8. In June 2008 total credit to the private sector in the United States was $24.4 trillion and bank deposits were $7 trillion. At the end of 2014 China's total private-sector credit was Rmb 122 trillion and bank deposits were Rmb 117 trillion (credit figures are from the Bank for International Settlements; deposit figures are from the FDIC for the United States and the People's Bank of China for China). Financial analysts often draw a distinction

between "liquidity" and "solvency" problems. You are insolvent when the true value of your assets is less than your liabilities; in this case an infusion of liquid funds can stave off the inevitable for a little while, but it cannot save you. Solvency, though, is a moving target, because the value of assets fluctuates. An argument in favor of bank bailouts during financial crises is that at such times the market value of assets falls far below their "true" or economic value, because everyone is selling assets at the same time. As a result, some banks or companies may appear to be insolvent even though they are really not, based on the long-run economic value of their assets. So it makes sense for the government to provide enough liquidity to rein in the fire sale of assets. In a fast-growing developing economy like China, the main systemic risk is lack of liquidity, not insolvency, because asset prices have a high chance of rising steeply over a five- to ten-year period. This means that even banks that are technically insolvent, as China's were in the late 1990s, can almost always return to solvency given some liquidity and time. The problem is that when such a country matures and shifts down to a lower trend growth rate, large rises in asset prices are no longer guaranteed, and insolvency starts to become a greater risk.

9. See Richard Koo, *The Holy Grail of Macroeconomics: Lessons from Japan's Great Recession* (John Wiley & Sons, 2009).

10. The banks transferred Rmb 1.4 trillion to the asset management companies, 18 percent of 1999 GDP as originally reported. (Subsequent revisions to GDP data mean the true ratio was about 15 percent, but that was not the number officials worked with at the time.) By 2009 the net remaining balance was Rmb 1.2 trillion, meaning that asset management companies recovered less than 15 percent of the loans' face value from the original borrowers.

11. Lardy 2014, 104–7.

12. Note that what matters for this calculation is the *nominal* GDP growth rate, since the principal value of debt is fixed in nominal terms. One of the reasons China wriggled out of its debt problems so easily in the 2000s was that nominal GDP grew at an average rate of nearly 17 percent a year from 2003 through 2011. Today, however, the nominal GDP growth rate is around 7 percent, and there seems little likelihood that this rate will increase substantially in the coming years. So in order for the debt-to-GDP ratio to stabilize, credit growth must slow from its current rate of around 14 percent to about half that.

13. The term "shadow banking" seems to have been coined in 2007 by Paul McCulley, the respected chief economist at the investment firm PIMCO. My own view is that the term as commonly used now is not really helpful, since it bunches together many different kinds of financial activity of widely varying levels of risk, and unfairly implies that it is all potentially nefarious.

14. See Financial Stability Board, *Global Shadow Banking Monitoring Report 2014*, available at http://www.financialstabilityboard.org/wp-content/uploads/r_141030.pdf. A credible analysis by Standard Chartered Bank puts the size of China's shadow sector at an even smaller 8 percent to 14 percent of GDP. See Stephen Green, Wei Li, and Lan Shan, "Your Map of the Expanding Credit Universe," Standard Chartered research note, March 3, 2014.

15. See Nicholas Borst, "Shadow Deposits as a Source of Financial Instability: Lessons from the American Experience for China," Peterson Institute for International Economics Policy Brief 13–14, May 2013, http://www.piie.com/publications/interstitial.cfm?ResearchID=2410.

16. In early 2015, the government announced its intention to amend the banking law to abolish the loan-to-deposit ratio cap, and stopped enforcing the cap.

17. At the end of 1993, the official exchange rate was 5.8 to the dollar; and the market-based "swap rate," which traders used, was 8.7 to the dollar. In January 1994 the official exchange rate was set at 8.7 and allowed to float fairly freely, and the separate swap rate was abolished.

18. Data on Rmb deposits, bond issuance, and Hong Kong from the Hong Kong Monetary Authority, http://www.hkma.gov.hk/eng/market-data-and-statistics/monthly-statistical-bulletin/.

19. For foreign exchange trading data, see Bank for International Settlements, "Triennial Survey of Foreign Exchange and Derivatives Market Activity in 2013," December 8, 2013, http://www.bis.org/publ/rpfx13.htm. For international bond market data, see http://www.bis.org/statistics/r_qa1412_hanx12a.pdf.

20. For a comprehensive discussion of the renminbi internationalization program and its relationship to economic reform, see Arthur Kroeber, "China's Global Currency: Lever for Financial Reform," Brookings Tsinghua Center for Public Policy, Monograph Series No. 3, April 2013, http://www.brookings.edu/research/papers/2013/04/china-global-currency-financial-reform-kroeber; and Eswar Prasad and Lei Ye, "The Renminbi's Role in the Global Monetary System," Brookings Institution, February 2012, http://www.brookings.edu/research/reports/2012/02/renminbi-monetary-system-prasad.

21. The IMF uses the SDR to denominate the loans it makes to member countries. Under the new formula approved by the IMF board on November 30, 2015, the renminbi has an 11 percent weight in the SDR, compared to 40 percent for the US dollar, 32 percent for the euro, and 9 percent each for the yen and the pound sterling. This weight mainly reflects China's importance as a trading country. The renminbi's share of global reserve assets is much lower, around 1 percent. See "China's Yuan in the SDR Basket," *Bloomberg China Brief*, November 30, 2015, http://newsletters.briefs.bloomberg.com/document/46z1i9i3mb3z15mu930/front.

22. A standard measure of financial openness is the Chinn-Ito index, according to which China has one of the most closed financial systems in the world. See http://econbrowser.com/archives/2014/08/chinn-ito-financial-openness-index-updated-to-2012. Another index found that of 100 countries surveyed, only six had more stringent capital controls than China; of these six only India could be considered a major economy. See Andres Fernandez et al., "Capital Control Measures: A New Dataset," NBER Working Papers No. 20970, February 2015; data available at http://www.columbia.edu/~mu2166/fkrsu/fkrsu.xls. For the renminbi to become a serious reserve currency, foreign investors need to be able to invest freely in financial assets—especially government bonds—in China's onshore markets (not just in Hong Kong), and to move their money in and out of China's markets from day to day as their needs change. Right now this is impossible, both because trading

on China's bond markets is so thin that there is no guarantee that you can make a large purchase or sale on a given day at a price you like; and because capital controls make it time consuming to move money out of China. Given the authorities' obsession with maintaining financial stability, it is unlikely that these conditions will change any time soon.

CHAPTER 8

1. This calculation is based on energy consumption data from the *BP Statistical Review of World Energy 2015*, and GDP data (at current exchange rates) from the World Bank's World Development indicators. The BP review presents energy consumption data in million metric tons of oil equivalent (mtoe), which I have converted into barrels at the standard rate of 1 ton = 7.33 barrels. China's energy intensity relative to GDP would look less dire if we used a purchasing-power parity (PPP) measure of GDP, which adjusted up the value of China's nontradable goods and services. But since the vast majority of energy in China goes into the production of tradable goods whose prices are more or less at global levels, GDP at the current exchange rate seems to me the more appropriate denominator.

2. Specifically, a power plant must burn about 10,500 British thermal units (BTUs) of coal to generate one kilowatt hour of electricity; for natural gas the figure is about 8,000 BTUs. See http://www.eia.gov/tools/faqs/faq.cfm?id=107&t=3. For the coal shares in power generation, see *China Statistical Yearbook 2014*, http://www.eia.gov/tools/faqs/faq.cfm?id=427&t=3; and http://www.eea.europa.eu/data-and-maps/indicators/electricity-production-by-fuel-1/electricity-production-by-fuel-assessment-3.

3. Daniel H. Rosen and Trevor Houser, *China Energy: A Guide for the Perplexed* (Peterson Institute for International Economics, 2007), 23.

4. For the relative efficiency of US and Chinese coal-fired power plants, see http://www.chinafaqs.org/library/wri-average-coal-fired-power-plant-fleet-efficiency-china-and-us. For Chinese vehicle fuel efficiency standards, see Hongyan H. Oliver et al., "China's Fuel Economy Standards for Passenger Vehicles: Rationale, Policy Process and Impacts," Discussion Paper 2009-03 (March 2009), Belfer Center for Science and International Affairs, Harvard Kennedy School.

5. For a detailed discussion of the major sources of inefficiencies, and potential efficiency gains, see Nan Zhou et al., "China's Energy and Emissions Outlook to 2050: Perspectives from Bottom-Up Energy End-Use Model," *Energy Policy* 53 (February 2013): 14ff.

6. Figures on energy mix from *BP Statistical Review 2015*; fuel breakdown of China's power production from the National Bureau of Statistics (NBS). For projections of the energy mix in 2050, see Zhou et al. (2013).

7. China originally reported that coal use declined by 2.9 percent in 2014, but a comprehensive revision of historical energy statistics showed that total coal consumption was about 16 percent higher than previously estimated, and that gross coal use in 2014 was essentially flat. On the other hand, the heat content of this previously hidden coal was very low, so the upward revisions to energy use and CO_2 emissions were smaller. The revisions

confirmed, however, that coal use grew little in 2012–2014; and the most recent data suggests that coal use did in fact decline in 2015. See Rosealea Yao, "Finding the Missing Coal," Gavekal Dragonomics research note, December 3, 2015.

8. Data on GHG emissions from World Resources Institute CAIT database. The six main greenhouse gases are CO_2, methane, nitrous oxide, and three fluorine-based gases. About three-quarters of global greenhouse gas emissions are CO_2, so China's emissions are more CO_2-heavy than the average. The CO_2 emissions of different fuels are at http://www.eia.gov/tools/faqs/faq.cfm?id=73&t=11.

9. On "Airpocalypse" and the general question of air pollution from $PM_{2.5}$ small particulates, note that while China's average $PM_{2.5}$ level of about 90 micrograms per cubic meter (μ/m^3) is often compared with the World Health Organization's (WHO) "safe" standard of 25 μ/m^3, the WHO in fact has a graded set of recommended levels (70, 50, and 30 μ/m^3), recognizing that developing countries are likely to have higher emissions in the early stages of industrialization. See WHO, http://whqlibdoc.who.int/hq/2006/WHO_SDE_PHE_OEH_06.02_eng.pdf, 12. For a dense but useful technical discussion of China's air pollution problems, progress so far, and policy prescriptions, see Chris P. Nielsen and Mun S. Ho, eds., *Clearing the Air* (MIT Press, 2007); and Chris P. Nielsen and Mun S. Ho, *Clearer Skies over China* (MIT Press, 2013).

10. For discussion of the Great Smog and a comparable disaster in Donora, Pennsylvania in 1948, see Stephen Mihm, http://www.bloombergview.com/articles/2013-11-06/londons-great-smog-provides-lessons-for-china.

11. The technical term for this relationship between income and environmental protection is the "Environmental Kuznets Curve" (EKC), so named because of the analogy with Simon Kuznets's theory that income inequality rises in the early stages of development but abates as a country grows richer (see chapter 11 for a discussion of inequality and the classic Kuznets curve). Like the traditional Kuznets curve for inequality, the EKC has been criticized on empirical grounds. See David I. Stern, "The Rise and Fall of the Environmental Kuznets Curve," *World Development* 32, no. 8 (2004): 1419–39, which argues that many developing countries are tackling environmental problems earlier than the classic EKC would predict.

12. For details on the issues and data discussed in this section, see Calvin Quek, "Bringing Back the Blue Sky Days," *China Economic Quarterly*, September 2014; Angel Hsu, "A Real War, More Ammo Required," *China Economic Quarterly*, September 2014; and Michal Meidan and Rosealea Yao, "King Coal's Long, Slow Decline," *China Economic Quarterly*, March 2014. On the primacy of coal in emissions, the Beijing office of Greenpeace estimates that coal combustion accounts for 45 percent to 50 percent of $PM_{2.5}$ emissions, while transport accounts for 15 percent to 20 percent (Quek 2014). Nielsen and Ho (2007, 57) find that a quarter of the health damage from air pollution came from the electricity sector, and another quarter from cement, chemicals, and steel. In their later work they find that the cement, brick, and glass industries account for 54 percent of total

particulate pollution, with electricity generation and metals smelting contributing another 14 percent. For sulfur dioxide emissions, power generation (51 percent) is the main culprit, with cement, brick, glass, and metals accounting for another 11 percent.

13. A good assessment of the industrial energy campaign is Jing Ke et al., "China's Industrial Energy Consumption Trends and Impacts of the Top-1000 Enterprises Energy-Saving Program and the Ten Key Energy-Saving Projects," *Energy Policy* 50 (November 2012), 562–69.

14. For energy price data, see *Key China Energy Statistics 2014* (Lawrence Berkeley National Laboratory China Energy Group, 2014).

CHAPTER 9

1. Yang Jisheng, *Tombstone: The Untold Story of Mao's Great Famine* (Allen Lane, 2012); and Judith Banister, *China's Changing Population* (Stanford University Press, 1987).

2. Guo Zhigang, "Family Planning Policy: Too Few By Far," *China Economic Quarterly* (June 2012): 22–26.

3. In 2014 China's labor force was 770 million people while that of the United States was 157 million. Figures from the CEIC database for China and from the Bureau of Labor Statistics for the United States. See http://data.bls.gov.

4. Wang Feng, "Demographic Transition: Racing towards the Precipice," *China Economic Quarterly* (June 2012): 17–21; and Judith Banister, "Labor Force: No Need to Panic," *China Economic Quarterly* (June 2012): 27–30.

5. Guo 2012.

6. Fertility data from the World Bank's World Development Indicators, http://data.worldbank.org. A comprehensive and scathing analysis of the one-child policy is Martin King Whyte, Wang Feng, and Yong Cai, "Challenging Myths About China's One-Child Policy," *China Journal* 74 (2015): 144–59.

7. Guo 2012.

8. Lardy 2014, 214–15.

9. Fang Cai, Albert Park, and Yaohui Zhao, "The Chinese Labor Market in the Reform Era," in Loren Brandt and Thomas G. Rawski, eds., *China's Great Economic Transformation* (Cambridge: Cambridge University Press, 2008), 171.

10. Oi 1999, 62–66; the term "collective" generally implies that an enterprise is controlled by a state entity at lower than the city level.

11. Cai et al. 2008, 176–77.

12. US nonfarm employment fell from a peak of 138.4 million in January 2008 to a trough of 129.7 million in December 2010. US manufacturing employment peaked at 19.5 million in 1979 and fell to 11.5 million in 2009. Data from the Bureau of Labor Statistics.

13. The official "registered urban unemployment" statistic, which has remained virtually static at just over 4 percent for more than a decade, is widely considered useless, since it excludes migrant workers and people who do not register for unemployment benefits. The 2013 unemployment rate of 5 percent was based on a survey published by the National

Development and Reform Commission; the government appears to conduct the survey regularly but usually does not publish the data. Various other estimates by government think tanks and independent scholars have come up with unemployment rates of anywhere from 6 percent to 10 percent since 2008. See "China Announces Survey-Based Unemployment Rate of Around 5 Pct," *Caijing*, August 2, 2013, http://english.caijing.com.cn/2013-08-02/113123807.html; and Yang Liu, "The Chinese Labour Market: High Unemployment Coexisting with a Labour Shortage," July 19, 2014, http://www.voxeu.org/article/china-s-unemployment-and-labour-shortage.

14. Cai et al. 2008, 179–82.
15. For the rise in the working-age population, see World Bank/DRC 2013, 277, fig. 4.5. For relative Chinese and Thai wage levels, see World Bank/DRC 2013, 349, fig. 5.12. The fall in the labor income share is from the flow of funds data in the national accounts. Two Chinese scholars, Bai Chong'en and Qian Zhenjie, found that the household share of national income (which includes financial income as well as wage income) fell from 67 percent in 1996 to 54 percent in 2005. See Bai and Qian, "Who Is the Predator, Who the Prey: An Analysis of Changes in the State of China's National Income Distribution," *Social Sciences in China* 30, no. 4 (November 2009): 179–205. Varying estimates of China's Gini coefficient are examined in more detail in chapter 11; all estimates agree that China's Gini rose substantially from 1995 to 2010. The figures cited here are from World Bank/DRC 2013, 275; and the National Bureau of Statistics.
16. The relevance of Lewis's work to China was first highlighted by an important Chinese labor economist, Cai Fang, in a 2008 book (*Lewis Turning Point: A Coming New Stage of China's Economic Development;* in Chinese), which was originally treated skeptically by government officials who assumed that China's overabundant labor supply was a permanent condition. Cai's views have since become widely accepted. For a summary in English, see Cai Fang, "Approaching a Triumphal Span: How Far Is China towards Its Lewisian Turning Point?" UNU-WIDER Research Paper No. 2008/09, February 2008, http://iple.cass.cn/upload/2012/06/d20120606103343081.pdf.
17. W. Arthur Lewis, "Economic Development with Unlimited Supplies of Labour," *Manchester School of Economic and Social Studies* 22 (1954): 139–91. Available at http://www.globelicsacademy.net/2008/2008_lectures/lewis%20unlimited%20labor%20supply%201954.pdf. A brief summary and explanation of its relevance to China is in World Bank/DRC 2014, 89. Lewis's detailed views are subject to various objections: in particular, some developing countries such as China have seen strong growth in nominal and real wages during the "unlimited labor" phase. But as a stylistic depiction of the dynamics of growth in a developing economy, and how they differ from those of rich countries, the Lewis model remains illuminating.
18. Specifically, from 230 million in 2010 to 150 million in 2023, a 35 percent decline. See Arthur Kroeber, "Economic Rebalancing: The End of Surplus Labor," *China Economic Quarterly* (March 2010): 35–46.
19. World Bank/DRC 2014, 180, shows migrant wages rose from 52 percent of urban hukou in 2007 to 65 percent in 2012, and the wage gap for comparable work has vanished.

20. For total migrant numbers, see Lardy 2014, 17. For the breakdown of migrant origins and destinations, see World Bank/DRC 2014, 98, table 1.4 and figure 1.11.
21. For estimates of rural surplus labor, see World Bank/DRC 2014, 100. For estimates of total migrant flows and ultimate urban population, see World Bank/DRC 2014, 114.
22. Child labor was legal in the United States until 1938, when the United States was by some measures more prosperous than China today. Federal restrictions on child labor still do not apply to agriculture.
23. Proof that this little sermonette is still needed comes from the extraordinary success of a January 2012 segment of the popular US radio program *This American Life*, in which performance artist Mike Daisey purported to document atrocious conditions at Chinese factories. The segment became the most downloaded one in the program's history. Daisey's account was quickly demolished by Western reporters in China, and the program devoted another hour-long segment to a full retraction (http://www.thisamerican-life.org/radio-archives/episode/460/retraction). A carefully reported and sensitive account of the lives and struggles of Chinese migrant workers is Leslie Chang, *Factory Girls: From Village to City in a Changing China* (Spiegel & Grau, 2008). For a well-informed view of China's many labor problems, see China Labor Bulletin, www.clb.org.hk.

CHAPTER 10

1. In the "expenditure" breakdown, GDP is made up of gross capital formation (investment), consumer spending, government spending, and net exports. There are two other ways of breaking down GDP. The "production approach" measures the economy as the sum of value added in agriculture, industry, construction, and services. The "income" approach divides it into wages, corporate profits, and government tax revenue. The expenditure approach is the one most commonly used by economists and government statisticians. China is unusual in that it mainly reports GDP in production terms, publishing expenditure data in much less detail and with a long lag.
2. The remaining 19 percent of GDP is made up of government spending, exports, and inventories, which are sometimes counted as part of investment. In this book I have used the narrower measure of investment, excluding inventory accumulation. This is because from 1980 to 1996 inventories were an unusually large share of the economy (7 percent on average), thanks to the huge number of inefficient state-owned factories producing goods no one wanted to buy. These inventories were liquidated under the SOE reforms of 1995–2005; since 2000 inventories have averaged around 2 percent of GDP. Including inventories substantially overstates the level of *productive* investment in the 1980s, and obscures the underlying trend of a steady increase in productive investment in the first two decades of reform. Including inventories, China's investment-to-GDP ratio has been around 48 percent since 2010.
3. See for this comparison Arthur Kroeber, "China's Consumption Paradox: Causes And Consequences," *Eurasian Geography and Economics* 52, no. 3 (2011):

330–46. Japan's consumption rate fell by 14 percentage points (pp) (66 percent to 52 percent) between 1955 and 1970; Taiwan's by 9 pp (62 percent to 53 percent) between 1974 and 1986; and South Korea's by an astonishing 30 pp (80 percent to 50 percent) between 1967 and 1988. In this context China's 16 pp decline (51 percent to 35 percent) between 1989 and 2010 seems far from extraordinary.

4. That is, $10,000 of per capita GDP, times 50 percent (the household income share of GDP), times 67 percent (the share of household income that is spent rather than saved).

5. The United States consumption ratio, at 68 percent, is unusually high. This is important to note, since US-centric economists often present the American economic structure as "normal" even though it is in fact rather abnormal. More relevant comparisons for China are its East Asian neighbors South Korea, Taiwan, and Japan, which have household consumption ratios of about 50 percent, 55 percent, and 60 percent respectively.

6. "Housing services" in economic jargon means the part of housing expenditure that represents consumption of the "service" of having a place to live, as opposed to investment in real estate. For renters, this is simply the amount of the rent they pay. For homeowners the calculation is more complicated, since their mortgage payments include both an implicit purchase of housing services and the purchase of an asset. Statisticians usually compute the services part by assigning an "imputed rent" to owner-occupied housing, based on average rental prices. In a country like China with a relatively small rental market for which data is poor, this is hard to do.

7. Lardy 2012, Appendix A, suggests that a proper accounting for housing services would add three to four percentage points to the consumption ratio. Thomas Gatley ("China's Missing Consumption," Gavekal Dragonomics research note, July 2013) argues that the official data undercounts not only housing services but also other household services and, surprisingly, purchases of cars and cell phones. Two Shanghai scholars, Zhu Tian and Zhang Jun, estimate that the consumption ratio should be adjusted up by 10 to 15 percentage points, thanks to unrecorded spending on these items and health and education; see Stephen Green, "China Is Not Really That Imbalanced," Standard Chartered Bank research note, September 24, 2013.

8. World Bank/DRC 2014, 104–5. The World Bank's income thresholds are in 2005 dollars at purchasing power parity (PPP). It found that about 20 percent of urban dwellers, but only 3 percent of rural residents, qualified as middle class.

9. These thresholds are adapted from Michael Silverstein, Abheek Singhi, Carol Liao, David Michael, and Simon Targett, *The $10 Trillion Prize: Captivating the Newly Affluent in China and India* (Harvard Business Review Press, 2012), using the procedure followed by Thomas Gatley, "Accelerating into Affluence," *China Economic Quarterly*, March 2013. The average household size in China is three people, so to convert these figures into per capita numbers one must divide by three. A household with annual income of $13,000 equates to three people each with a per capita income of $4,333.

10. Ernan Cui, "Consumer Outlook and Thematic Review," Gavekal Dragonomics research note, November 2014.
11. In the fourth quarter of 2014, Lenovo, Huawei, and Xiaomi combined for 17 percent of global smartphone sales by volume. Samsung and Apple each had a market share of around 20 percent. See http://www.idc.com/prod-serv/smartphone-market-share.jsp.
12. Gatley 2013.
13. These figures are the five-year moving average of annual growth in per-capita consumer spending in US dollars at purchasing power parity, using the World Bank data used to generate Figure 10.1. Using Chinese national accounts data, and deflating household spending by the consumer price index, yields figures of 7.2 percent in 2001, 9.2 percent in 2008, and 10.5 percent in 2013.
14. Bai and Qian 2009.
15. See World Bank/DRC 2014, 198–214, for an excellent discussion of social welfare issues; also Thomas Gatley and Andrew Batson, "China's Welfare State: Mission Accomplished?" Gavekal Dragonomics research note, March 19, 2013.

CHAPTER 11

1. Gini index estimates vary because to calculate income inequality precisely would require knowing the exact income of every person in the country. In practice, Ginis are calculated using income surveys, and results can vary depending on the underlying survey data. For a good survey of private Gini estimates for China, see Yu Xie and Xiang Zhou, "Income Inequality in Today's China," *Proceedings of the National Academy of Sciences*, February 20, 2014, www.pnas.org/cgi/doi/10.1073/pnas.1403158111. For the comparison between China's high inequality and the relatively low inequality of other East Asian countries, see Martin King Whyte, "Soaring Income Gaps: China in Comparative Perspective," *Daedalus* 143, no. 2 (Spring 2014): 39–52. The World Bank Gini estimates for all countries are at http://data.worldbank.org/indicator/SI.POV.GINI; although note that its latest estimate of the Gini for China (0.41 for 2010) falls far below most private estimates and the Chinese government's own figures.
2. The data in Figure 11.1 comes from Christoph Lakner and Branko Milanovic, "Global Income Distribution: From the Fall of the Berlin Wall to the Great Recession," World Bank Policy Research Working Paper 6719, December 2013. Milanovic's work includes some of the most accessible cross-country comparisons of inequality over time. Note that the Gini index is an imperfect measure, because it is unable to provide a more detailed picture of how income or wealth might be concentrated in the top 1 percent or 10 percent of the population. For a critique of the Gini and other measures of inequality, such as the Theil index, see Thomas Piketty, *Capital in the Twenty-First Century* (Harvard University Press, 2014), 266–69.
3. Wide discussion of "mass incidents" began in 2006 with the publication of data from the Public Security Ministry indicating that mass incidents rose from under 20,000 a year in the late 1990s to 87,000 in 2005. Since then the

government has published no systematic data, nor has it offered definitions or breakdowns that would enable analysis of the existing data. For a good review of the problems, see this entry in the Zonaeuropa blog, http://www.zonaeuropa.com/20061115_1.htm; and Austin Strange, "Mass Incidents in Central China: Causes, Historical Factors and Implications for the PAP," *Monitor* 17, no. 2 (Summer 2012), http://web.wm.edu/so/monitor/issues/17-2/3-strange.pdf. For a summary of a 2012 report on mass incidents by the *Legal Daily* newspaper, which appears to reflect recent official thinking, see http://www.danwei.com/a-report-on-mass-incidents-in-china-in-2012/

4. Martin Whyte and Dong-Kyun Im, "Is the Social Volcano Still Dormant? Trends in Chinese Attitudes toward Inequality," *Social Science Research* 48 (2014): 62–76, http://scholar.harvard.edu/files/martinwhyte/files/pdf_0.pdf. Also, Martin Whyte, *Myth of the Social Volcano* (Stanford University Press, 2010). For Pew data, see http://www.pewglobal.org/database/. The Pew survey data are actually compiled by Horizon Research, the leading independent polling firm in China.

5. In 2013 China's total budgeted spending on domestic security at all levels of government was Rmb 769 billion, more than the Rmb 741 billion budgeted for the People's Liberation Army (PLA) (see "China Hikes Defense Budget, To Spend More on Domestic Security," Reuters, March 5, 2013). Full data for subsequent years are not available. Total military spending almost certainly exceeds the official PLA budget, so it may not be the case (as some journalistic accounts allege) that domestic security spending exceeds the national defense budget.

6. See World Bank/DRC 2014, 105.

7. Andrew Batson, "The Rise of the Middling," Gavekal Dragonomics research note, October 10, 2012.

8. The estimate of the top 10 percent's share of assets is from World Bank/DRC 2014, 16. For the rising public concern about inequality, see http://www.pewglobal.org/2012/10/16/growing-concerns-in-china-about-inequality-corruption/. In Pew's most recent (2015 survey), inequality continued to rank third, behind corruption and pollution. A majority of respondents expected the corruption problem to lessen in coming years, but were more pessimistic about pollution and inequality: http://www.pewglobal.org/2015/09/24/corruption-pollution-inequality-are-top-concerns-in-china/.

9. Simon Kuznets, "Economic Growth and Income Inequality," *American Economic Review* 45, no. 1 (1955): 1–28, available at https://www.aeaweb.org/aer/top20/45.1.1-28.pdf. Many researchers dispute Kuznets's hypothesis, noting that survey-based studies of income inequality over time in many countries fail to support it. Whyte (2014) exemplifies the skeptics. A detailed defense of Kuznets's basic insight, which I find persuasive, is James K. Galbraith, *Inequality and Instability: A Study of the World Economy Just before the Great Crisis* (Oxford University Press, 2012).

10. Andrew Batson and Thomas Gatley, "Inequality Is Improving, Discontent Is Not," Gavekal Dragonomics research note, November 4, 2013.

11. See Naughton 2007, 384–85.

12. For a vivid picture of official corruption in China's railway industry, see Evan Osnos, "Boss Rail," *New Yorker*, October 22, 2012, http://www.newyorker.com/magazine/2012/10/22/boss-rail.

13. A well-documented example is the 2007 IPO of Ping An Insurance, which proved immensely profitable to relatives of Premier Wen Jiabao. See David Barboza, "Lobbying, a Windfall, and a Leader's Family," *New York Times*, November 25, 2012.

14. For the China rich list, see http://www.hurun.net/EN/HuList.aspx. For Wen Jiabao's family wealth, see David Barboza, "Billions Amassed in the Shadows by the Family of China's Premier," *New York Times*, October 26, 2012. For that of Xi Jinping's family and other top leaders, see "Xi Jinping Millionaire Relations Reveal Fortunes of Elite," Bloomberg News, June 29, 2012; and "Heirs of Mao's Comrades Rise as New Capitalist Nobility," Bloomberg News, December 27, 2012. On Zhou Yongkang's wealth, there is no independent confirmation of the vast sums supposedly confiscated by police, and there is an ancient tradition in China of lurid and probably exaggerated accounts of the financial and sexual misdeeds of disgraced officials. When Zhou was actually tried, he was charged with accepting a mere $118,000 in bribes, and prosecutors alleged his family accumulated assets of $300 million. See http://www.wsj.com/articles/chinas-former-security-chief-zhou-yongkang-sentenced-to-life-in-prison-1434018450.

15. The best expression of this view is Pei 2006.

16. For a colorful account of this scandal, see Oliver August, *Inside the Red Mansion: On the Trail of China's Most Wanted Man* (Houghton Mifflin Harcourt, 2007).

17. A superb discussion of corruption in the reform era, on which I have drawn heavily, is Andrew Wedeman, *Double Paradox: Rapid Growth and Rising Corruption in China* (Cornell University Press, 2012).

18. "In order to promote the nation's governance system and modernize governance capacity, achieve the targets of the 'two one-hundred-year' struggles [i.e., a "moderately prosperous society" by 2021, the 100th anniversary of the founding of the Chinese Communist Party; and completing China's development as a strong, democratic, civilized, harmonious modern socialist state by 2049, the 100th anniversary of the founding of the People's Republic] and the great rejuvenation of the Chinese people and the China Dream ... it is necessary to persevere in having the party manage the party strictly, and to deepen the struggle for clean governance and anti-corruption." From "The 2013–2017 Work Plan to Establish a Robust System for Punishing and Preventing Corruption," http://news.xinhuanet.com/politics/2013-12/25/c_118708522.htm (in Chinese). The obscurity of this turgid prose is a good reminder of why deciphering the intentions of the Communist Party leadership remains such a specialized skill, even among Chinese people.

CHAPTER 12

1. See Andrew Batson and Janet Zhang, Capital Stock: How Much Is Too Much?" *China Economic Quarterly* (September 2011): 46–49. Using different depreciation rates yields a capital stock of anywhere from 2.1 to 2.9 times GDP in 2010; either way, the conclusion is that China does not have an unreasonably large capital stock.

2. This larger estimate of the stimulus is drawn from Victor Shih, "Local Government Debt: Big Rock Candy Mountain," *China Economic Quarterly* (June 2010): 26–32. It represents the total increase in credit over a hypothetical "business as usual" scenario. Rmb 11 trillion was about 15 percent of combined 2009–2010 GDP.

3. OECD, *Economic Survey of China 2015*, 26, fig. 12.

4. A good summary of the latest rules on the Internet is Hu Yong, "China's Tough New Internet Rules Explained," ChinaFile, September 10, 2014, http://www.chinafile.com/reporting-opinion/viewpoint/china-tough-new-internet-rules-explained.

5. The classic description of China's censorship system is Perry Link, "China: The Anaconda in the Chandelier," *New York Review of Books*, April 11, 2002.

6. See Alice Miller, "More Already on the Central Committee's Leading Small Groups," *China Leadership Monitor* No. 44 (July 28, 2014) (http://www.hoover.org/research/more-already-central-committees-leading-small-groups.)

7. By party protocol, the first plenary session or plenum of each five-year party congress session elects the new leadership team. The second, held a few months later, deals with other personnel issues. The third, held about a year after the first, is the traditional venue for the new leadership team to unveil its policy agenda.

8. See Batson, "Small Business to the Rescue?" *China Economic Quarterly* (September 2014): 40–44.

9. Examples include Minxin Pei, *China's Trapped Transition* (Harvard University Press, 2006); and Will Hutton, *The Writing on the Wall* (Free Press, 2006).

CHAPTER 13

1. See US Department of Defense, Base Structure Report, Fiscal Year 2009 Baseline (http://www.defense.gov/pubs/pdfs/2009Baseline.pdf).

2. In other words, so long as it is properly managed, the large national debt of the US is a strength, not a weakness. Alexander Hamilton recognized this over two centuries ago when he advocated the creation of a permanent debt in his *First Report on the Public Credit* in 1790, http://www.milestonedocuments.com/documents/view/alexander-hamiltons-first-report-on-public-credit/. The unique position of the US dollar was decried by Valéry Giscard d'Estaing, Charles De Gaulle's finance minister, as an "exorbitant privilege." John Connally, President Nixon's treasury secretary, boasted of this privilege when he told his European counterparts that the dollar "is our currency and your problem." For a full explanation of the dollar's role as the global reserve currency, see Barry Eichengreen, *Exorbitant Privilege: The Rise and Fall of the Dollar and the Future of the International Monetary System* (Oxford University Press, 2011). For a brief summary, see Arthur Kroeber, "Debt, Innovation and the Durable Dollar," *China Economic Quarterly* (December 2008): 50–55.

3. Strictly speaking, the European Union is the world's biggest economic unit. But this technical fact is not of much relevance in discussions of global political and economic power. Economically, despite its formal freedom of flows of labor and capital, the EU remains fragmented among its twenty-eight

member economies, which maintain separate governance structures, separate fiscal and financial systems, and in some cases currencies other than the euro (not to mention different languages). Politically and militarily, European force projection capacity is severely undermined by this fragmentation, and the geopolitical influence of "Europe" as a whole is arguably less significant than that of its most powerful member state, Germany.

4. In 2014 headline-writers jumped on a study by the World Bank reckoning that, adjusting for purchasing power parity (PPP), China's economy was already the biggest in the world. This conclusion ought not to be taken seriously. PPP is a technical tool economists use to account for the different prices of nontradable goods in countries with different labor costs. The classic example is a haircut, which might cost $5 in Shanghai and $30 in New York, because labor in China is so much cheaper. Therefore a Shanghainese with $5 has the same purchasing power, in regard to haircuts, as a New Yorker with $30 (assuming the quality of the two haircut experiences is identical, which can be doubtful). PPP is useful for comparing average living standards across countries with differing wage rates. It is useless for comparing the size of whole economies, whose relative importance is determined by their international, not their domestic, purchasing power. Obviously, the Shanghainese who moves to New York with $5 will purchase far fewer haircuts than the New Yorker who moves to Shanghai with $30. For similar reasons, efforts by defense analysts to inflate China's military spending using PPP adjustments are bogus: all these estimates tell you is how much China *would* spend on its military if it paid its soldiers and officers as much as the US military does. See George J. Gilboy and Eric Heginbotham, *Chinese and Indian Strategic Behavior: Growing Power and Alarm* (Cambridge University Press, 2012).

5. For a pessimistic view of China's long-run growth prospects, see Lant Pritchett and Lawrence H. Summers, "Asiaphoria Meets Regression to the Mean," NBER Working Paper 20573, October 2014 (http://www.nber.org/papers/w20573). For a more optimistic prognosis, see Dwight H. Perkins and Thomas G. Rawski, "Forecasting China's Economic Growth to 2025," in Loren Brandt and Thomas G. Rawski, eds., *China's Great Economic Transformation* (Cambridge: Cambridge University Press, 2008): 829–86; and Dwight Perkins, "Understanding the Slowing Growth Rate of the People's Republic of China," *Asian Development Review* 32, no. 1 (2015): 1–30.

6. Out of China's total exports of $2.34 billion in 2014, $661 million or 28 percent were classified by the General Administration of Customs as "new or high technology" goods.

7. This detailed product list is for the iPhone 3G, but there is no evidence that Chinese suppliers have had any success in producing components for later generations of the iPhone. See https://technology.ihs.com/389273/iphone-3g-s-carries-17896-bom-and-manufacturing-cost-isuppli-teardown-reveals; and Yuqing Xing and Neal Detert, "How the iPhone Widens the United States Trade Deficit with the People's Republic of China," ADBI Working Paper Series No. 257, December 2010.

8. See Loren Brandt, Thomas G. Rawski, and John Sutton, "China's Industrial Development," in Brandt and Rawski 2008, 569–632.

9. For the threat posed by Chinese SOEs, see Jim McGregor, *No Ancient Wisdom, No Followers: The Challenges of Chinese Authoritarian Capitalism* (Prospecta Press, 2012). The problem with his argument is that we are invited to believe that SOEs are both an unstoppable juggernaut, which threaten to upset the rules of international investment, and a group of stagnant dinosaurs whose inefficiency threatens to bring down the Chinese economy. One cannot have it both ways.

10. The exact connotation of this phrase is subject to dispute. Western defense analysts sometimes assume it implies that China should conceal its strength until an opportune moment arises to display it. Chinese scholars often contend that it simply means China should be cautious and pursue limited goals in its international engagements. Given that Deng popularized the phrase at a time when China was poor, weak, and diplomatically isolated, the Chinese interpretation seems to me more plausible. Zha Daojiong, a professor of international relations at Peking University, says that the phrase literally means that "a person with a weakened physical situation should not take that as cause for despair." (Personal communication.)

11. Official Chinese data put the stock of China's outward direct investment at $532 billion at the end of 2012; since then it has certainly increased. See "Investment Abroad: The Dragon Steps Out," *China Economic Quarterly* (March 2014): 9–33; Rhodium Group China Investment Tracker, http://www.rhgroup.net/china-investment-monitor/; and Heritage Foundation China Global Investment Tracker, http://www.heritage.org/research/projects/china-global-investment-tracker-interactive-map.

12. A landmark was a 2005 speech by then Deputy Secretary of State Robert Zoellick suggesting that China should become a "responsible stakeholder" in the global order: http://www.ncuscr.org/files/2005Gala_RobertZoellick_Whither_China1.pdf.

13. Details of the comparison between China's pre-1980 and post-1980 record, and between China and India, can be found in Gilboy and Heginbotham 2012. The authors find that total military spending in China (including items outside the formal defense budget) has consistently been lower, both as a share of the government budget and of GDP, than in India (117–19), and that the frequency of the use of force in international affairs has been identical for the two countries since 1980 (76–79). Obviously, since China's economy is much larger than India's, its spending is larger in absolute terms. But the claim that China devotes an unusually large proportion of government spending to the military is not borne out by the facts.

14. The claim that China's increasingly bellicose attitude requires the United States to respond with a modified strategy of containment, analogous to its Cold War policy against the Soviet Union, is advanced by Robert Blackwill and Ashley Tellis, "Revising U.S. Grand Strategy Toward China," Council on Foreign Relations Special Report No. 72, March 2015. A convincing rebuttal is Jeffrey A. Bader, "Changing China Policy: Are We in Search of Enemies?" Brookings Institution, June 2015.

15. An analysis of the potential lending capacity of these new funds is Arthur Kroeber, "Financing China's Global Dreams," *China Economic Quarterly* (November 2015): 27–36.

16. See ADB, "Public Private Partnerships Key to Meeting Asia's $8 Trillion Infrastructure Needs," May 30, 2012, http://www.adb.org/news/public-private-partnerships-key-meeting-asias-8-trillion-infrastructure-needs-study.

17. China's own reliance on World Bank expertise is still considerable. In 2013 and 2014 the World Bank and the Chinese government's main think tank, the Development Research Council (DRC) jointly published two major reports respectively outlining a comprehensive economic reform strategy and a program for a new approach to urbanization. (Both reports are extensively cited in this book.) It is inconceivable that the government of the United States or any other major Western nation would solicit outside advice of this kind in forming economic policy.

18. Erica S. Downs, "Inside China, Inc: China Development Bank's Cross-Border Energy Deals," Brookings Institution China Center Monograph, March 21, 2011; and Michael Forsythe and Henry Sanderson, *China's Superbank* (Bloomberg Press, 2013).

19. See Justin Y. Lin, "Flying Geese, Leading Dragons and Africa's Potential," May 23, 2011 (http://blogs.worldbank.org/developmenttalk/flying-geese-leading-dragons-and-africa-s-potential); and Vandana Chandra, Justin Y. Lin, and Yan Wang, "Leading Dragons Phenomenon: New Opportunities for Catch-Up in Low-Income Countries," World Bank Policy Research Working Paper No. 6000, March 1, 2012.

20. The classic exposition of Southeast Asia's failure to fully replicate the northeast Asian growth model is Studwell 2012.

21. A cogent articulation of this point is Lin's final blog post at the World Bank: http://blogs.worldbank.org/developmenttalk/let-s-be-pragmatic-my-final-post-as-world-bank-chief-economist.

22. See this excellent infographic in the online magazine Quartz: http://qz.com/181056/globalization-really-means-countries-just-trade-with-their-neighbors/.

23. The trade surplus in the first 10 months of 2015 was $485 billion; a figure of at least $600 billion is likely for the full year. The reason the current account surplus is smaller than the trade surplus is the explosion in outflows of spending on services, which mainly reflects Chinese international tourism.

24. A nice interactive map of Chinese direct investment in the United States is at http://rhg.com/interactive/china-investment-monitor.

25. The US mechanism is a body called the Commission on Foreign Investment in the United States (CFIUS), which was established in the late 1980s to defuse political pressure over a wave of Japanese direct investment.

26. For a balanced and realistic view of China's impact on Africa, see Deborah Brautigam, *The Dragon's Gift: The Real Story of China in Africa* (Oxford University Press, 2011). For a consideration of Chinese aid in Africa, see Bradley C. Parks and Austin M. Strange, "Aid to Africa: Helpful or Harmful?" *China Economic Quarterly* (June 2014): 29–33.

27. For the influence of South Korean popular culture in China, see Amy Qin, "China's Love Affair with Irresistible Korean TV," *New York Times*, July 21, 2015.

28. For the impact on US manufacturing employment, see David H. Autor et al., "The China Syndrome: Local Labor Market Effects of Import Competition in the United States," *American Economic Review* 103, no. 6 (2013): 2121–68. For the labor income share, see Michael W. L. Elsby, Bart Hobin, and Aysegul

Sahin, "The Decline of the U.S. Labor Share," *Brookings Papers on Economic Activity,* Fall 2013. See also Avraham Ebenstein, Ann Harrison, and Margaret McMillan, " Why Are American Workers Getting Poorer? China, Trade and Offshoring," NBER Working Paper 21027, March 2015 (http://www.nber.org/papers/w21027).

29. Specifically, a one-percentage-point increase in competition from Chinese exports was found to reduce European export volumes by 0.3 to 0.55 percentage points. See Matthias Flueckiger and Markus Ludwig, "Chinese Export Competition, Declining Exports and Adjustments at the Industry and Regional Level in Europe," MPRA Paper No. 48878, August 2013.

30. See, e.g., "Interview: Li Keqiang on China's Challenges," *Financial Times,* April 15, 2015. The introduction cites the decision of many American allies to join the China-sponsored Asian Infrastructure Investment Bank as "a striking example of how the centre of geopolitical power is shifting east."

31. See the Pew Global Attitudes and Trends Survey (2015), http://www.pewglobal.org/2015/06/23/2-views-of-china-and-the-global-balance-of-power/.

32. Improved in the sense that the United States has figured out how to exercise effective global hegemony without incurring the high fixed costs of actually occupying vast swaths of foreign territory.

APPENDIX

1. See Carsten Holz, "Can We Trust The Numbers?" *China Economic Quarterly* (March 2014): 43–50. Holz finds no evidence of deliberate falsification and estimates that China's average GDP growth rate since 1978 is probably accurate to within plus or minus one percentage point.

2. "China's Growth and Productivity Performance Debate Revisited: Accounting for China's Sources of Growth with a New Data Set," The Conference Board Economics Program Working Paper Series #14-01, January 2014, https://www.conference-board.org/pdf_free/workingpapers/EPWP-1401.pdf.

INDEX

Accountability, local government, 113, 124, 277n3
Ad hoc financing (fees), 117, 121
Africa: China emulation, 247–248; Chinese involvement, 252
Aging population: demographic transition to, 166, 167f; impact on labor force and economic growth, 166–169, 168f, 284n3
Agribusiness land leases, 36, 269–270n9
Agricultural Bank of China, 129
Agricultural Development Bank of China, 279n5
Agricultural reform, 27–29; land to tiller, 11, 28–29
Agriculture: brigades, 27; communes, 1980s end, 13, 27–29; GDP, current share of, 27; in industrialization, 13, 27; large-scale, 39; work teams, 27
Agriculture, land, and rural economy, 27–42. *See also* Farmers and farming; *specific topics*; agriculture communes' end, 13, 27–29; food self-sufficiency/security, 40–42, 40f, 270n17; land ownership, farmers', 35–37, 269–270n9, 270n11; land rights improvement, rural, 37–39, 270nn12–14; rural-urban inequality, 30–32, 269n6; rural-urban inequality, government policies on, 32–35, 33f,

34f, 269n8; township and village enterprises, 29–30, 269n5
Aircraft industry, 58
Airpocalypse, 155–156, 159, 161–162, 283n9
Air pollution. *See also specific sources*: coal, 152–153, 159–160, 283n12; reduction, 161–162
Airports: construction, 211; vanity, 86
Alibaba, 55, 189, 240
Allies, international, 253–254
American System, 13
Anticorruption campaigns, 112, 276n1; Xi Jinping, 208–209, 222–223, 290n18
Asian Infrastructure Investment Bank (AIIB), 246
Asset management companies: loan transfers, 136–137, 280n10; SOE transfer, 110
Authoritarian regimes. *See also specific regimes*: centralized control, 5–6; economic growth priority, 6 (*See also* Growth, economic); resilient, 253
Auto industry: failures, 57–58; joint ventures, 57; local manufacturers, 114; producers, 57; *vs.* South Korea and Japan, 57
Autonomous regions, 22–23, 269n21
Autonomy: innovation *vs.*, 64–65, 272n22; local government, 4

Pragmatism, 249
Precautionary savings, 190–191
Price reform: 1990s, 48, 49f;
Deng Xiaoping, 47–49, 49f; on
electricity, 161; on energy, Third
Plenum, 226; on environmental
problems, 161
Price system, two-track, 203, 206
Prime ministers. *See also specific
individuals*: as economic
strategists, 17–18
Private sector (firms): bank loan access,
107–108; "crony capitalism," 90;
evolution, 105–106, 276n18;
importance, 104–105, 276n17; retreats,
vs. state advances, 106–107, 107t;
return on assets, 108, 108f; *vs.* state,
balance of power, 108–110, 108f; *vs.*
state-owned enterprises, 89–90
Privatization, farming, 27
Privatization, urban housing, 37, 50;
impact, 76–79, 273nn15–16; urban
bias, 78
Production chains,
internationalization, 15
Productivity. *See also*
Efficiency: worker, 168–169
Property Law, 2007, 35
Property ownership, urban: 1990s,
32; housing privatization, 37, 50;
housing privatization, impact, 76–79,
273nn15–16
Property rights: male ownership, 39,
270n14; rural, improvement, 37–39,
270nn12–14; rural, ownership by
farmers, 35–37, 269–270n9; rural *vs.*
urban discrepancy, 36–37, 78–79,
270n11; urban leaseholds, 37, 270n11
Property tax, 123
Provinces, 22–23, 269n21;
decentralization, 111–112, 112t;
experimentation, 23
Public order disturbances, 198
Public-private partnerships, debt
restructuring, 122–123
Purchasing power parity (PPP), 292n4

Railroads, high-speed passenger, 84,
85–86, 274nn25–26
Red line, arable land, 38, 270n12
"Reform and opening," 5, 45
Registered urban unemployment
statistic, 284–285n13
Renminbi, international
currency: likelihood, 146–148,
281nn21–22; rationale,
144–146, 281n19
Rent, imputed, 287n6
Replacement rate, 165
Repression, financial, 12, 131–133, 133f,
140, 279n7
Residence permit, 75, 87
Residence registration (hukou) system,
72–74, 273n10; reforms, 74–75, 273n12
Resource mobilization, *vs.*
efficiency, 22
Resource use, efficiency, 210–211
Retiree, working-age persons per,
166, 167f
Retirement, leadership: mandatory, 3;
succession, 2–3
Return on assets (ROA), SOEs *vs.*
private firms, 108, 108f
Return on capital, 218–221, 220f
Revenue collection, local
government, 112
"Revitalize the Northeast," 50
Round-tripping, 55, 271n11
Rural banks, 131
Rural construction land, 38, 270n12
Rural economy. *See* Agriculture, land,
and rural economy
Rural Land Contracting Law of
2004, 35
Rural land rights: improvement, 37–39,
270nn12–14; ownership by farmers,
35–37, 269–270n9; *vs.* urban, 36–37,
78–79, 270n11
Rural population, 27
Rural to urban land reclassification, 71
Rural-urban inequality: 1989+, 30–32,
269n6; 2000s, government on, 32–35,
33f, 34f, 269n8